TUTOR DELIVERY PACK

ENGLISH LANGUAGE

— GCSE —

GRADES 5-9

AQA ENGLISH — Grades 5-9

Contents

Page		Learning Objectives
3	How to use this pack	
5	Information for parents and guardians	
7	Specification guidance	
8	Preparing for the exam	
11	Needs analysis	
13	*Revise* mapping guide	
15	Progress report	
16	End-of-lesson report	
17	Source texts	
23	1 Diagnostic: Reading and writing *3.1.1*	• To self-assess reading skills • To evaluate critical reading skills • To evaluate writing skills
	Reading	
29	2 Tackling an unseen text *3.1.1*	• To be able to cope with unfamiliar language • To be able to question the text • To be able to recognise different possible readings • To be familiar with information retrieval questions
35	3 Explicit and implicit information *3.1.1*	• To be able to identify and explore patterns of inference • To be able to gather a range of evidence
41	4 Summarising using evidence *3.1.1*	• To be able to summarise the key points of a text • To be able to embed evidence in a summary
47	5 Comparative summary *3.1.1*	• To be able to identify similarities and differences in two texts • To be able to structure a comparison of two texts
53	6 Analysing words, phrases and language features 1 *3.1.1*	• To be able to identify the writer's intention • To be able to identify patterns of vocabulary choice
59	7 Analysing words, phrases and language features 2 *3.1.1*	• To be able to identify significant language choices • To be able to explore language and mood • To be able to explore a range of responses to language choice
65	8 Analysing words, phrases and language features 3 *3.1.1*	• To be able to analyse the writer's language choices in depth and detail • To be able to structure an effective response
71	9 Analysing sentence forms 1 *3.1.1*	• To be able to identify significant sentence forms • To be able to analyse the impact of sentence forms
77	10 Analysing sentence forms 2 *3.1.1*	• To be able to identify significant sentence forms • To be able to analyse the impact of sentence forms
83	11 Developing language analysis *3.1.1*	• To be able to identify significant features of a text • To be able to comment on the writer's choices of words, phrases, language features and sentence forms • To be able to structure an effective analysis
89	12 Exploring whole text structure 1 *3.1.1*	• To be able to track the development of ideas through a text • To be able to explore how the writer's ideas interact
95	13 Exploring whole text structure 2 *3.1.1*	• To be able to analyse the intention and impact of whole text structure
101	14 Exploring whole text structure 3 *3.1.1*	• To be able to analyse the intention and impact of whole text structure • To be able to write a critical response analysing text structure
107	15 Beginning an evaluation *3.1.1*	• To be able to identify the writer's intentions • To be able to explore the success of the writer's intentions
113	16 Writing an evaluative response *3.1.1*	• To be able to develop critical engagement with, and evaluation of, a text • To be able to structure an effective evaluation
119	17 Developing critical evaluation *3.1.1*	• To be able to develop critical engagement with, and evaluation of, a text • To be able to structure an effective evaluation

CONTENTS

PAGE		LEARNING OBJECTIVES
125	18 Planning a comparison 3.1.1	• To be able to identify significant points of comparison in two texts • To be able to compare the writer's choices in two texts
131	19 Developing a comparison 3.1.1	• To be able to analyse and compare pace and tone in two texts • To be able to craft a cohesive comparison of two texts
137	20 Writing a comparison 3.1.1	• To be able to analyse and compare ideas and perspectives in two texts • To be able to plan and structure a comparison of two texts
	DESCRIPTIVE AND NARRATIVE WRITING	
143	21 Gathering ideas 3.1.2	• To be able to gather ideas for a descriptive writing task • To be able to gather ideas for a narrative writing task
149	22 Structuring ideas 3.1.2	• To be able to structure and sequence ideas for impact
155	23 Beginnings and endings 3.1.2	• To be able to plan effective openings • To be able to plan effective endings
161	24 Structuring paragraphs for effect 3.1.2	• To be able to structure paragraphs for effect
167	25 Structuring sentences 3.1.2	• To be able to structure sentences in a variety of ways
173	26 Structuring sentences for effect 3.1.2	• To be able to manipulate sentence structure for effect
179	27 Vocabulary for impact 3.1.2	• To be able to select vocabulary for clarity, precision and impact
185	28 Consolidation 3.1.2	• To be able to plan and write an effective piece of descriptive or narrative writing
	WRITING TO PRESENT A VIEWPOINT	
191	29 Gathering ideas 3.1.2	• To be able to identify the appropriate form, purpose and audience for a writing task • To be able to gather ideas to present a viewpoint
197	30 Structure and shape 3.1.2	• To be able to structure and shape an argument text
203	31 Introductions and conclusions 3.1.2	• To be able to craft an effective introduction • To be able to craft an effective conclusion
209	32 Building a paragraph 3.1.2	• To be able to structure a paragraph to present a viewpoint with clarity and impact
215	33 Paragraph and sentence forms for impact 3.1.2	• To be able to structure paragraphs for impact • To be able to structure sentences for impact
221	34 Selecting vocabulary for impact 3.1.2	• To be able to select vocabulary for clarity and impact
227	35 Planning a response 3.1.2	• To be able to plan and write an effective response to present a viewpoint
	SPaG	
233	36 Punctuation for clarity 3.1.2	• To be able to use a range of punctuation accurately
239	37 Punctuation for effect 3.1.2	• To be able to use a range of punctuation for effect
245	38 Spelling 3.1.2	• To be able to spell commonly misspelt words

How to use this pack

The *Tutors' Guild* AQA English Language Tutor Delivery Pack gives you all of the tools you need to deliver effective English Language lessons to GCSE students who are aiming for grades 5–9 in the 9–1 GCSE. Everything in this pack is available for you to download as an editable file. This means that every lesson can be edited to suit the needs of your student, but also that you can print off each resource as many times as you need.

Lessons

There are 38 one-hour, six-page lessons in this Tutor Delivery Pack. Most tutors working for a full year will have around 38 lessons with a student. If you have less contact time, you can choose which lessons are most important to the student and build your own course, using the customisable digital version of this pack. Each lesson is standalone and can be taught independently from those preceding it.

If you have more than 38 lessons together, or your lessons are longer than one hour, you can incorporate assessment from the accompanying Tutor Assessment Pack (ISBN: 9781292195384). There is an *end-of-topic test* for every lesson in this pack, as well as *checkpoint challenges* and a *practice paper*. All of the papers can also be given as homework, used as diagnostic tests or incorporated into revision.

Lesson plans

The first page of each lesson is your *lesson plan*. It is designed specifically for tutors and is intended to guide you through a one-hour session in either a one-to-one or small group setting. It is not designed to be student-facing.

Learning objectives and specification links

At the top of each lesson plan, you will find two lists. The first – *learning objectives* – is a list of your aims for the lesson. The learning objectives will be informed by the specification but may have been rephrased to make sure they are accessible to and useful for everyone. You can discuss these with the student or use them for your own reference when tracking progress. The second list – *specification links* – shows you where in the specification you can find the objectives relevant to the lesson. You can find out more about the specification on pages 7–10.

Activities

The first five minutes of your lesson should be spent reviewing the previous week's homework. You should not mark the homework during contact time: instead, use the time to talk through what the student learned and enjoyed, and any difficulties they encountered.

The final five minutes should be used to set homework for the forthcoming week. There are three ways to do this: using the *end-of-lesson report* on page 16; orally with a parent or guardian; or simply using the *homework activity sheet* on the fifth page of each lesson.

In each lesson plan, you will find four types of activities.
- *Starter activities* are 5–10 minutes each and provide an introduction to the topic.
- *Main activities* are up to 40 minutes long and are more involved, focussing on the main objectives of the lesson.
- *Plenary activities* are 5–10 minutes each, require little to no writing and recap the main learning points or prepare for the homework.
- *Homework activities* can be up to an hour long and put learning into practice.

In the lesson plan, you will find a page reference (where the activity is paper-based), a suggested timeframe and teaching notes for each activity. The teaching notes will help to guide you in delivering the activity and will also advise you on any common misconceptions associated with the topic.

ENGLISH
Grades 5-9

HOW TO USE THIS PACK

SUPPORT AND EXTENSION IDEAS
This pack is aimed at students who are targeted grades 5–9, but every student is different: some will struggle with activities that others working at the same level find straightforward. In these sections, you will find ideas for providing some differentiation throughout the activities.

PROGRESS AND OBSERVATIONS
This section is left blank for you to use as appropriate. You can then use the notes you make to inform assessment and future lessons, as well as to inform *progress reports* to parents.

ACTIVITIES
There are four student-facing *activity sheets* for each lesson: one for the starter activities; two for the main activities and one for the homework activity. On each sheet, you'll find activity-specific lesson objectives, an equipment list and a suggested timeframe. All activities are phrased for one-to-one tutoring but are equally as appropriate for small group settings. If you have a small group and the task asks you to work in pairs or challenge each other, ask the students to pair up while you observe and offer advice as necessary. Where appropriate, answers can be found on the sixth page of the lesson.

DIAGNOSTICS
The first lesson in this pack is a diagnostic lesson, designed to help you find out more about your student: their likes and dislikes; strengths and weaknesses; and personality traits. As well as the diagnostic lesson, the *needs analysis* section (pages 11–12) allows you, the student and the student's parents to investigate together which areas of the subject will need greater focus. Together, these sections will help you deliver the most effective, best value tuition.

PROGRESS REPORT
This can be used to inform parents or for your own planning as frequently or infrequently as is useful for you. Spend some time discussing the statements on the report with the student. Be prepared, though – some students will tell you there isn't anything that they enjoy about the subject!

END-OF-LESSON REPORT
Parent participation will vary greatly. The *end-of-lesson* report is useful for efficiently feeding back to parents who prefer an update after each lesson. There is space to review completed homework and achievements in the lesson, as well as space for the student to explain how confident they feel after the lesson. Finally, there is a section on what steps, including homework, the parent and student can take to consolidate learning or prepare for the following week. The *end-of-lesson* report may also be useful for communicating with some parents who speak English as a second language, as written information may be easier to follow.

CERTIFICATES
In the digital version of this pack, you will find two customisable certificates. These can be edited to celebrate achievements of any size.

ENGLISH
Grades 5–9

INFORMATION FOR PARENTS AND GUARDIANS

INTRODUCTION

Your son or daughter's tutor will often make use of resources from the *Tutors' Guild* series. These resources have been written especially for the new 9–1 GCSEs and are tailored to the AQA GCSE (9–1) English Language specification. The tutor will use their expert knowledge and judgement to assess your son or daughter's current needs. This will allow them to target areas for improvement, build confidence levels and develop skills as quickly as possible to ensure the best chance of success.

Just as a classroom teacher might do, the tutor will use lesson plans and activities designed to prepare your son or daughter for the 9–1 GCSEs. Each set of resources has been designed by experts in GCSE English Language and reviewed by tutors to ensure it offers great quality, effective and engaging teaching. All *Tutors' Guild* resources are flexible and fully adaptable, so you can be confident that the tuition your son or daughter receives is tailored to his or her needs.

GETTING STARTED

Before tuition can begin, the tutor will need to know more about your motives for employing them in order to set clear, achievable goals. They will also try to learn more about your son or daughter to ensure lessons are as useful and as engaging as possible.

To gather this information, the tutor will work through the *needs analysis* pages of this pack with you. It shouldn't take too long, but it will really maximise the value of the tuition time you pay for. You could also take this opportunity to discuss with the tutor any questions or concerns you may have.

LESSONS AND HOMEWORK

Each lesson will have the same structure: there will be a starter, which is a quick introduction to the topic; some main activities, which will look at the topic in greater detail; and a plenary activity, which will be used to round off the topic. Throughout the year, your son or daughter will become increasingly confident with the content of the specification, but will also improve his or her speaking, writing, reading, listening and co-ordination skills through a carefully balanced range of activities.

At the end of each lesson, the tutor will set some homework, which should take no longer than an hour to complete. If you don't want the tutor to set homework, please let them know. If you are happy for homework to be given, they will either discuss the homework task with you at the end of the lesson or give you an end-of-lesson report. All of the homework activities are designed to be completed independently, but if you would like to help with completion of homework, the tutor will be able to tell you what you can do.

FURTHER SUPPORT

Parents often ask a tutor what else they can do to support their son or daughter's learning or what resources they can buy to provide extra revision and practice. As a Pearson resource, *Tutors' Guild* has been designed to complement the popular *Revise* series. Useful titles you may wish to purchase include:
- *Revise* AQA GCSE (9–1) English Language Revision Guide 9781447988052
- *Revise* AQA GCSE (9–1) English Language Revision Workbook 9781447987833
- *Revise* AQA GCSE (9–1) English Language Revision Cards 9781292182056.

Using pages 13–14 of this pack, the tutor will be able to tell you which pages of the resources are appropriate for each lesson. If you purchase a set of Revision Cards, each card has a page reference in the top corner.

ENGLISH
Grades 5-9

AQA

INFORMATION FOR PARENTS AND GUARDIANS

WHAT'S IN THE TEST?

You may have heard a lot about the new 9–1 GCSEs from your son or daughter's school, from other parents or in the media. Here is a breakdown of the AQA GCSE (9–1) English Language exam.

Your son or daughter will sit two tests that assess learning against the AQA GCSE (9–1) English Language specification.

Paper 1: *Explorations in creative reading and writing (50% of the total marks)*
> Students are given 1 hour and 45 minutes to complete Paper 1. It comprises two sections: Section A, which assesses reading comprehension using one 'unseen' 20th- or 21st-century fiction text, and Section B, which assesses Students' descriptive or narrative writing ability. 'Unseen' means that the text will not have been studied in class prior to the exam and 'descriptive or narrative writing' is what we often think of as creative writing.

Paper 2: *Writers' viewpoints and perspectives (50% of the total marks)*
> Students are given 1 hour and 45 minutes to complete Paper 2. It, again, comprises two sections: Section A, which assesses reading comprehension using two 'unseen' non-fiction texts, and Section B, which assesses students' transactional writing ability. Types of non-fiction texts include letters, journals, obituaries, reference books, speeches and reviews. One non-fiction text will be from the 20th century and one will be from the 21st century. Transactional writing generally aims to inform, explain or review, although it can have other purposes too.

It is recommended that the 1 hour and 45 minutes' exam time for each paper is spent as follows:
- 15 minutes reading for Section A (read the questions, then skim read the text(s), and then read the text(s) again more thoroughly, annotating useful sections)
- 45 minutes answering Section A
- 10 minutes planning and checking for Section B
- 35 minutes writing for Section B.

SPELLING, PUNCTUATION AND GRAMMAR

The new AQA GCSE (9–1) English Language exam awards 20% of the total marks available to accurate spelling, punctuation and grammar. These marks are awarded in Section B of each paper. Accurate spelling, punctuation and grammar in the writing tasks could, therefore, contribute 36 marks to your son or daughter's overall mark. If you think that this is an area for improvement, you may wish to support tuition with extra practice through the Revise GCSE Spelling, Punctuation and Grammar series (Revision Guide ISBN: 9781292211527, Revision Workbook ISBN: 9781292211497).

RESULTS AND GRADES

GCSE results day is typically the third or fourth Thursday in August. It is the same day across the country, so you can find out the exact date online. On results day, your son or daughter will be given a slip of paper (or one per exam board, if the school hasn't collated them) with an overall grade for each GCSE. Grades for the 9–1 GCSE in English Language are given as numbers (9–1) instead of letters (A*–U). The diagram below shows roughly how the old-style grades translate to the new ones.

A*	A	B	C	D	E	F	G	U
9	8	7	6	5	4	3	2	1	U

As you can see, the new grade 9 is pitched higher than an A,* and there is a wider spread of grades available for students who would previously have been targeted a B/C. English Language is not a tiered exam (there are no Foundation and Higher papers) so all of the above grades are available to your son or daughter.

ENGLISH
Grades 5-9

SPECIFICATION GUIDANCE

The new AQA GCSE (9–1) English Language qualification was introduced for first teaching in 2015 and first assessment in 2017.

Assessment of the specification is no longer tiered. This means that every student should cover the same subject content and will sit the same paper. There will be no Foundation or Higher papers. It also means that every student has the opportunity to attain any grade that can be awarded. This Tutor Delivery Pack is tailored for the needs of students aiming for grades 5–9, but its content is provided in an adaptable format to allow you to stretch or support your student as necessary. More information about the new grading structure can be found in the Tutors' Guild AQA GCSE (9–1) English Language Tutor Assessment Pack.

If you are new to tutoring GCSE (9–1) English Language, this page will give you a brief introduction to the qualification before you move on to pages 8–10. Further guidance on particular areas of the specification – including common misconceptions and barriers to learning – can be found in the lesson plans throughout this book. Full details of the specification can be found at http://www.aqa.org.uk/subjects/english/gcse/english-language-8700.

KEY FACTS

Scope of study
There are three main skills-based content areas in the new 9–1 GCSE.

- **Critical reading and comprehension**: The reading component is worth 50% of the total marks for the GCSE. Topics within this content area are critical reading and comprehension (for example, interpretation of themes, ideas and information); summary and synthesis (for example, summarising information from one text or bringing together analysis of themes in more than one text); evaluation of writer's choice of vocabulary, form, grammatical and structural features (for example, explanation of the contribution of linguistic features to the overall impact of a text, with accurate use of linguistic terms); and comparing texts (using all of the skills learnt to critically compare two or more texts).
- **Writing**: The writing component is also worth 50% of the total marks available. It is split into two main topics: producing clear and coherent text (for example, appropriately identifying and writing for a specific purpose and audience, and maintaining consistency and coherence throughout), and writing for impact (for example, effective selection and structuring of ideas delivered through creative use of language). Also within the writing component (and thus a part of its 50% weighting) are spelling, punctuation and grammar. The government has stated that spelling, punctuation and grammar must be worth 20% of the overall marks for the 9–1 GCSE, which is a significant increase on past GCSEs. This reflects the government's commitment to improving literacy skills in general.
- **Spoken language**: Speaking and listening skills are no longer awarded a mark. Spoken language will be assessed by your student's teacher and graded as *pass*, *merit* or *distinction*. Although spoken language is not specifically dealt with in this pack, your student will have ample opportunity to practise oral responses. If you or your student's parents feel that more practice is needed, the guidelines in the specification are very clear.

Each lesson plan in this pack highlights which areas of the specification it covers. As the pack is not intended to replace classroom teaching, it will not cover all 9–1 GCSE content in full detail. It will instead focus on the most important areas and those students struggle with the most, in order to maximise your student's chances of success.

Exam papers
AQA GCSE (9–1) English Language is not a tiered exam, so all students will sit the same two papers:
- **Paper 1: Explorations in Creative Reading and Writing**
    - 1 hour 45 minutes; 80 marks; 50% of GCSE
    - Section A: Reading (one fiction text, four mandatory questions); Section B: Writing (one extended writing question from a choice of two)
- **Paper 2: Writers' Viewpoints and Perspectives**
    - 1 hour 45 minutes; 80 marks; 50% of GCSE
    - Section A: Reading (one non-fiction text and one literary non-fiction text, four mandatory questions); Section B: Writing (one mandatory extended writing question).

You can find further information about the exam itself in the accompanying AQA GCSE English (5–9) Tutor Assessment Pack (ISBN: 9781292195384).

ENGLISH
Grades 5–9
AQA

PREPARING FOR THE EXAM

The structure of the AQA GCSE (9–1) English Language exams is prescriptive. There are two papers, each with four reading questions and one writing question. Paper 1 provides a choice of two writing questions, one of which is accompanied by a prompt image, whereas there is no choice in Paper 2. The questions appear in a set order (from low to high demand), test specific assessment objectives and even have specific wording.

READING (SECTION A)

It's important that you understand which skills will be tested in which papers, and therefore on which text types. Note that there will be little variation in the question stems used in the exam, so you should base your own questions on those below.

Paper 1
Paper 1 will be accompanied by one prose fiction extract from either the 20th or 21st century. It will be from the beginning, end or a transitional point within the story. Encourage your student to read as much post-1900 literature as possible.

Question 1: Identify explicit ideas and information within a specific section of the extract (AO1).
Example question stem: *List four things from this part of the text…*

Point out an explicit idea within a small section of the text (for example, what we learn about a setting) and challenge your student to find four pieces of information about it within that section. Question 1 won't ask your student to explain their response, simply to list the information they find – quoting or paraphrasing is acceptable.

Question 2: Explain and analyse the writer's use of language within a specific section of the extract (AO2).
Example question stem: *How does the writer use of language to…?*
        You could include the writer's choice of:
- *words and phrases*
- *language features and techniques*
- *sentence forms.*

This question explores how language is used to explain something about the idea identified in Question 1. For example, if your student noted information about a setting, they may now look at how language creates atmosphere in that setting.

Students will need to look at a range of aspects of language as suggested by the supporting bullet points in the question, remembering to use subject terminology accurately. However, it is not enough for your student to simply identify a word or phrase and name it appropriately. They must be able to analyse and explain the effect of its use.

For Question 2, students should not consider the text holistically. The question will ask them to look at a small section of the source (around 10 lines), so comments should be at word, phrase and sentence level, not paragraph or whole text level.

Question 3: Explain and analyse the writer's use of structure across the whole extract (AO2).
Example question stem: *This text is from…*
        How has the writer structured the text to interest you as a reader?
        You could write about:
- *what the writer focuses your attention on at the beginning*
- *how and why the writer changes this focus as the source develops*
- *any other structural features that interest you.*

This is a new approach to structural analysis, but it's actually very similar to the approach to language analysis in Question 2. Your student's discussion should include analysis of three levels of structure:
- whole text level – beginnings, ends, shifts in perspective (for example, from one character to another)
- paragraph level – cohesion and change of time period, topic or speaker
- sentence level – comment should only be made on sentences that affect the overall structure of the source. For example, it would be appropriate to discuss a sentence used to introduce a shift in perspective or further the reader's understanding of the whole text.

ENGLISH
— Grades 5-9 —

PREPARING FOR THE EXAM

The phrase 'to interest you as a reader' reminds students that they must explain the effect of the structural devices, while allowing them the freedom to explain in what way the text is interesting. As with Question 2, it is important that your student remembers to use subject terminology and pick relevant examples that enhance and support their points.

Question 4: Evaluate a specific section of the extract critically (AO4).
Example question stem: *A student, having read this section of the text said: '...'*
To what extent do you agree?
In your response, you could:
- *consider your own impression of...*
- *evaluate how the writer creates...*
- *support your opinions with references to the text.*

Critical evaluation assesses your student synoptically; it requires them to bring together a range of skills: inference, analysis and evaluation. Your student should focus their response on the statement made in the question: how and why is the text effective or ineffective at what is claimed? It is acceptable to agree or disagree entirely with the statement. However, a more perceptive response might partially agree, discussing how the text is both successful and potentially unsuccessful in achieving its aim. Remind your student that the question is asking for their own opinion and thoughts.

Bullet points are provided within the question to support students in formulating a response. If your student seems a little daunted at first, point out that this question draws together observations from Questions 1–3 and has bullet points to help them structure their response. If they note down their answers to each point, they should find it much easier to pull those notes together into a coherent and structured evaluation.

Paper 2
Paper 2 will be accompanied by two texts: one non-fiction and one literary non-fiction. Non-fiction text types that students may find in the exam include newspaper or magazine articles, reviews, letters and leaflets. A literary non-fiction text, such as a diary, a piece of travel writing, a biography or a retelling of a historical event, is still factual in content but uses literary devices you would find in fictional prose. To help students practise the skills required, ensure they have access to a range of the text types listed above. On Paper 2, there will be some synthesis and comparison of texts, skills that are not tested in Paper 1.

Question 1: Identify and interpret explicit and implicit ideas within a specific section of the extract (AO1).
Example question stem: *Choose four statements below which are TRUE.*
- *Shade the boxes of the ones that you think are true.*
- *Choose a maximum of four statements.*

The skills needed to answer this question are similar to those for Question 1 on Paper 1. The difference here, however, is that your student will need to be able to interpret implicit information to decide whether some of the statements are correct.

Students who are generally risk-averse often find multiple-choice questions difficult to answer because they spend time finding a reason why each statement is either true or false. If they have read and digested the text, their 'gut feeling' is likely to be correct. Set some practice questions for your student under timed conditions and, if it looks as though their reasoning is sound, encourage them to listen to their instincts and use the text to verify their answers rather than to work them out.

Question 2: Synthesise implicit and explicit ideas (AO1) from two extracts.
Example question stem: *You need to refer to Source A and Source B for this question.*
Use details from both Sources. Write a summary of the differences between...

The example above asks students to summarise the differences between two texts, but could equally ask about the similarities. This question requires the most extended response of those assessing AO1, and for many students will be the most inaccessible. The key differences between this question and the other AO1 questions are that students need to bring together information from two texts throughout and refer to each text as a whole. To be successful, your student will need to work on and regularly practise the following skills:
- recognising what is to be summarised, for example the similarities between two people

ENGLISH
Grades 5-9

PREPARING FOR THE EXAM

- locating appropriate evidence within each text and identifying what it tells them in relation to the question
- synthesising (bringing together) inferences and evidence to form a cohesive response.

Note that, although it asks for a comparison, Question 2 is only worth 8 marks and does not require in-depth analysis.

Question 3: Explain and analyse the writer's use of language throughout the whole extract (AO2).
Example question stem: *How does Henry use language to…?*

The principles of this question are similar to those in Paper 1, Question 2: analysing the use of various linguistic features at word, phrase and sentence level. However, it will not provide suggestions of what the students' answers could include. Furthermore, your student will need to look at language use in the whole extract, provide a broader range of examples and discuss these in more detail.

Having a clear idea of how to structure a response will help your student to approach the question in an organised manner. Give them an example question and ask them to identify the linguistic features they would like to discuss, and what they show. Then, ask them to categorise their ideas in a logical way: for example, grouping similar features or themes.

Question 4: Compare writers' ideas and perspectives and how they are conveyed throughout two extracts (AO3).
Example question stem: *Compare how the two writers convey their different attitudes to…*
   In your answer, you could:
   - *compare their different attitudes*
   - *compare the methods they use to convey their attitudes*
   - *support your ideas with references to both texts.*

This is the one reading question for which AQA suggests that students factor in planning time, as it is perhaps the most demanding of the reading questions. Fortunately, students will have practised many of the skills needed in Questions 1–3, such as writing about two texts together, discussing the methods used to convey an idea and providing evidence.

Students need to be able to identify the attitudes and viewpoints of both writers and support their ideas with evidence of the writers' methods, such as language and structure techniques. Identification of audience, purpose and form is essential, as these influence the writers' choices. Your student may need support and practice identifying tone and voice, skills which demand a sophisticated understanding of the holistic impact of the writers' craft.

Students will then need to compare the texts in more depth than in Question 2 and will have the freedom to choose what to compare. This can be daunting. For example, one student may choose to compare how two writers use similes to portray an enthusiastic attitude, looking at the word choices in those figurative devices. Another may compare how writers create an enthusiastic tone in a different way – though energetic verb choices or through rhetorical questions, for example. The skill is being able to juggle both texts, while demonstrating a sophisticated understanding of the writer's craft.

Start preparing your student for this question with texts in which the writers use similar methods to convey clearly similar, or different, attitudes towards a topic. This practice with the core skills will increase their confidence. Then develop more perceptive comments by building up to texts in which the writers show broadly the same attitude, but for different reasons and in different ways. Remember, the student is asked to 'compare' so they should look for similarities *and* differences.

WRITING (SECTION B)

Paper 1: Question 5 offers students two creative writing tasks – with one written and one visual stimulus – closely linked to the theme of the source text in Section A. One task will require descriptive writing and the other will require narrative writing. While it will be useful to encourage your student to think critically about their own work and in which area their strengths lie, dissuade them from deciding definitively which question they are going to answer before reading the tasks.

Paper 2: Question 5 of Paper 2 does not offer a choice of writing tasks. The theme will be linked to that of the source texts in Section A, and the audience, purpose and form will be specified. Students will have to write to explain, instruct/advise, argue or persuade through a letter, article, leaflet, speech or essay, using characteristic linguistic, structural and presentational devices. Analysing good examples of each form together will increase your student's familiarity with its features.

ENGLISH
Grades 5-9

NEEDS ANALYSIS

FOR PARENTS

We have a tutor because...
(Briefly explain why you have employed a tutor.)

Where we are currently...
(Briefly explain your son or daughter's current progress. Do you have access to reports and predicted grades?)

FOR STUDENTS

Use this space to tell your tutor about yourself.

I am...
Tell your tutor what type of person you think you are. Are you quiet or outgoing? Are you confident about your abilities?

I like...
Explain to your tutor how you like to work. Do you like to work independently or with more guidance? Do you like to write your answers down or talk through them first? Do you like to be creative?

How I feel about English...

ENGLISH
Grades 5–9
AQA

NEEDS ANALYSIS

OUR GOALS

Work together to set small, achievable goals for the year ahead. Make them as positive as you can and don't limit your goals to areas of English – think about personal development too. Together, look back at this list often to see how you are progressing.

TICK OFF EACH GOAL WHEN YOU'VE ACHIEVED IT

In four weeks' time, I will…

- ☐ ....
- ☐ ....
- ☐ ....
- ☐ ....
- ☐ ....
- ☐ ....

In three months' time, I will…

- ☐ ....
- ☐ ....
- ☐ ....
- ☐ ....
- ☐ ....
- ☐ ....

By the time I sit my exam, I will…

- ☐ ....
- ☐ ....
- ☐ ....
- ☐ ....
- ☐ ....
- ☐ ....

AQA ENGLISH — Grades 5–9

REVISE MAPPING GUIDE

Pearson's *Revise* series provides simple, clear support to students preparing for their GCSE (9–1) exams. Parents may ask you if you know of any independent study resources that they can work through with their child, or you may wish to provide such resources yourself.

We have provided below a mapping guide for each lesson in this pack to a corresponding page in the *Revise* series, to make such recommendations easier for you. See page 5 for a list of recommended titles for students studying AQA GCSE (9–1) English Language.

The Revision Guides and Revision Workbooks for each level correspond page-for-page, so the page references are the same for both.

REVISE AQA GCSE (9–1) ENGLISH LANGUAGE

Lesson		Page
1	Diagnostic: Reading and writing	Find out what the student knows; Find out their preferences and attitudes
2	Tackling an unseen text	Covered throughout Revision Guide
3	Explicit and implicit information	Explicit information and ideas 13–14
4	Summarising using evidence	Skimming for the main idea 7; Annotating the sources 8; Point-Evidence-Explain 16; Writing about two texts 39; Selecting evidence for synthesis 40
5	Comparative summary	Writing about two texts 39; Selecting evidence for synthesis 40; Answering a synthesis question 41; Looking closely at language 42; Planning to compare language 43; Comparing language 44; Comparing structure 45; Comparing ideas 46; Comparing perspective 47; Answering a comparison question 48
6	Analysing words, phrases and language features 1	Word classes 19; Connotations 20; Figurative language 21; Creation of character 22; Creating atmosphere 23; Narrative voice 24; Rhetorical devices 1 27; Rhetorical devices 2 28
7	Analysing words, phrases and language features 2	Word classes 19; Connotations 20; Figurative language 21; Creation of character 22; Creating atmosphere 23; Narrative voice 24; Rhetorical devices 1 27; Rhetorical devices 2 28
8	Analysing words, phrases and language features 3	Word classes 19; Connotations 20; Figurative language 21; Creation of character 22; Creating atmosphere 23; Narrative voice 24; Rhetorical devices 1 27; Rhetorical devices 2 28
9	Analysing sentence forms 1	Identifying sentence types 31; Commenting on sentences 32
10	Analysing sentence forms 2	Identifying sentence types 31; Commenting on sentences 32
11	Developing language analysis	Inference 15; Point-Evidence-Explain 16; 19; Connotations 20; Figurative language 21; Creation of character 22; Creating atmosphere 23; Narrative voice 24; Rhetorical devices 1 27; Rhetorical devices 2 28; Identifying sentence types 31; Commenting on sentences 32; Looking closely at language 42; Planning to compare language 43
12	Exploring whole text structure 1	Whole text structure: fiction 29
13	Exploring whole text structure 2	Whole text structure: fiction 29
14	Exploring whole text structure 3	Whole text structure: fiction 29
15	Beginning an evaluation	Evaluating a fiction text 1 35; Evaluating a fiction text 2 36; Using evidence to evaluate 37
16	Writing an evaluative response	Evaluating a fiction text 1 35; Evaluating a fiction text 2 36; Using evidence to evaluate 37
17	Developing critical evaluation	Evaluating a fiction text 1 35; Evaluating a fiction text 2 36; Using evidence to evaluate 37
18	Planning a comparison	Writing about two texts 39; Selecting evidence for synthesis 40; Answering a synthesis question 41; Looking closely at language 42; Planning to compare language 43

ENGLISH
Grades 5-9

REVISE MAPPING GUIDE

REVISE AQA GCSE (9–1) ENGLISH LANGUAGE

	LESSON	PAGE
19	Developing a comparison	Writing about two texts **39**; Selecting evidence for synthesis **40**; Answering a synthesis question **41**; Looking closely at language **42**; Planning to compare language **43**; Comparing language **44**; Comparing structure **45**; Comparing ideas **46**; Comparing perspective **47**; Answering a comparison question **48**
20	Writing a comparison	Answering a comparison question **48**
21	Gathering ideas	Writing for a purpose: creative 1 **54**; Writing for a purpose: creative 2 **55**
22	Structuring ideas	Writing for a purpose: creative 1 **54**; Writing for a purpose: creative 2 **55**; Ideas and planning: creative **65**; Structure: creative **66**; Beginnings and endings: creative **67**
23	Beginnings and endings	Beginnings and endings: creative **67**
24	Structuring paragraphs for effect	Paragraphing **74**; Linking ideas **75**
25	Structuring sentences	Sentence variety 1 **87**; Sentence variety 2 **88**
26	Structuring sentences for effect	Sentences for different effects **89**
27	Vocabulary for impact	Vocabulary for effect: synonyms **79**; Vocabulary for effect: creative **80**
28	Consolidation	Writing questions: an overview **50**; Writing questions: Paper 1 **51**; Writing questions: time management **53**; Language for different effects 1 **82**; Language for different effects 2 **83**; Language for different effects 3 **84**
29	Gathering ideas	Writing for a purpose: viewpoint 1 **56**; Writing for a purpose: viewpoint 2 **57**
30	Structure and shape	Writing for a purpose: viewpoint 1 **56**; Writing for a purpose: viewpoint 2 **57**; Writing for an audience **58**; Form: articles **61**; Form: letters and reports **62**; Form: speeches **63**; Ideas and planning: viewpoint 1 **69**; Ideas and planning: viewpoint 2 **70**
31	Introductions and conclusions	Openings: viewpoint **71**; Conclusions: viewpoint **72**
32	Building a paragraph	Paragraphing **74**; Linking ideas **75**
33	Paragraph and sentence forms for impact	Paragraphing **74**; Sentence variety 1 **87**; Sentence variety 2 **88**; Sentences for different effects **89**
34	Selecting vocabulary for impact	Vocabulary for effect: viewpoint **81**; Language for different effects 1 **82**; Language for different effects 2 **83**; Language for different effects 3 **84**
35	Planning a response	Writing questions: an overview **50**; Writing questions: Paper 2 **52**; Writing questions: time management **53**; Formality and standard English 1 **77**; Formality and standard English 2 **78**; Language for different effects 3 **84**
36	Punctuation for clarity	Ending a sentence **91**; Commas **92**; Apostrophes and speech punctuation **93**
37	Punctuation for effect	Colons, semi-colons, dashes, brackets and ellipses **94**
38	Spelling	Common spelling errors 1 **96**; Common spelling errors 2 **97**; Common spelling errors 3 **98**; Proofreading **99**

PROGRESS REPORT

Fill in the boxes below with help from your tutor.

My strengths are ...
Which areas of English do you think you've done well in recently? List at least three.

My favourite English topic is...
Which English topic is your favourite? It doesn't have to be the one you're best at!

because...

The areas of English I need to work on are...
In which areas of English do you think you need more practice?

To improve these areas, we are going to...
This space is for your tutor to explain how he/she is going to help you become confident in these areas.

ENGLISH
Grades 5-9

END-OF-LESSON REPORT

We have looked at last week's homework and my tutor thinks...
This space is for your tutor to give feedback on last week's homework.

Today, we worked on...
This space is for you to list all of the topics and skills that you and your tutor have worked on today.

I feel...
This space is for you to explain how you feel about today's lesson. Did you enjoy it? Do you feel confident?

My tutor thinks...
This space is for your tutor to explain how the lesson went.

At home this week, we can...
This space is for your tutor to explain what your homework is and give you other ideas for extra revision and practice.

Source A: Non-fiction text

The food writer, M F K Fisher, describes memories of her childhood.

The Gastronomical Me

The first thing I remember tasting and then wanting to taste again is the grayish-pink fuzz my grandmother skimmed from a spitting kettle of strawberry jam. I suppose I was about four.

Women in those days made much more of a ritual of their household duties than they do now. Sometimes it was indistinguishable from a dogged if unconscious martyrdom. There were times for This, and other equally definite times for That. There was one set week a year for "the sewing woman." Of course, there was Spring Cleaning. And there were other periods, almost like festivals in that they disrupted normal life, which were observed no matter what the weather, finances, or health of the family.

Many of them seem odd or even foolish to me now, but probably the whole staid rhythm lent a kind of rich excitement to the housebound flight of time.

With us, for the first years of my life, there was a series, every summer, of short but violently active cannings. Crates and baskets and lug-boxes of fruits bought in their prime and at their cheapest would lie waiting with opulent fragrance on the screened porch, and a whole battery of enameled pots and ladles and wide-mouthed funnels would appear from some dark cupboard.

All I knew then about the actual procedure was that we had delightful picnic meals while Grandmother and Mother and the cook worked with a kind of drugged concentration in our big dark kitchen, and were tired and cross and at the same time oddly triumphant in their race against summer heat and processes of rot.

Now I know that strawberries came first, mostly for jam. Sour red cherries for pies and darker ones for preserves were a little later, and then came the apricots. They were for jam if they were very ripe, and the solid ones were simply "put up." That, in my grandmother's language, meant cooking with little sugar, to eat for breakfast or dessert in the winter which she still thought of in terms of northern Iowa.

She was a grim woman, as if she had decided long ago that she could thus most safely get to Heaven. I have a feeling that my father might have liked to help with the cannings, just as I longed to. But Grandmother, with that almost joyfully stern bowing to duty typical of religious women, made it clear that helping in the kitchen was a bitter heavy business forbidden certainly to men, and generally to children. Sometimes she let me pull stems off the cherries, and one year when I was almost nine I stirred the pots a little now and then, silent and making myself as small as possible.

But there was no nonsense anyway, no foolish chitchat. Mother was still young and often gay, and the cook too... and with Grandmother directing operations they all worked in a harried muteness... stir, sweat, hurry. It was a pity. Such a beautifully smelly task should be fun, I thought.

In spite of any Late Victorian asceticism, though, the hot kitchen sent out tantalizing clouds, and the fruit on the porch lay rotting in its crates, or readied for the pots and the wooden spoons, in fair glowing piles upon the juice-stained tables. Grandmother, saving always, stood like a sacrificial priestess in the steam, "skimming" into a thick white saucer, and I, sometimes permitted and more often not, put my finger into the cooling froth and licked it. Warm and sweet and odorous. I loved it, then.

SOURCE B: NON-FICTION TEXT

In 1860, the writer Charles Dickens watched a warship, the Achilles, being built in Chatham Dockyard.

The Uncommercial Traveller

Ding, Clash, Dong, BANG, Boom, Rattle, Clash, BANG, Clink, BANG, Dong, BANG, Clatter, BANG BANG BANG! What on earth is this! This is, or soon will be, the Achilles, iron armour-plated ship. Twelve hundred men are working at her now; twelve hundred men working on stages over her sides, over her bows, over her stern, under her keel, between her decks, down in her hold, within her and without, crawling and creeping into the
5   finest curves of her lines wherever it is possible for men to twist. Twelve hundred hammerers, measurers, caulkers, armourers, forgers, smiths, shipwrights; twelve hundred dingers, clashers, dongers, rattlers, clinkers, bangers bangers bangers! Yet all this stupendous uproar around the rising Achilles is as nothing to the reverberations with which the perfected Achilles shall resound upon the dreadful day when the full work is in hand for which this is but note of preparation – the day when the scuppers[1] that are now fitting like great, dry,
10 thirsty conduit-pipes, shall run red. All these busy figures between decks, dimly seen bending at their work in smoke and fire, are as nothing to the figures that shall do work here of another kind in smoke and fire, that day. These steam-worked engines alongside, helping the ship by travelling to and fro, and wafting tons of iron plates about, as though they were so many leaves of trees, would be rent[2] limb from limb if they stood by her for a minute then. To think that this Achilles, monstrous compound of iron tank and oaken chest, can ever
15 swim or roll! To think that any force of wind and wave could ever break her! To think that wherever I see a glowing red-hot iron point thrust out of her side from within – as I do now, there, and there, and there! – and two watching men on a stage without, with bared arms and sledge-hammers, strike at it fiercely, and repeat their blows until it is black and flat, I see a rivet being driven home, of which there are many in every iron plate, and thousands upon thousands in the ship!

20 How such a prodigious mass as the Achilles can ever be held by such comparatively little anchors as those intended for her and lying near her here, is a mystery of seamanship. For my own part, I should as soon have thought of tethering an elephant to a tent-peg, or the larger hippopotamus in the Zoological Gardens to my shirt-pin. Yonder in the river, alongside a hulk, lie two of this ship's hollow iron masts. THEY are large enough for the eye, I find, and so are all her other appliances. I wonder why only her anchors look small.

1: *scuppers* – for draining water from the deck of a ship
2: *rent* – torn

Source C: Non-fiction text

In this newspaper article, written for the *Guardian*, Oliver Wainwright describes the offices of some well-known technology companies.

Inside Facebook and Friends

From the fifth-floor putting green of Samsung's Silicon Valley headquarters, looking out at a rolling horizon of sun-scorched mountains, it's quite easy to forget you're at work. An executive is practising tai chi by the cactus garden, while another jiggles in a robotic massage chair nearby. A volleyball match is in full swing in the lush-planted courtyard below, while raucous shrieks of table football emerge from the Chill Zone, next to a row of space-age nap pods. "Meet by the
5   ping-pong tables," reads a sign stuck on the window. "Today's spinning class will be on the terrace! :)"

With its new $300m office block, which stands like a stack of gleaming white hard drives at an intersection north of San Jose, the South Korean electronics giant is plunging headlong into the holiday camp workplace culture of the Bay Area tech scene. [....]

Samsung's fun-filled office-cum-wellness-centre is just the latest in a wave of new flagship headquarters in the San
10 Francisco Bay Area. [....]

Stretching across 40,000 square metres, [...] Facebook headquarters, [....] housing the biggest continuous office floor in the world, seating around 3,000 workers in an open-plan jumble, [...] is a suitably gargantuan home for a social network that now counts one fifth of the world's population in its membership. Walking the office floor feels like exploring a techie jungle, where lianas of cables dangle from the seven-metre-high ceiling, servicing 'pods' of programmers, while
15 novelty helium balloons sway above their adjustable standing desks. [....]

At the top of a dog-leg staircase, in a moment of Alice in Wonderland revelation, we come to a nine-acre rooftop park, a bucolic idyll of sloping lawns and wireless-enabled wildflower meadows that look out across the marshy rust-coloured flats of the bay. [....]

"No one pays attention to how much you're at your desk," says my guide. "As long as you get your work done, you can be
20 lying on the lawn or sitting at the grilled cheese bar." [....]

A few blocks away, one of the region's fastest growing companies is rapidly filling the floors of a former paper factory, where it has converted the industrial spaces into a theatrical playground of themed work zones. At Airbnb, you can have your meetings in a log cabin or a Milanese loft apartment, a bedouin tent or a replica ramen cafe – each space meticulously recreated from the website's holiday rental listings. [....]

25 Out on the street, [...] you're confronted with a stark symbol of one of the symptoms of the success of this room-letting behemoth, in the form of a type of enclosure that doesn't make it into the themed office landscape: the tents of a homeless encampment, huddled beneath the flyover.

It is a reminder of the side-effects that the booming tech industry is having on the immediate context outside its hermetically sealed, candy-coated walls. The recent influx of companies from the valley to the city, lured here by
30 considerable tax incentives, is not only increasing rents but bringing other unexpected consequences.

"Tech offices can have a kind of deadening effect on the city," says Allison Arieff of SPUR, a non-profit urban research centre. "Because they now provide their employees with everything on site for free – from coffee to dry-cleaning to haircuts – local businesses are often forced to close down when they move in."

ENGLISH
— Grades 5-9 —

Source D: Fiction text

This is the opening of the novel, *One Hundred Years of Solitude* by Gabriel Garcia Marquez.

One Hundred Years of Solitude

Many years later as he faced the firing squad, Colonel Aureliano Buendía was to remember that distant afternoon when his father took him to discover ice. At that time Macondo was a village of twenty adobe houses, built on the bank of a river of clear water that ran along a bed of polished stones, which were white and enormous, like prehistoric eggs. The world was so recent that many things lacked names, and in order to
5 indicate them it was necessary to point. Every year during the month of March a family of ragged gypsies would set up their tents near the village, and with a great uproar of pipes and kettledrums they would display new inventions. First they brought the magnet. A heavy gypsy with an untamed beard and sparrow hands, who introduced himself as Melquíades, put on a bold public demonstration of what he himself called the eighth wonder of the learned alchemists of Macedonia. He went from house to house dragging two metal
10 ingots and everybody was amazed to see pots, pans, tongs, and braziers tumble down from their places and beams creak from the desperation of nails and screws trying to emerge, and even objects that had been lost for a long time appeared from where they had been searched for most and went dragging along in turbulent confusion behind Melquíades' magical irons. "Things have a life of their own," the gypsy proclaimed with a harsh accent. "It's simply a matter of waking up their souls." José Arcadio Buendía, whose unbridled
15 imagination always went beyond the genius of nature and even beyond miracles and magic, thought that it would be possible to make use of that useless invention to extract gold from the bowels of the earth. Melquíades, who was an honest man, warned him: "It won't work for that." But José Arcadio Buendía at that time did not believe in the honesty of gypsies, so he traded his mule and a pair of goats for the two magnetized ingots. Úrsula Iguarán, his wife, who relied on those animals to increase their poor domestic
20 holdings, was unable to dissuade him. "Very soon we'll have gold enough and more to pave the floors of the house," her husband replied. For several months he worked hard to demonstrate the truth of his idea. He explored every inch of the region, even the riverbed, dragging the two iron ingots along and reciting Melquíades' incantation aloud. The only thing he succeeded in doing was to unearth a suit of fifteenth century armour which had all of its pieces soldered together with rust and inside of which there was the hollow
25 resonance of an enormous stone-filled gourd. When José Arcadio Buendía and the four men of his expedition managed to take the armour apart, they found inside a calcified skeleton with a copper locket containing a woman's hair around its neck.

In March the gypsies returned. This time they brought a telescope and a magnifying glass the size of a drum, which they exhibited as the latest discovery of the Jews of Amsterdam. They placed a gypsy woman at one end
30 of the village and set up the telescope at the entrance to the tent. For the price of five reales, people could look into the telescope and see the gypsy woman an arm's length away. "Science has eliminated distance," Melquíades proclaimed. "In a short time, man will be able to see what is happening in any place in the world without leaving his own house." A burning noonday sun brought out a startling demonstration with the gigantic magnifying glass: they put a pile of dry hay in the middle of the street and set it on fire by
35 concentrating the sun's rays. José Arcadio Buendía, who had still not been consoled for the failure of big magnets, conceived the idea of using that invention as a weapon of war. Again Melquíades tried to dissuade him, but he finally accepted the two magnetized ingots and three colonial coins in exchange for the magnifying glass.

SOURCE E: FICTION TEXT

This is the opening of the novel *The Ocean at the End of the Lane,* by Neil Gaiman.

The Ocean at the End of the Lane

I wore a black suit and a white shirt, a black tie and black shoes, all polished and shiny: clothes that normally would make me feel uncomfortable, as if I were in a stolen uniform, or pretending to be an adult. Today they gave me comfort, of a kind. I was wearing the right clothes for a hard day.

5   I had done my duty in the morning, spoken the words I was meant to speak, and I meant them as I spoke them, and then, when the service was done, I got in my car and I drove, randomly, without a plan, with an hour or so to kill before I met more people I had not seen for years and shook more hands and drank too many cups of tea from the best china. I drove along winding Sussex country roads I only half remembered, until I found myself headed towards the town centre, so I turned, randomly, down another road, and took a left, and a right. It was only then that I realised where I was going, where I had been going all along, and I grimaced at my own foolishness.

10 I had been driving towards a house that had not existed for decades.

I thought of turning around, then, as I drove down a wide street that had once been a flint lane beside a barley field, of turning back and leaving the past undisturbed. But I was curious.

The old house, the one I had lived in for seven years, from when I was five until I was twelve, that house had been knocked down and was lost for good. The new house, the one my parents had built at the bottom of the garden,
15 between the azalea bushes and the green circle in the grass we called the fairy ring, that had been sold thirty years ago.

I slowed the car as I saw the new house. It would always be the new house in my head. I pulled up into the driveway, observing the way they had built out on the mid-seventies architecture. I had forgotten that the bricks of the house were chocolate brown. The new people had made my mother's tiny balcony into a two-storey sunroom. I stared at the house, remembering less than I had expected about my teenage years: no good times, no bad times. I'd lived in that
20 place, for a while, as a teenager. It didn't seem to be any part of who I was now.

I backed the car out of their driveway.

It was time, I knew, to drive to my sister's bustling, cheerful house, all tidied and stiff for the day. I would talk to people whose existence I had forgotten years before and they would ask me about my marriage (failed a decade ago, a relationship that had slowly frayed until eventually, as they always seem to, it broke) and whether I was seeing anyone
25 (I wasn't; I was not even sure that I could, not yet), and they would ask about my children (all grown up, they have their own lives, they wish they could be here today), and work (doing fine, thank you, I would say, never knowing how to talk about what I do. If I could talk about it, I would not have to do it. I make art, sometimes I make true art, and sometimes it fills the empty places in my life. Some of them. Not all). We would talk about the departed; we would remember the dead.

30 The little country lane of my childhood had become a black tarmac road that served as a buffer between two sprawling housing estates. I drove further down it, away from the town, which was not the way I should have been travelling, and it felt good.

The slick black road became narrower, windier, became the single-lane track I remembered from my childhood, became packed earth and knobbly, bone-like flints.

35 Soon I was driving slowly, bumpily, down a narrow lane with brambles and briar roses on each side, wherever the edge was not a stand of hazels or a wild hedgerow. It felt like I had driven back in time.

Source F: Non-fiction text

From the 1840s to the 1860s, Henry Mayhew studied and recorded how working people in London lived. He published his findings in *London Labour and the London Poor*.

London Labour and the London Poor

First, as to the number of stalls in the streets of London, I caused personal observations to be made; and in a walk of 46 miles, 632 stalls were counted, which is at the rate of very nearly 14 to the mile. This, too, was in bad weather, was not on a Saturday night, and at a season when the fruit-sellers all declare that "things is dull". [...]

5   The miscellaneous stalls include peas-soup, pickled whelks, sweetmeats, toys, tin-ware, elder-wine, and jewellery stands. [...]

The stalls occupied by costermongers[1] for the sale of fish, fruit, vegetables, etc., are chiefly constructed of a double cross-trestle or moveable frame, or else of two trestles, each with three legs, upon which is laid a long deal board, or tray. Some of the stalls consist merely of a few boards resting upon two baskets, or upon
10   two herring-barrels. The fish-stalls are mostly covered with paper – generally old newspapers or periodicals – but some of the street-fishmongers, instead of using paper to display their fish upon, have introduced a thin marble slab, which gives the stall a cleaner, and, what they consider a high attribute, a "respectable" appearance.

Most of the fruit-stalls are, in the winter time, fitted up with an apparatus for roasting apples and chestnuts;
15   this generally consists of an old saucepan with a fire inside; and the woman who vends them, huddled up in her old faded shawl or cloak, often presents a picturesque appearance, in the early evening, or in a fog, with the gleam of the fire lighting up her half somnolent figure. Within the last two or three years, however, there has been so large a business carried on in roasted chestnuts, that it has become a distinct street-trade, and the vendors have provided themselves with an iron apparatus, large enough to roast nearly half a
20   bushel[2] at a time. At the present time, however, the larger apparatus is less common in the streets, and more frequent in the shops, than in the previous winter.

There are, moreover, peculiar kinds of stalls such as the hot eels and hot peas-soup stalls, having tin oval pots, with a small chafing-dish containing a charcoal fire underneath each, to keep the eels or soup hot. The early breakfast stall has two capacious tin cans filled with tea or coffee, kept hot by the means before
25   described, and some are lighted up by two or three large oil-lamps; the majority of these stalls, in the winter time, are sheltered from the wind by a screen made out of an old clothes horse covered with tarpaulin. The cough-drop stand, with its distilling apparatus, the tin worm curling nearly the whole length of the tray, has but lately been introduced. The nut-stall is fitted up with a target at the back of it. The ginger-beer stand may be seen in almost every street, with its French-polished mahogany frame and bright polished taps, and
30   its foot-bath-shaped reservoir of water, to cleanse the glasses. The hot elder wine stand, with its bright brass urns, is equally popular.

The sellers of plum-pudding, "cake, a penny a slice," sweetmeats, cough-drops, pin-cushions, jewellery, chimney ornaments, tea- and tablespoons, make use of a table covered over, some with old newspapers, or a piece of oil-cloth, upon which are exposed their articles for sale.

1: *costermongers* – people who sell fruit and vegetables from a stall or handcart
2: *half a bushel* – a measure of volume equivalent to approximately 18 litres

AQA ENGLISH — Grades 5-9

1 Diagnostic: Reading and writing

Learning objectives
- To self-assess reading skills
- To evaluate critical reading skills
- To evaluate writing skills

Specification links
- 3.1.1 critical reading and comprehension

Starter activity
- **Reading self-assessment; 5 minutes; page 24**
Ask the student to complete the self-assessment sheet. You may need to illustrate some of the skills by showing an example of an exam question that requires them. Discuss any barriers to confidence in areas the student identifies as weaknesses, e.g. the clarity of the concept, applying it to a text, structuring a response, etc.

Main activities
- **Responding to a text; 20 minutes; page 25**
Ask the student to read Source A: *The Gastronomical Me* (page 17). Explain that they are going to complete a short activity to help you assess and develop their reading skills in future sessions. Ask them to share their thought processes with you as they complete the task.
- **Critical writing; 20 minutes; page 26**
Ask the student to complete the task independently. Note the pace at which they respond and write as an indicator of confidence and ability. After completion, ask them to explain how they approached the task. Note the elements that present the greatest challenge as priorities for future learning.

Plenary activity
- **Review; 5 minutes**
Ask the student to review the lesson's activities and then negotiate three key targets to work on. Note them to guide future learning and self- and teacher-assessment.

Homework activity
- **Writing; 45 minutes; page 27**
Explain that the key aims of the task are to produce an effective piece of writing and to show awareness of how/why it is effective. Explain that you will use their planning, writing and self-assessment to identify future learning needs.

Support ideas
- **Responding to a text** Guide the student with prompts, noting where confidence or understanding is lost. If the student still struggles with a question even when prompted, note that area as a priority for future learning.
- **Critical writing** Check the student is familiar with the structure of the exam. If necessary, show them the sample assessment material and ask them to summarise each question on both papers. Practice papers can be found on the AQA website or in the Tutors' Guild AQA GCSE (9–1) English Foundation Assessment Pack.

Extension idea
- **Responding to a text** Challenge the student to identify two or more quotations, word choices etc. that contribute cumulatively to a specific response, impression or mood.

Progress and observations

ENGLISH
— Grades 5-9 —

AQA

STARTER ACTIVITY: READING SELF-ASSESSMENT   **TIMING: 5 MINS**

LEARNING OBJECTIVES
- To self-assess reading skills

EQUIPMENT
- sample exam papers

How would you rate your reading skills?
Tick the box that best describes how you feel about each of these key skills.

1. Finding key information in a text

I'm not sure what this means. | I find this difficult. | I'm pretty good at this. | I'm really confident with this.

☐ ─── ☐ ─── ☐ ─── ☐

2. Choosing relevant evidence from a text

I'm not sure what this means. | I find this difficult. | I'm pretty good at this. | I'm really confident with this.

☐ ─── ☐ ─── ☐ ─── ☐

3. Commenting on the writer's use of words and phrases

I'm not sure what this means. | I find this difficult. | I'm pretty good at this. | I'm really confident with this.

☐ ─── ☐ ─── ☐ ─── ☐

4. Commenting on the writer's use of sentence forms

I'm not sure what this means. | I find this difficult. | I'm pretty good at this. | I'm really confident with this.

☐ ─── ☐ ─── ☐ ─── ☐

5. Commenting on the writer's use of whole text structure

I'm not sure what this means. | I find this difficult. | I'm pretty good at this. | I'm really confident with this.

☐ ─── ☐ ─── ☐ ─── ☐

6. Evaluating a text

I'm not sure what this means. | I find this difficult. | I'm pretty good at this. | I'm really confident with this.

☐ ─── ☐ ─── ☐ ─── ☐

7. Comparing texts

I'm not sure what this means. | I find this difficult. | I'm pretty good at this. | I'm really confident with this.

☐ ─── ☐ ─── ☐ ─── ☐

ENGLISH
Grades 5-9

MAIN ACTIVITY: RESPONDING TO A TEXT | **TIMING: 20 MINS**

LEARNING OBJECTIVES
- To evaluate critical reading skills

EQUIPMENT
- Source A: *The Gastronomical Me*
- highlighter

1. Understanding – summarise the text in one sentence. What is it about?

   ....

   ....

2. Intention – these are the opening paragraphs of a food writer's autobiography. Discuss why you think she chose to begin her story in this way.

3. Ideas and perspectives – discuss the impressions the writer creates of herself, her childhood and her family.

4. Mood – give one word to describe the mood the writer creates in the text.

   ....

5. Reader's responses – discuss with your tutor how two different readers might respond in different ways to the text.

6. Selecting evidence – circle two quotations in Source A that support one of your answers to question 3, 4 or 5.

7. Words and phrases – look at the writer's use of words, phrases and language features in your selected quotations. Underline two words, phrases or language features that contribute to one or more of the following:
   - the text's mood
   - the writer's intention
   - the reader's response.

8. Sentence forms – look at the writer's use of sentence forms in one of the quotations you have chosen. Highlight one sentence form that contributes to one or more of the following:
   - the text's mood
   - the writer's intention
   - the reader's response.

9. Evaluation – discuss whether the text is successful. Give reasons for your answer.

ENGLISH
Grades 5-9

MAIN ACTIVITY: CRITICAL WRITING **TIMING: 20 MINS**

LEARNING OBJECTIVES
- To evaluate writing skills

EQUIPMENT
- Source A: *The Gastronomical Me*
- coloured pens/pencils

1. Write one paragraph in response to the question below.

   > What impressions does the writer create of her grandmother in Source A: *The Gastronomical Me*?
   >
   > [8 marks]

   _____

   _____

   _____

   _____

   _____

   _____

   _____

2. Think carefully about the different features of a successful piece of critical writing. Which have you included in your response? Identify and label them.

AQA ENGLISH — Grades 5-9

HOMEWORK ACTIVITY: WRITING **TIMING: 45 MINS**

LEARNING OBJECTIVES
- To evaluate writing skills

EQUIPMENT
none

Look at the Paper 1, Section B exam-style writing task below.

> Describe an event from your childhood that you remember very clearly.
> [40 marks]

1. **Write a plan for your response.**

   ------

2. **On a separate piece of paper, write the opening paragraph of your response.**
   Make sure you:
   - give the reader a clear impression of the people and the event you are describing
   - write 100–125 words.

3. **How have you tried to create a clear impression of the people and the event in your writing? Note down three ways.**

   ------

1 Answers

Starter activity: Reading self-assessment
1. Student's own answers

Main activity: Responding to a text
Examples:
1. The writer describes her grandmother's approach to fruit preserving and other household duties and explains her own introduction to the pleasures of food.
2. The extract describes the writer's first memory of pleasure in food – suggesting this was a particularly formative moment in her childhood. The powerful character of her grandmother is engaging and entertaining.
3. The extract is dominated by the impressions the writer creates of her grandmother as an intimidating, controlling and 'grim woman'.
4. Humorous
5. Some readers might be entertained by the portrayal of the writer's grandmother; others might be interested in the routines and habits of women in this period.
6. Accept any valid selection.
7. Accept any valid response.
8. Accept any valid response.
9. Accept any valid response supported with relevant evidence.

Main activity: Critical writing
1. Look for responses that feature a clear focus on, and keywords from, the question; focused, relevant evidence; and detailed analysis of the writer's intention, the choices that support it and their impact.
2. Look for labels to the above features.

Homework activity: Writing
1. See exam-style mark scheme on pages 251–253.
2. See exam-style mark scheme on pages 251–253.
3. Student's own answer

Glossary

Evidence
A quotation from a text or an observation of a particular event or point of view that is used to support an argument or perspective

Evaluation
Judging, as a reader, how successful a particular aspect of a text is, with an explanation

Compare
Identifying similarities and differences between two or more texts

AQA ENGLISH — Grades 5-9

2 READING: TACKLING AN UNSEEN TEXT

LEARNING OBJECTIVES
- To be able to cope with unfamiliar language
- To be able to question the text
- To be able to recognise different possible readings
- To be familiar with information retrieval questions

SPECIFICATION LINKS
- 3.1.1 critical reading and comprehension

STARTER ACTIVITY
- **Unfamiliar words; 5 minutes; page 30**
  Explain to the student that, particularly in nineteenth century texts, there may be language they are not familiar with. Some terms may be glossed on the exam paper, but others will not. Fold the worksheet to conceal question two. Ask the student to complete question one, warning them that they may find it tricky! Reveal question two. Ask the student to complete it and then discuss whether seeing the words in context helped them to deduce meaning.

MAIN ACTIVITIES
- **Questioning the source; 20 minutes; page 31**
  Ask the student to read Source B: *The Uncommercial Traveller* (page 18) and complete the task. Explain that these questions are relevant to any text and will help them become familiar with a source in preparation for responding to exam questions.
- **Different readings; 20 minutes; page 32**
  Note that the ability to recognise different possible readings is a high-level skill and a significant feature of the most successful exam responses.

PLENARY ACTIVITY
- **Review; 5 minutes**
  Ask the student to review their familiarity with the content of the text and the writer's intention, and discuss how the approach outlined in the lesson helped them to feel confident about their understanding.

HOMEWORK ACTIVITY
- **Information retrieval; 30 minutes; page 33**
  Explain to the student that the false answers should be plausible and based on possible misunderstandings or misreadings.

SUPPORT IDEA
- **Unfamiliar words** Discuss whether the student would still be able to understand the text if they failed to deduce the meaning of one or more of the words. Emphasise that they should not let challenging vocabulary affect their confidence when tackling an unseen text.

EXTENSION IDEA
- **Different readings** Challenge the student to identify further evidence to support each interpretation and/or further examples of different possible readings.

PROGRESS AND OBSERVATIONS

ENGLISH
Grades 5-9

AQA

| **Starter activity: Unfamiliar words** | **Timing: 5 mins** |

| **Learning objectives** | **Equipment** |
| • To be able to cope with unfamiliar language | none |

1. Can you guess what these words mean? Write a definition beneath each one.

   a) caulker

   ....

   b) scupper

   ....

   c) conduit-pipes

   ....

   --fold--

2. Read the extract, and then see if you can improve your definitions.

   > In 1860, the writer Charles Dickens watched a warship, the Achilles, being built in Chatham Dockyard.
   >
   > ***The Uncommercial Traveller***
   >
   > Ding, Clash, Dong, BANG, Boom, Rattle, Clash, BANG, Clink, BANG, Dong, BANG, Clatter, BANG BANG BANG! What on earth is this! This is, or soon will be, the Achilles, iron armour-plated ship. Twelve hundred men are working at her now; twelve hundred men working on stages over her sides, over her bows, over her stern, under her keel, between her decks, down in her hold, within her and without, crawling and creeping into the finest curves of her lines wherever it is possible for men to twist. Twelve hundred hammerers, measurers, (caulkers,) armourers, forgers, smiths, shipwrights; twelve hundred dingers, clashers, dongers, rattlers, clinkers, bangers bangers bangers! Yet all this stupendous uproar around the rising Achilles is as nothing to the reverberations with which the perfected Achilles shall resound upon the dreadful day when the full work is in hand for which this is but note of preparation – the day when the (scuppers) that are now fitting like great, dry, thirsty (conduit-pipes) shall run red.

   a) caulker

   ....

   b) scupper

   ....

   c) conduit-pipes

   ....

30

ENGLISH
Grades 5-9

MAIN ACTIVITY: QUESTIONING THE SOURCE   **TIMING: 20 MINS**

LEARNING OBJECTIVES
- To be able to question the text

EQUIPMENT
- Source B: *The Uncommercial Traveller*

When you first read a source, you can ask yourself some key questions to check and develop your understanding of it. This is a good way to prepare for writing about it.

1. Read Source B: *The Uncommercial Traveller* and then fill in the spider diagram below.

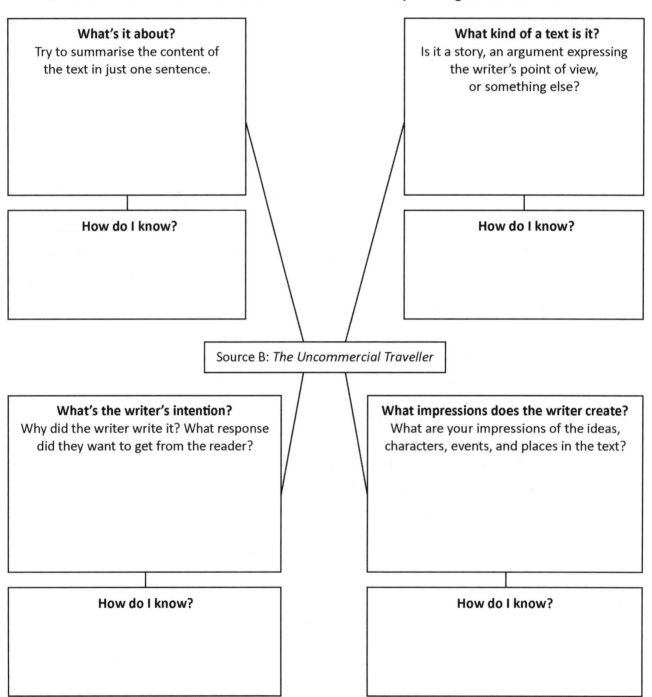

ENGLISH
— Grades 5-9 —

AQA

| MAIN ACTIVITY: DIFFERENT READINGS | TIMING: 20 MINS |

LEARNING OBJECTIVES
- To be able to recognise different possible readings

EQUIPMENT
- Source B: *The Uncommercial Traveller*

Readers may respond in different ways to the same text. Similarly, a writer may present two conflicting opinions or impressions of a situation, event, character or idea. Being able to identify and explore differing readings of a text is a key feature of successful critical writing.

Compare these four extracts from Source B: *The Uncommercial Traveller*.

A. ...all this stupendous uproar around the rising Achilles is as nothing to the reverberations with which the perfected Achilles shall resound upon the dreadful day when the full work is in hand for which this is but note of preparation – the day when the scuppers that are now fitting like great, dry, thirsty conduit-pipes, shall run red.

B. To think that this Achilles, monstrous compound of iron tank and oaken chest, can ever swim or roll! To think that any force of wind and wave could ever break her!

C. Twelve hundred hammerers, measurers, caulkers, armourers, forgers, smiths, shipwrights; twelve hundred dingers, clashers, dongers, rattlers, clinkers, bangers bangers bangers!

D. How such a prodigious mass as the Achilles can ever be held by such comparatively little anchors as those intended for her and lying near her here, is a mystery...

1. What different impressions of the Achilles does Dickens create in these extracts? Write down at least two of them.

2. How might different readers respond in different ways to them? Write two or three sentences explaining your ideas.

32

AQA ENGLISH — Grades 5-9

HOMEWORK ACTIVITY: INFORMATION RETRIEVAL

TIMING: 30 MINS

LEARNING OBJECTIVES
- To be familiar with information retrieval questions

EQUIPMENT
none

When you have read and questioned the source, you should be ready to answer an information retrieval question.

In Paper 2, Section A of the exam, the non-fiction information retrieval question will ask you to identify four true statements from a list of eight.

1. **Complete the Paper 2, Section A exam-style question below.**
   You should add:
   - four pieces of information about the ship that *can* be found in the extract and are **true**
   - four pieces of information about the ship that *cannot* be found in the extract and are **false**.

Read Source B: *The Uncommercial Traveller* again. Choose four statements below which are TRUE.

- Shade the boxes of the ones that you think are true.
- Choose a maximum of four statements.

A. _____ ☐

B. _____ ☐

C. _____ ☐

D. _____ ☐

E. _____ ☐

F. _____ ☐

G. _____ ☐

H. _____ ☐

[4 marks]

ENGLISH
Grades 5-9

2 ANSWERS

STARTER ACTIVITY: UNFAMILIAR WORDS

1. a) Caulker: a person who applies caulk, a waterproofing sealant.
b) Scupper: a drain to remove water from the deck of a ship.
c) Conduit-pipes: drainpipes.
2. Check the student has improved their definitions.

MAIN ACTIVITY: QUESTIONING THE SOURCE

1. What it's about: observations on the building of a vast warship, e.g. 'This is, or soon will be, the Achilles, iron armour-plated ship.'
What kind of text: a description, e.g. 'great', 'dry', 'thirsty'
The writer's intention: to convey the power and scale of the ship, e.g. 'prodigious mass'
The impressions the writer creates: the ship is both impressively vast and terrifyingly powerful, e.g. 'monstrous compound of iron tank and oaken chest'

MAIN ACTIVITY: DIFFERENT READINGS

1. The ship is presented as both invincible ('To think that any force of wind and wave could ever break her!') and vulnerable ('such comparatively little anchors'). The ship is 'stupendous', yet this is undercut with the writer's reservations about its 'dreadful' purpose as a warship when its scuppers will 'run red' with the blood of its sailors.
2. Student's own answer

HOMEWORK ACTIVITY: INFORMATION RETRIEVAL

1. Ensure the student has written four statements that are true and four that are false.

GLOSSARY

Retrieval
To find something within a text

ENGLISH
Grades 5–9

3 READING: EXPLICIT AND IMPLICIT INFORMATION

LEARNING OBJECTIVES
- To be able to identify and explore patterns of inference
- To be able to gather a range of evidence

SPECIFICATION LINKS
- 3.1.1 critical reading and comprehension

STARTER ACTIVITY
- **Inferring ideas; 5 minutes; page 36**
  Ensure the student understands the difference between explicit and implicit information.

MAIN ACTIVITIES
- **Patterns of inference; 20 minutes; page 37**
  Ask the student to read Source C: *Inside Facebook and Friends* (page 19). Explain that the most sophisticated critical responses identify connections and relationships between a range of evidence in order to support a point. Ask the student to complete the task, verbalising their thought process as they identify a relevant pattern of inference in the extract.
- **Accumulating inferences; 20 minutes; page 38**
  Explain to the student that inferences made at different points in a text can work cumulatively, influencing the reader's response to the text and to its subject matter.

PLENARY ACTIVITY
- **Review; 5 minutes**
  Ask the student to summarise and evaluate their skills of inference, and ability to identify patterns of inference and their cumulative impact.

HOMEWORK ACTIVITY
- **Gathering evidence; 30 minutes; page 39**
  Ensure the student appreciates the importance of annotating the text to gather a range of relevant evidence.

SUPPORT IDEAS
- **Inferring ideas** If the student is struggling, clarify the difference between explicit and implicit information by modelling how to complete the task.
- **Patterns of inference; Accumulating inferences** Focus the student on one or two particularly relevant sentences in each extract, first eliminating any parts that are not relevant to the task, then focusing on the implications of those that are.

EXTENSION IDEA
- **Patterns of inference; Accumulating inferences** Challenge the student to gather as wide a range of evidence from the extracts as possible.

PROGRESS AND OBSERVATIONS

ENGLISH
Grades 5-9

| STARTER ACTIVITY: INFERRING IDEAS | TIMING: 5 MINS |

LEARNING OBJECTIVES
- To be able to identify and explore patterns of inference

EQUIPMENT
none

Information and ideas can be:
- **explicitly** stated in a text
- **implicitly** suggested in a text, leaving the reader to **infer** them.

Read this extract from Source C: *Inside Facebook and Friends*

> Stretching across 40,000 square metres, Facebook headquarters, housing the biggest continuous office floor in the world, seating around 3,000 workers in an open-plan jumble, is a suitably gargantuan home for a social network that now counts one fifth of the world's population in its membership.

1. **Underline one part of the extract that explicitly states information about Facebook.**

2. **Circle one part of the extract that does not clearly state, but implies information about Facebook.**

ENGLISH
Grades 5-9

MAIN ACTIVITY: PATTERNS OF INFERENCE   **TIMING: 20 MINS**

LEARNING OBJECTIVES
- To be able to identify and explore patterns of inference
- To be able to gather a range of evidence

EQUIPMENT
- Source C: *Inside Facebook and Friends*

Writers often imply ideas throughout a text, or a section of a text.

Look carefully at the extract from Source C: *Inside Facebook and Friends* below. In this extract, the writer implies his view of Samsung's headquarters.

> From the fifth-floor putting green of Samsung's Silicon Valley headquarters, looking out at a rolling horizon of sun-scorched mountains, it's quite easy to forget you're at work. An executive is practising tai chi by the cactus garden, while another jiggles in a robotic massage chair nearby. A volleyball match is in full swing in the lush-planted courtyard below, while raucous shrieks of table football emerge from the Chill Zone, next to a row of space-age nap pods. "Meet by the ping-pong tables," reads a sign stuck on the window. "Today's spinning class will be on the terrace! :)"
>
> With its new $300m office block, which stands like a stack of gleaming white hard drives at an intersection north of San Jose, the South Korean electronics giant is plunging headlong into the holiday camp workplace culture of the Bay Area tech scene.
>
> Samsung's fun-filled office-cum-wellness-centre is just the latest in a wave of new flagship headquarters in the San Francisco Bay Area.

At the end of the extract, he talks about 'the holiday camp workplace culture' and describes it as a 'fun-filled office-cum-wellness-centre'.

1. What do these two descriptions imply about Samsung and other technology companies in California? Write at least two sentences explaining your ideas.

   ----

2. What other details and information does the writer use in this extract to imply this view? Underline them.

ENGLISH
Grades 5-9

MAIN ACTIVITY: ACCUMULATING INFERENCES **TIMING: 20 MINS**

LEARNING OBJECTIVES
- To be able to identify and explore patterns of inference
- To be able to gather a range of evidence

EQUIPMENT
none

Writers sometimes use a range of details and information to imply an idea or point of view. Often these ideas or points of view will work together, or accumulate, to imply a further idea or point of view.

1. Annotate the extracts from Source C: *Inside Facebook and Friends* below, identifying where and what the writer is implying about the place they are describing.

    A. Facebook's offices

    > At the top of a dog-leg staircase, in a moment of Alice in Wonderland revelation, we come to a nine-acre rooftop park, a bucolic idyll of sloping lawns and wireless-enabled wildflower meadows that look out across the marshy rust-coloured flats of the bay.

    B. AirBnB's offices

    > A few blocks away, one of the region's fastest growing companies is rapidly filling the floors of a former paper factory, where it has converted the industrial spaces into a theatrical playground of themed work zones. At Airbnb, you can have your meetings in a log cabin or a Milanese loft apartment, a bedouin tent or a replica ramen cafe – each space meticulously recreated from the website's holiday rental listings.

    C. The homeless encampment

    > Out on the street, you're confronted with a stark symbol of one of the symptoms of the success of this room-letting behemoth, in the form of a type of enclosure that doesn't make it into the themed office landscape: the tents of a homeless encampment, huddled beneath the flyover.

2. Look carefully at your annotations above. Think about how the writer's implied ideas and views throughout the whole source work together. What might he be trying to imply about the technology companies featured in this article? Write two or three sentences on a separate piece of paper explaining your ideas.

AQA ENGLISH — Grades 5-9

| HOMEWORK ACTIVITY: GATHERING EVIDENCE | TIMING: 30 MINS |

LEARNING OBJECTIVES
- To be able to identify and explore patterns of inference
- To be able to gather a range of evidence

EQUIPMENT
- Source A: *The Gastronomical Me*
- coloured pens/pencils

Read Source A: *The Gastronomical Me*.

1. Now read the questions below. Annotate the source, identifying relevant evidence you could use to support your answers.

2. What does the writer imply about her family? Write two or three sentences, summing up your ideas and supporting them with a range of evidence from the source.

3. What does the writer imply about herself? Write two or three sentences, summing up your ideas and supporting them with a range of evidence from the source.

3 Answers

STARTER ACTIVITY: INFERRING IDEAS
1. Example: Facebook has a large office: 'the biggest continuous office floor in the world'.
2. Example: Facebook is an enormous, and extremely successful, company: 'counts one fifth of the world's population in its membership'.

MAIN ACTIVITY: PATTERNS OF INFERENCE
1. The writer implies a possibly derogatory view that technology companies' offices are not serious places of work. The descriptions also imply that these companies value their employees highly.
2. Examples: 'putting green', 'tai chi', 'cactus garden', 'massage chair', 'volleyball'.

MAIN ACTIVITY: ACCUMULATING INFERENCES
1. Examples:
A. wonder, beauty: 'Alice in Wonderland', 'bucolic idyll'
B. ostentation and pretense: 'theatrical playground', 'Milanese loft apartment'
C. vulnerability and poverty: 'huddled beneath the flyover'.
2. The writer implies that technology companies are extravagant, with little regard for the lives of, or their impact on, people outside their luxurious offices.

HOMEWORK ACTIVITY: GATHERING EVIDENCE
1. Student's own answer. Ensure relevant evidence is identified in the source.
2. Student's own answer. Ensure response is supported with a range of evidence from question 1.
3. Student's own answer. Ensure response is supported with a range of evidence from question 1.

GLOSSARY

Explicit
Stated clearly and in detail, leaving no room for confusion or doubt

Implicit
Suggested but not directly expressed

Infer
To read between the lines

AQA ENGLISH — Grades 5-9

4 READING: SUMMARISING USING EVIDENCE

LEARNING OBJECTIVES
- To be able to summarise the key points of a text
- To be able to embed evidence in a summary

SPECIFICATION LINKS
- 3.1.1 summary and synthesis

STARTER ACTIVITY
- **A brief summary; 5 minutes; page 42**
  Explore the elements of the modelled summary: the key point of the extract, illustrated and supported with a very short, embedded quotation. Ask the student to complete the tasks to achieve a summary featuring the same elements.

MAIN ACTIVITIES
- **Summarising; 20 minutes; page 43**
  Ask the student to complete the task. Emphasise to the student that their summaries should be written in complete sentences, not in note form. Point out that this task is intended to hone their summary skills in preparation for next lesson's focus on summarising and synthesising information from two texts for comparison.
- **Embedding evidence; 20 minutes; page 44**
  Encourage the student to select short quotations. Pause to review their first choice of quotation: can its length be reduced to improve focus/relevance?

PLENARY ACTIVITY
- **Review; 5 minutes**
  Ask the student to review and evaluate the skills of summarising using carefully selected and embedded evidence.

HOMEWORK ACTIVITY
- **Summarising and embedding; 30 minutes; page 45**
  Explain to the student that the task will help them to practise the skills developed in this lesson, and prepare them for next lesson in which they will be comparing Source D: *London Labour and the London Poor* (page 20) and Source A: *The Gastronomical Me* (page 17).

SUPPORT IDEAS
- **Summarising** Do not restrict sentence length too much. Focus on reviewing summaries once written to explore ways in which they could be edited down.
- **Embedding evidence** Focus the student on selecting one relevant quotation only.

EXTENSION IDEAS
- **Summarising** Challenge the student to produce the shortest possible summaries without loss of accuracy or key information, and while still writing in a complete sentence.
- **Embedding evidence** Challenge the student to embed quotations of only one or two words.

PROGRESS AND OBSERVATIONS

ENGLISH
— Grades 5-9 —

STARTER ACTIVITY: A BRIEF SUMMARY   TIMING: 5 MINS

LEARNING OBJECTIVES
- To be able to summarise the key points of a text
- To be able to embed evidence in a summary

EQUIPMENT
none

This is a short extract from Source F: *London Labour and the London Poor* in which the writer describes how working people lived in Victorian London. The source focuses on the food stalls around London.

> First, as to the number of stalls in the streets of London, I caused personal observations to be made; and in a walk of 46 miles, 632 stalls were counted, which is at the rate of very nearly 14 to the mile. This, too, was in bad weather, was not on a Saturday night, and at a season when the fruit-sellers all declare that "things is dull."

Read this summary of the short extract.

> There were hundreds of food stalls in Victorian London, the writer counting 'very nearly 14 to the mile'.

Now read another short extract from Source F: *London Labour and the London Poor*.

> Most of the fruit-stalls are, in the winter time, fitted up with an apparatus for roasting apples and chestnuts; this generally consists of an old saucepan with a fire inside; and the woman who vends them, huddled up in her old faded shawl or cloak, often presents a picturesque appearance, in the early evening, or in a fog, with the gleam of the fire lighting up her half somnolent figure.

1. Write a sentence, summarising this extract.

....

....

2. Underline a short, relevant quotation in the extract that supports and/or illustrates your summary.

3. Rewrite your summary, embedding your chosen quotation in it.

....

....

....

ENGLISH
Grades 5-9

MAIN ACTIVITY: SUMMARISING

TIMING: 20 MINS

LEARNING OBJECTIVES
- To be able to summarise the key points of a text

EQUIPMENT
- Source F: *London Labour and the London Poor*

Read Source F: *London Labour and the London Poor*.

1. There are six paragraphs in the source. Note the most important piece of key information in each paragraph in the space below.

1.	2.
3.	4.
5.	6.

2. Look at your notes on paragraphs 1–3. Summarise them in one complete sentence of 5–15 words.

------

3. Look at your notes on paragraphs 4–6. Summarise them in one complete sentence of 5–15 words.

------

4. Look at your summaries of paragraphs 1–3 and paragraphs 4–6. Write one complete sentence of 5–15 words, summarising the whole source.

ENGLISH
Grades 5-9

MAIN ACTIVITY: EMBEDDING EVIDENCE

TIMING: 20 MINS

LEARNING OBJECTIVES
- To be able to embed evidence in a summary

EQUIPMENT
- Source F: *London Labour and the London Poor*

Look again at your summary of the whole of Source F: *London Labour and the London Poor*.

1. Identify and write down three key quotations from the source that support and/or illustrate your summary.

a)

b)

c)

2. Underline one or two key phrases in your quotations that are particularly effective in supporting and/or illustrating your summary.

3. Rewrite your summary, embedding some or all of your chosen key phrases in it.

....

....

....

....

....

....

ENGLISH
Grades 5-9

HOMEWORK ACTIVITY: SUMMARISING AND EMBEDDING	TIMING: **30** MINS

LEARNING OBJECTIVES	EQUIPMENT
• To be able to summarise the key points of a text • To be able to embed evidence in a summary	• Source A: *The Gastronomical Me*

Read Source A: *The Gastronomical Me.*

1. Note the most important piece of key information in each paragraph.

1.	2.	3.
4.	5.	6.
7.	8.	9.

2. Write a summary of the source in one sentence.

....

....

3. Underline key quotations in the source to support and/or illustrate your summary.

4. Re-write your summary, embedding in it key words or phrases from your chosen quotations.

....

....

....

....

4 Answers

Starter activity: A brief summary

1. Example: The fruit stalls sold roasted apples and chestnuts in winter, roasted in a pan.
2. Check that an appropriate quotation is underlined in the source text.
3. Example: The fruit stalls sold roasted apples and chestnuts in winter, roasted in 'an old saucepan with a fire inside'.

Main activity: Summarising

1. Examples:
    1. There were hundreds of food stalls in Victorian London.
    2. There were many different things available from the stalls.
    3. The stalls were not sophisticated constructions.
    4. Roasted apples and chestnuts were cooked in an old saucepan.
    5. Stalls had specific equipment to produce the food and drink that they sold.
    6. Some stalls were covered with newspapers and oil-cloth.
2. There were hundreds of makeshift stalls selling a huge range of produce in Victorian London.
3. Some stalls were more sophisticated than others.
4. A huge range of produce was sold from hundreds of stalls in Victorian London.

Main activity: Embedding evidence

1. Student's own answer
2. Student's own answer
3. Example: A huge range of produce from 'hot eels' to 'ginger beer' was sold from hundreds of stalls, 'very nearly 14 to the mile', in Victorian London.

Homework activity: Summarising and embedding

1. Examples might include:
    1. The writer enjoyed her grandmother's jam from an early age.
    2. Household jobs were done at specific times of the year.
    3. The writer found this added excitement to her childhood.
    4. Every summer the writer's family would preserve fruit.
    5. The writer's mother and grandmother worked hard to preserve the fruit.
    6. Different fruits were preserved in different ways.
    7. The writer's grandmother was a 'grim' woman.
    8. The writer's grandmother made them work hard.
    9. The writer loved the jam.
2. Examples might include: The writer enjoyed helping her grandmother make jam.
3. Check that appropriate evidence is underlined in the source text.
4. Examples might include: The writer enjoyed helping her 'grim' grandmother to make 'warm and sweet and odorous' jam.

Glossary

Summary
A concise and clear description presenting the main facts or ideas of a text

46

AQA ENGLISH — Grades 5-9

5 READING: COMPARATIVE SUMMARY

LEARNING OBJECTIVES
- To be able to identify similarities and differences in two texts
- To be able to structure a comparison of two texts

SPECIFICATION LINKS
- 3.1.1 summary and synthesis

STARTER ACTIVITY
- **First thoughts; 10 minutes; page 48**
  The student will have read the two sources in previous lessons. If necessary, give them a few minutes to remind themselves.

MAIN ACTIVITIES
- **Parallels and differences; 20 minutes; page 49**
  Explain that looking for parallels in the two texts is a good way to identify significant differences. Encourage the student to identify parallels that are relevant to the exam-style question in the starter activity, e.g. the purpose of the food preparation, the kinds of food referred to, etc.
- **Structuring a comparison; 15 minutes; page 50**
  Ask the student to complete the task, selecting a different pair of points to that used in question three of the previous activity. Emphasise the value of synthesising a range of evidence from each text to support a point. Highlight the difference between conjunctions (*whereas/while*), which can link clauses but not sentences, and adverbials (*however, on the other hand*) which can link both clauses and sentences.

PLENARY ACTIVITY
- **Review; 5 minutes**
  Ask the student to review, summarise and evaluate their understanding of the skills and content required to be successful in this kind of task.

HOMEWORK ACTIVITY
- **Complete your response; 30 minutes; page 51**
  Ensure the student is aware of the time constraints in the exam. Explain that their speed in planning and writing responses to this type of question will increase with practice. The success criteria are meant only as a guide to assess the student's progress throughout the lesson – a full mark scheme is provided in the corresponding Assessment Pack to this title.

SUPPORT IDEA
- **Structuring a comparison** The student can re-use the pair of points and evidence they chose in question three of the *Parallels and differences* sheet.

EXTENSION IDEA
- **Structuring a comparison** Challenge the student to experiment with different ways of structuring the paragraph, e.g. comparing points and then comparing evidence.

PROGRESS AND OBSERVATIONS

ENGLISH
Grades 5-9

Starter Activity: First Thoughts

Timing: 10 mins

Learning Objectives
- To be able to identify similarities and differences in two texts

Equipment
none

Read this Paper 2, Section A exam-style question.

> You need to refer to Source F: *London Labour and the London Poor* and Source A: *The Gastronomical Me* for this question.
>
> The food prepared on stalls in Victorian London and the food prepared in M F K Fisher's kitchen are different.
>
> Use details from **both** sources to write a summary of the differences.
>
> **[8 marks]**

Now compare these short extracts from the two sources below.

Source A: *The Gastronomical Me*

> The first thing I remember tasting and then wanting to taste again is the grayish-pink fuzz my grandmother skimmed from a spitting kettle of strawberry jam. I suppose I was about four.

Source B: *London Labour and the London Poor*

> The miscellaneous stalls include peas-soup, pickled whelks, sweetmeats, toys, tin-ware, elder-wine, and jewellery stands.
>
> The stalls occupied by costermongers for the sale of fish, fruit, vegetables, etc., are chiefly constructed of a double cross-trestle or moveable frame, or else of two trestles, each with three legs, upon which is laid a long deal board, or tray.

1. **What similarities can you identify?**

2. **What differences can you identify?**

Discuss your ideas with your tutor.

AQA ENGLISH — Grades 5-9

Main activity: Parallels and differences

Timing: 20 mins

Learning objectives
- To be able to identify similarities and differences in two texts

Equipment
- Source A: *The Gastronomical Me*
- Source F: *London Labour and the London Poor*

In Paper 2 of your exam, you will be asked to compare the content of two texts and identify any relevant differences. In order to do this, you first need to identify some parallel features. Firstly, you need to consider the key points in one text.

Look at one student's notes on Source F: *London Labour and the London Poor*.

Source F
- food for sale
- many different kinds of food
- food laid out/prepared on newspapers, barrels and old saucepans
- prepared in cold foggy London
- little detail given of people who make and sell

Source A
a) Is the food for sale?
b) Are there many different kinds of food?
c) How is the food laid out/prepared?
d) Where is it prepared?
e) Is there much detail about people making the food?

1. Now answer the questions above, identifying parallel points in Source A: *The Gastronomical Me* and noting any differences.

2. Which of the pairs of points above would you include in your comparison of the two texts? Highlight them.

3. Choose one of the pairs you highlighted and mark it with an asterisk*. Note down two short quotations you could use to support each of the points in your chosen pair.

Source F	Source A
1	1
2	2

ENGLISH
Grades 5-9

MAIN ACTIVITY: STRUCTURING A COMPARISON **TIMING: 15 MINS**

LEARNING OBJECTIVES
- To be able to structure a comparison of two texts

EQUIPMENT
- Source A: *The Gastronomical Me*
- Source F: *London Labour and the London Poor*

> You need to refer to Source F: *London Labour and the London Poor* and Source A: *The Gastronomical Me* for this question.
>
> The food prepared on stalls in Victorian London and the food prepared in M F K Fisher's kitchen are different.
>
> Use details from **both** sources to write a summary of the differences.
>
> [8 marks]

The key elements in a paragraph in response to this kind of Paper 2, Section A exam question are shown below.

| Source 1
A key point | Source 1
1 or 2 quotations | An adverbial or conjunction, signalling comparison

...whereas...
...while...
However
In contrast
On the other hand | Source 2
A comparable key point | Source 2
1 or 2 quotations |

1. Use the space above to plan a paragraph in response to the exam-style question. Base it on one of the pairs of points you identified in the *Parallels and differences* activity.

2. Use your notes to write a paragraph in response to the exam-style question.

....

....

....

....

....

....

....

AQA ENGLISH — Grades 5-9

HOMEWORK ACTIVITY: COMPLETE YOUR RESPONSE

TIMING: 30 MINS

LEARNING OBJECTIVES
- To be able to identify similarities and differences in two texts
- To be able to structure a comparison of two texts

EQUIPMENT
- Source A: *The Gastronomical Me* and Source F: *London Labour and the London Poor*

1. On a separate piece of paper, write a full response to the Paper 2, Section A exam-style question below. Use the checklist to remind yourself of the things you need to achieve in your response.

> You need to refer to Source F: *London Labour and the London Poor* and Source A: *The Gastronomical Me* for this question.
>
> The food prepared on stalls in Victorian London and the food prepared in M F K Fisher's kitchen are different.
>
> Use details from **both** sources to write a summary of the differences.
>
> [8 marks]

2. When you have written your response, check you have achieved all of the success criteria below.

   a) Tick all the criteria you feel you have achieved.

   - ☐ identified at least three significant differences
   - ☐ used a range of relevant evidence synthesised from **each** text to support **each** point
   - ☐ clearly signalled comparisons using adverbials and conjunctions, e.g. 'but', 'whereas', 'however', etc.
   - ☐ written in paragraphs
   - ☐ carefully checked for accurate spelling and punctuation, and clear written expression

   b) Look at any of the criteria you feel you have not achieved. Add to and improve your response so that you can tick all of them.

5 Answers

Starter activity: First thoughts

1. They both talk about food.
2. Example: one focuses on fruit and jam, the other on a variety of foods available from stalls in Victorian London.

Main activity: Parallels and differences

1. a) No, it is being preserved for the family to eat.
b) Not many – they are preserving fruit (strawberries, cherries, apricots)
c) Using enamelled pots, ladles, funnels
d) In a hot, dark kitchen
e) The writer creates a clear impression of her grandmother.
2. Student's own answer
3. Student's own answer

Main activity: Structuring a comparison

1. Student's own answer
2. Student's own answer. Check that the response includes all the key elements, clearly and fluently structured.

Homework activity: Complete your response

1.

Marks	Criteria
7–8 marks	<ul><li>Insightful inferences from both texts</li><li>A carefully selected range of relevant, focused evidence from both texts</li><li>A range of insightful differences between texts</li></ul>
5–6 marks	<ul><li>Clear inferences from both texts</li><li>A range of relevant, focused textual evidence from both texts</li><li>Clear differences between texts</li></ul>
3–4 marks	<ul><li>Some inference from one or both texts</li><li>Relevant and focused textual evidence from one or both texts</li><li>Significant differences between texts</li></ul>
1–2 marks	<ul><li>Largely literal understanding, rather than inferential</li><li>Largely relevant textual evidence from one or both texts</li><li>Simple differences between texts</li></ul>
No marks	<ul><li>No creditable response</li></ul>

2. Student's own answer. Ensure they have achieved all of the success criteria.

Glossary

Synthesise
To combine a number of things into a coherent whole

AQA ENGLISH — Grades 5-9

6 READING: ANALYSING WORDS, PHRASES AND LANGUAGE FEATURES 1

LEARNING OBJECTIVES
- To be able to identify the writer's intention
- To be able to identify patterns of vocabulary choice

SPECIFICATION LINKS
- 3.1.1 evaluation of a writer's choice of vocabulary, form, grammatical and structural features

STARTER ACTIVITY
- **Intentions; 10 minutes; page 54**
  Ensure understanding of form, purpose and intention. Explain that the writer's intention is achieved through their selection of ideas and their use of language, working in tandem. Encourage the student to talk through their thought processes as they arrange forms, purposes and intentions in different ways.

MAIN ACTIVITIES
- **Identifying intentions; 15 minutes; page 55**
  Ask the student to number the paragraphs in the source, sharing and explaining their thought processes. Ensure the writer's intentions in each paragraph are noted as succinctly as possible, avoiding duplication.
- **Identifying patterns of language; 20 minutes; page 56**
  Ensure focus on the relationship between intention and language choice.

PLENARY ACTIVITY
- **Review; 5 minutes**
  Ask the student to evaluate their understanding of intention and language choices, and assess their confidence in their ability to complete the homework task.

HOMEWORK ACTIVITY
- **Annotating the text; 30 minutes; page 57**
  Ensure the student understands that the task is to annotate the text in preparation for writing a response, not to write a full response to the question.

SUPPORT IDEA
- **Identifying intention** Use the examples of intention in the starter activity to prompt thoughts about the writer's intentions in the source, e.g. to introduce a character, to create a sense of mystery, etc.

EXTENSION IDEAS
- **Intentions** Challenge the student to suggest other intentions that the writer of a specific form/purpose might have.
- **Identifying patterns of language** Challenge the student to explore the writer's choices further, e.g. why does the writer not explicitly refer to the funeral?

PROGRESS AND OBSERVATIONS

ENGLISH
Grades 5-9

STARTER ACTIVITY: INTENTIONS   **TIMING: 10 MINS**

LEARNING OBJECTIVES
- To be able to identify the writer's intention

EQUIPMENT
- scissors

A text always has:
- a **form** – the kind of text it is
- at least one **purpose** – the point of writing it
- at least one **intention** – the impact the writer wants their ideas and language choices to have on the reader.

1. Cut out the examples of form, purpose and intention below. Match them together in as many different ways as you can.

Form

| a novel | a newspaper article | an encyclopaedia entry |

Purpose

| to describe | to argue | to inform | to explain | to entertain |

Intention

| to create a sense of mystery | to create a vivid image | to prompt questions in the reader | to suggest the writer's expertise and authority |

| to influence the reader's opinion | to engage the reader's interest | to introduce a character |

54

ENGLISH
Grades 5-9

MAIN ACTIVITY: IDENTIFYING INTENTIONS

TIMING: 15 MINS

LEARNING OBJECTIVES
- To be able to identify the writer's intention

EQUIPMENT
- Source E: *The Ocean at the End of the Lane*

Read Source E: *The Ocean at the End of the Lane*.

1. Reread the source, thinking carefully about the impact the writer is aiming to achieve in each paragraph. Complete the summary below, circling the relevant paragraph numbers and noting the writer's different intentions.

In paragraph(s):   1   2   3   4   5   6   7   8   9   10   11
The writer's intention is to:
- ....
- ....

In paragraph(s):   1   2   3   4   5   6   7   8   9   10   11
The writer's intention is to:
- ....
- ....

In paragraph(s):   1   2   3   4   5   6   7   8   9   10   11
The writer's intention is to:
- ....
- ....

In paragraph(s):   1   2   3   4   5   6   7   8   9   10   11
The writer's intention is to:
- ....
- ....

ENGLISH
— Grades 5-9 —

MAIN ACTIVITY: IDENTIFYING PATTERNS OF LANGUAGE   **TIMING: 20 MINS**

LEARNING OBJECTIVES
- To be able to identify patterns of vocabulary choice

EQUIPMENT
none

Source E is the opening of a novel, and is set on the day of a family funeral. However, the writer does not state this directly.

1. Underline any words or phrases in the extract below from which you can infer that it is set on the day of a funeral.

> I wore a black suit and a white shirt, a black tie and black shoes, all polished and shiny: clothes that normally would make me feel uncomfortable, as if I were in a stolen uniform, or pretending to be an adult. Today they gave me comfort, of a kind. I was wearing the right clothes for a hard day.
>
> I had done my duty in the morning, spoken the words I was meant to speak, and I meant them as I spoke them, and then, when the service was done, I got in my car and I drove, randomly, without a plan, with an hour or so to kill before I met more people I had not seen for years and shook more hands and drank too many cups of tea from the best china.

2. Now read the extract again, circling any words or phrases that suggest the narrator's thoughts and feelings about the funeral.

3. Annotate the words and phrases you have circled, thinking about the writer's intention and what their language choices suggest about the narrator's thoughts and feelings about the funeral.

4. Can you identify any patterns or connections between the language choices you have noted? Write two or three sentences below, explaining your ideas.

AQA ENGLISH — Grades 5-9

Homework activity: Annotating the text

Timing: 30 mins

Learning objectives
- To be able to identify patterns of vocabulary choice

Equipment
- Source E: *The Ocean at the End of the Lane*

Read this Paper 1, Section A exam-style question.

Look in detail at this extract from **lines 22 to 29** of the source.

> It was time, I knew, to drive to my sister's bustling, cheerful house, all tidied and stiff for the day. I would talk to people whose existence I had forgotten years before and they would ask me about my marriage (failed a decade ago, a relationship that had slowly frayed until eventually, as they always seem to, it broke) and whether I was seeing anyone (I wasn't; I was not even sure that I could, not yet), and they would ask about my children (all grown up, they have their own lives, they wish they could be here today), and work (doing fine, thank you, I would say, never knowing how to talk about what I do. If I could talk about it, I would not have to do it. I make art, sometimes I make true art, and sometimes it fills the empty places in my life. Some of them. Not all). We would talk about the departed; we would remember the dead.

How does the writer use language to present the narrator to the reader?

You could include the writer's choice of:

- words and phrases
- language features and techniques
- sentence forms.

[8 marks]

---

1. Circle any relevant words, phrases and language features you could comment on in a response to the question.

2. Annotate the words and phrases you have circled, thinking about the writer's intention and what their language choices suggest about the narrator.

3. Can you see any patterns or connections between the language choices you noted? Write two or three sentences below, explaining your ideas.

ENGLISH
— Grades 5-9 —

6 ANSWERS

STARTER ACTIVITY: INTENTIONS
1. Examples: a novel, to entertain, to engage the reader's interest; a newspaper article, to argue, to influence the reader's opinion; an encyclopaedia entry, to inform, to suggest the writer's expertise and authority.

MAIN ACTIVITY: IDENTIFYING INTENTIONS
1. Examples:
In paragraphs 1, 2, 5, 6, 7 and 8, the writer's intention is to introduce character and setting.
In paragraphs 3, 4, 9, 10 and 11, the writer's intention is to intrigue the reader and create a sense of mystery.

MAIN ACTIVITY: IDENTIFYING PATTERNS OF LANGUAGE
1. Examples: 'black suit', 'black tie and black shoes', 'a hard day', 'service'
2. Examples: 'uncomfortable', 'comfort', 'a hard day', 'duty', 'randomly'
3. Student's own answers
4. Examples: The emotional impact of the funeral on the narrator ('comfort', 'A hard day', 'randomly') contrasts with the sense of unemotional formality and duty ('duty', 'shook more hands', 'best china').

HOMEWORK ACTIVITY: ANNOTATING THE TEXT
1. Examples: 'failed', 'frayed', 'broke', 'their own lives', 'empty places'
2. Student's own answers
3. Examples: difficult emotional issues, perhaps loneliness, are suggested by 'failed', 'frayed', 'broke'; his children have 'their own lives'; his life has 'empty places'.

GLOSSARY

Writer's intention
The impact or influence that the writer wants their text to have on the reader

58

AQA ENGLISH — Grades 5–9

7 READING: ANALYSING WORDS, PHRASES AND LANGUAGE FEATURES 2

LEARNING OBJECTIVES
- To be able to identify significant language choices
- To be able to explore language and mood
- To be able to explore a range of responses to language choice

SPECIFICATION LINKS
- 3.1.1 evaluation of a writer's choice of vocabulary, form, grammatical and structural features

STARTER ACTIVITY
- **Rich language; 5 minutes; page 60**
  Work with the student to identify significant, rich language choices that might be worth further investigation. Which have been chosen to convey explicit meaning, and which to achieve the writer's intention?

MAIN ACTIVITIES
- **Connotation and mood; 20 minutes; page 61**
  Ensure understanding of connotation and mood, referring to the Glossary definitions if required.
- **Different responses; 20 minutes; page 62**
  Ensure the student considers two or more possible responses.

PLENARY ACTIVITY
- **Review; 5 minutes**
  Ask the student to consider why Dickens chose to refer to bloodshed indirectly, rather than use the word 'blood'. How does this choice affect the mood created? How would the word 'blood' alter it? How might it provoke different responses from a range of readers?

HOMEWORK ACTIVITY
- **Write your response; 30 minutes; page 63**
  Explain that in the exam, this style of question will also ask for comment on sentence forms (which will be the focus of lessons 9 and 10), but in this task the student need focus on words and phrases only. The success criteria are meant only as a guide to assess the student's progress throughout the lesson – a full mark scheme is provided in the corresponding Assessment Pack to this title.

SUPPORT IDEAS
- **Rich language** Begin by eliminating non-lexical vocabulary, e.g. 'what', 'is'; then focus on lexical vocabulary, e.g. 'ding', 'clash', 'iron', 'armour-plated'.
- **Connotation and mood** Focus on identifying representative language choices rather than complete range. Prompt with suggestions of possible moods created in the extract, e.g. tension, danger, chaos, busyness, etc.

EXTENSION IDEA
- **Throughout** Challenge the student to consider the widest possible range of responses and explore them in depth.

PROGRESS AND OBSERVATIONS

ENGLISH
Grades 5-9

STARTER ACTIVITY: RICH LANGUAGE　　　　　　　　　**TIMING: 5 MINS**

LEARNING OBJECTIVES
- To be able to identify significant language choices

EQUIPMENT
none

Look at the opening sentences of Source B: *The Uncommercial Traveller*. The writer is describing a warship, the Achilles, being built.

> Ding, Clash, Dong, BANG, Boom, Rattle, Clash, BANG, Clink, BANG, Dong, BANG, Clatter, BANG BANG BANG! What on earth is this! This is, or soon will be, the Achilles, iron armour-plated ship.

1. Underline any choices of words, phrases or language features that you might be able to comment on.

AQA ENGLISH
Grades 5-9

MAIN ACTIVITY: CONNOTATION AND MOOD   **TIMING: 20 MINS**

LEARNING OBJECTIVES
- To be able to identify significant language choices
- To be able to explore language and mood
- To be able to explore a range of responses to language choice

EQUIPMENT
- highlighters

Look closely at this opening section of Source B: *The Uncommercial Traveller*.

> Ding, Clash, Dong, BANG, Boom, Rattle, Clash, BANG, Clink, BANG, Dong, BANG, Clatter, BANG BANG BANG! What on earth is this! This is, or soon will be, the Achilles, iron armour-plated ship. Twelve hundred men are working at her now; twelve hundred men working on stages over her sides, over her bows, over her stern, under her keel, between her decks, down in her hold, within her and without, crawling and creeping into the finest curves of her lines wherever it is possible for men to twist. Twelve hundred hammerers, measurers, caulkers, armourers, forgers, smiths, shipwrights; twelve hundred dingers, clashers, dongers, rattlers, clinkers, bangers bangers bangers!

1. **Highlight the text to identify significant language choices.**
   - use one colour for the words used to describe the ship itself
   - use another colour for the words used to describe the building of the ship
   - use another colour for the words used to describe the ship-builders.

2. **Think about the connotations of those language choices – the ideas and impressions that each word and phrase creates.**

    a) Annotate the words and phrases you have marked, noting what each suggests about the ship and the people building it.
    b) Write two or three sentences summarising your ideas about the writer's use of language in this section.

----

3. **How would you describe the mood or atmosphere created in the extract? Write two or three different words to describe it.**

----

4. **Which words in the extract contribute most powerfully to the mood, or moods, you have noted? Tick up to five.**

ENGLISH
Grades 5-9

MAIN ACTIVITY: DIFFERENT RESPONSES **TIMING: 20 MINS**

LEARNING OBJECTIVES
- To be able to explore language and mood
- To be able to explore a range of responses to language choice

EQUIPMENT
none

Now read the next section of Source B: *The Uncommercial Traveller*.

> Yet all this stupendous uproar around the rising Achilles is as nothing to the reverberations with which the perfected Achilles shall resound upon the dreadful day when the full work is in hand for which this is but note of preparation – the day when the scuppers that are now fitting like great, dry, thirsty conduit-pipes, shall run red.

1. Has the mood changed? Write two or three words to describe the mood in this section of the source.

2. Find four language choices in the extract that make a powerful contribution to the mood. Write one in the middle of each spider diagram.

3. Now think about the connotations of each word or phrase you have written below. Complete the spider diagrams with ideas about the ideas and impressions conjured up by each one. Add more legs if you need to.

ENGLISH
Grades 5-9

HOMEWORK ACTIVITY: WRITE YOUR RESPONSE **TIMING: 30 MINS**

LEARNING OBJECTIVES
- To be able to explore language and mood
- To be able to explore a range of responses to language choice

EQUIPMENT
none

1. Write your response to this Paper 2, Section A exam-style question on a separate piece of paper.

> You now need to refer to Source B: *The Uncommercial Traveller*, from **lines 1 to 11**.
>
> How does Dickens use language to make you, the reader, feel as though you are in the shipyard, watching the building of the Achilles?
>
> [12 marks]

2. When you have written your response, check you have achieved all of the success criteria below.

   a) Tick all the criteria you feel you have achieved.

   - ☐ focused on the writer's language choices
   - ☐ commented on the connotations of the writer's language choices
   - ☐ commented on the impact of the writer's language choices
   - ☐ commented on the moods created in the extract
   - ☐ explored different possible responses to the writer's language choices
   - ☐ written in paragraphs
   - ☐ carefully checked for accurate spelling and punctuation, and clear written expression

   b) Look at any of the criteria you feel you have not achieved. Add to and improve your response so that you can tick all of them.

7 ANSWERS

STARTER ACTIVITY: RICH LANGUAGE

1. Examples: 'Ding, Clash, Dong, BANG, Boom, Rattle... Clatter', 'iron armour-plated ship'

MAIN ACTIVITY: CONNOTATION AND MOOD

1. Student's own answers
2. a) Student's own answers
b) Examples: The writer suggests the chaotic noise of the shipyard and his enthusiasm for it through an almost child-like overuse of onomatopoeia. He conveys the strength, scale and beauty of the ship through the number and variety of people building her, and his description of the 'finest curves of her lines'. The workers are belittled, 'crawling... creeping', reinforcing the scale of the vessel.
3. Examples: chaotic, enthusiastic.
4. Student's own answers

MAIN ACTIVITY: DIFFERENT RESPONSES

1. Examples: serious, frightening, threatening.
2. Examples: 'stupendous uproar', 'dreadful day', 'run red'.
3. Student's own answers

HOMEWORK ACTIVITY: WRITE YOUR RESPONSE

1.

Marks	Criteria
10–12 marks	• Clear and detailed analysis of the effect of the writer's language choices • A carefully selected range of relevant, focused textual evidence • A range of subject terminology to achieve clarity and precision
7–9 marks	• Clear comments on the effect of the writer's language choices • A range of relevant, focused textual evidence • A range of subject terminology to achieve clarity
4–6 marks	• Some comments on the effect of the writer's language choices • Relevant and focused textual evidence • Largely accurate subject terminology
1–3 marks	• Straightforward comments on the effect of the writer's language choices • Largely relevant textual evidence • Some use of subject terminology, with inconsistent accuracy
No marks	• No creditable response

2. Ensure the student has achieved all, or the majority of, the success criteria.

GLOSSARY

Connotation
The ideas or feelings that vocabulary choices can suggest to the reader

Mood
The atmosphere, tone or overall impression created through the writer's language choice

AQA ENGLISH — Grades 5-9

8 READING: ANALYSING WORDS, PHRASES AND LANGUAGE FEATURES 3

LEARNING OBJECTIVES
- To be able to analyse the writer's language choices in depth and detail
- To be able to structure an effective response

SPECIFICATION LINKS
- 3.1.1 evaluation of a writer's choice of vocabulary, form, grammatical and structural features

STARTER ACTIVITY
- **First thoughts; 5 minutes; page 66**
  Give the student two minutes to read the exam-style question and extract, then discuss how they might begin to approach it. Direct the student to identify and consider the impact of relevant and significant language choices in the text. The student will need to refer to this exam-style question throughout the lesson.

MAIN ACTIVITIES
- **Developing analysis; 20 minutes; page 67**
  Explain to the student that this activity consolidates the analysis skills they have developed over the last two lessons. Focus them on one row at a time: first considering the broad impact of the writer's choices, then refining that response to focus on specific vocabulary choices and, finally, a variety of possible responses.
- **Structuring a response; 20 minutes; page 68**
  Note that Student A's paragraph follows a very formulaic 'Point, Evidence, Explain' structure, while Student B's achieves all the same features (and more) from a focus on the writer's intention and the impressions created in the extract. Point out that these paragraphs are taken from quite extreme ends of the spectrum: from competent to exceptional.

PLENARY ACTIVITY
- **Review; 5 minutes**
  Ask the student to review, summarise and evaluate their learning in the lesson and their confidence in successfully completing the homework task.

HOMEWORK ACTIVITY
- **Write your response; 30 minutes; page 69**
  Explain that in the exam, this style of question will also ask for comment on sentence forms (which will be the focus of lessons 9 and 10), but in this task they need focus on words and phrases only.

SUPPORT IDEA
- **Structuring a response** Use Student B's response to model and develop understanding of those elements that the student felt less confident in achieving in the previous activity.

EXTENSION IDEA
- **Developing analysis** Encourage the student to use the second and third layers of analysis to focus on those ideas noted in the first.

PROGRESS AND OBSERVATIONS

ENGLISH
Grades 5–9

STARTER ACTIVITY: FIRST THOUGHTS

TIMING: 5 MINS

LEARNING OBJECTIVES
- To be able to analyse the writer's language choices in depth and detail

EQUIPMENT
none

Read this Paper 1, Section A exam-style question. How would you begin to approach it?

> Look in detail at this extract from **lines 1 to 14** of Source D: *One Hundred Years of Solitude*
>
> Many years later as he faced the firing squad, Colonel Aureliano Buendía was to remember that distant afternoon when his father took him to discover ice. At that time Macondo was a village of twenty adobe houses, built on the bank of a river of clear water that ran along a bed of polished stones, which were white and enormous, like prehistoric eggs. The world was so recent that many things lacked names, and in order to indicate them it was necessary to point. Every year during the month of March a family of ragged gypsies would set up their tents near the village, and with a great uproar of pipes and kettledrums they would display new inventions. First they brought the magnet. A heavy gypsy with an untamed beard and sparrow hands, who introduced himself as Melquíades, put on a bold public demonstration of what he himself called the eighth wonder of the learned alchemists of Macedonia. He went from house to house dragging two metal ingots and everybody was amazed to see pots, pans, tongs, and braziers tumble down from their places and beams creak from the desperation of nails and screws trying to emerge, and even objects that had been lost for a long time appeared from where they had been searched for most and went dragging along in turbulent confusion behind Melquíades' magical irons. 'Things have a life of their own,' the gypsy proclaimed with a harsh accent. 'It's simply a matter of waking up their souls.'
>
> How does the writer use language here to describe the lives of the people of Macondo?
>
> You could include the writer's choice of:
> - words and phrases
> - language features and techniques
> - sentence forms.
>
> **[8 marks]**

AQA ENGLISH
Grades 5-9

MAIN ACTIVITY: DEVELOPING ANALYSIS   **TIMING: 20 MINS**

LEARNING OBJECTIVES
- To be able to analyse the writer's language choices in depth and detail

EQUIPMENT
- *First thoughts* starter activity

1. Focus your analytical skills on the writer's language choices in quotation A or B below – or select another quotation that makes a significant contribution to the description of the lives of the people of Macondo and write it in box C.

A. a river of clear water that ran along a bed of polished stones, which were white and enormous, like prehistoric eggs

B. 'Things have a life of their own,' the gypsy proclaimed with a harsh accent. 'It's simply a matter of waking up their souls.'

C.

2. Use the space below to gather your ideas about the writer's language choices and their impact in your chosen quotation.

The writer's intentions	Impressions created	Mood created

Patterns of vocabulary choice	Connotations	Impact

Different possible responses

ENGLISH
— Grades 5-9 —

AQA

MAIN ACTIVITY: STRUCTURING A RESPONSE	TIMING: 20 MINS

LEARNING OBJECTIVES
- To be able to structure an effective response

EQUIPMENT
- *First thoughts* starter activity

Compare these two paragraphs, taken from two students' responses to the exam-style question.

Student A

> The writer shows how the people of Macondo think and live: 'The world was so recent that many things lacked names'. The word 'recent' sounds like this all happened at the beginning of time. It suggests how primitive and naïve the people of Macondo are, so it is not surprising that they are easily taken in by Melquiades selling them magnets.

Student B

> The writer creates the atmosphere of a myth in the extract, suggesting that the people of Macondo lived in a distant past. The writer describes the world as 'recent', suggesting it is newly made and that everything is waiting to be discovered and named. This is reflected in the image of the rocks at the bottom of the river being compared to 'prehistoric eggs', creating an impression of a new world waiting to be hatched. However, it could also suggest the primitive naivety of the people of Macondo who 'point' because so 'many things lacked names' and believe that magnets are 'magical'.

1. Which paragraph is more effective? Why? Write a sentence or two explaining your ideas.

....
....
....
....
....

2. Now think about the structure of each paragraph. Underline where each student achieves some or all of the features below, labelling the underlined text a, b, c etc.

   a) makes a clear point
   b) supports with evidence
   c) analyses intention and impressions
   d) analyses impact and connotations of vocabulary choices
   e) identifies and analyses patterns of vocabulary
   f) explores different responses

AQA ENGLISH
Grades 5-9

HOMEWORK ACTIVITY: WRITE YOUR RESPONSE **TIMING: 30 MINS**

LEARNING OBJECTIVES
- To be able to analyse the writer's language choices in depth and detail
- To be able to structure an effective response

EQUIPMENT
none

1. Write your response to this Paper 1, Section A exam-style question on a separate piece of paper.

> Look in detail at this extract from **lines 1 to 14** of Source D: *One Hundred Years of Solitude*
>
> > Many years later as he faced the firing squad, Colonel Aureliano Buendía was to remember that distant afternoon when his father took him to discover ice. At that time Macondo was a village of twenty adobe houses, built on the bank of a river of clear water that ran along a bed of polished stones, which were white and enormous, like prehistoric eggs. The world was so recent that many things lacked names, and in order to indicate them it was necessary to point. Every year during the month of March a family of ragged gypsies would set up their tents near the village, and with a great uproar of pipes and kettledrums they would display new inventions. First they brought the magnet. A heavy gypsy with an untamed beard and sparrow hands, who introduced himself as Melquíades, put on a bold public demonstration of what he himself called the eighth wonder of the learned alchemists of Macedonia. He went from house to house dragging two metal ingots and everybody was amazed to see pots, pans, tongs, and braziers tumble down from their places and beams creak from the desperation of nails and screws trying to emerge, and even objects that had been lost for a long time appeared from where they had been searched for most and went dragging along in turbulent confusion behind Melquíades' magical irons. 'Things have a life of their own,' the gypsy proclaimed with a harsh accent. 'It's simply a matter of waking up their souls.'
>
> How does the writer use language here to describe the lives of the people of Macondo?
>
> You could include the writer's choice of:
> - words and phrases
> - language features and techniques
> - sentence forms.
>
> [8 marks]

2. When you have written your response, check you have achieved all of the success criteria below.

   a) Tick the criteria you feel you have achieved.
   - ☐ focused on the writer's language choices
   - ☐ analysed the writer's intentions and the impressions they have created in the text
   - ☐ analysed the impact and connotations of the writer's language choices
   - ☐ analysed patterns of language choices
   - ☐ explored different possible responses to the writer's language choices
   - ☐ written in paragraphs
   - ☐ carefully checked for accurate spelling and punctuation, and clear written expression

   b) Look at any of the criteria you feel you have not achieved. Add to and improve your response so that you can tick all of them.

8 ANSWERS

STARTER ACTIVITY: FIRST THOUGHTS

Student's own answers

MAIN ACTIVITY: DEVELOPING ANALYSIS

1. Exam-style mark scheme:

AO2
- Explain, comment on and analyse how writers use language and structure to achieve effects and influence readers, using relevant subject terminology to support their views

This question focuses on language only.

Level	Skills descriptors
Level 4 7–8 marks	• Clear and detailed analysis of the effect of the writer's language choices • A carefully selected range of relevant, focused textual evidence • A range of subject terminology to achieve clarity and precision
Level 3 5–6 marks	• Clear comments on the effect of the writer's language choices • A range of relevant, focused textual evidence • A range of subject terminology to achieve clarity
Level 2 3–4 marks	• Some comments on the effect of the writer's language choices • Relevant and focused textual evidence • Largely accurate use of subject terminology
Level 1 1–2 marks	• Straightforward comments on the effect of the writer's language choices • Largely relevant textual evidence • Some use of subject terminology, with inconsistent accuracy
Level 0 No marks	• No comments on the writer's use of language • No rewardable response

2. Examples:

The writer creates an impression of pure and simple beauty, describing the 'clear water', the 'polished stones'.

The comparison to 'prehistoric eggs' suggests an ancient, even alien landscape in which life is about to develop.

The gypsy's claims suggest the naïve credulity of the people of Macondo or, perhaps, their primitive animistic beliefs in the 'life' and 'soul' within inanimate objects.

MAIN ACTIVITY: STRUCTURING A RESPONSE

1. Student B's paragraph features much greater depth and detail of analysis.
2. Student A:
a) The writer shows how people in Macondo think and live
b) 'The world was so recent that many things lacked names.'
d) It suggests how primitive...
Student B:
b) The writer describes the world as 'recent'
c) The writer creates an atmosphere...
d) ...creating an impression of a new world waiting to be hatched.
e) This is reflected in the image of...
f) However, it could also suggest...

HOMEWORK ACTIVITY: WRITE YOUR RESPONSE

1. See exam-style mark scheme for *Main activity: Developing analysis* question 1.
2. Student's own answer. Ensure they have achieved all, or the majority of, the success criteria.

AQA ENGLISH — Grades 5–9

9 READING: ANALYSING SENTENCE FORMS 1

LEARNING OBJECTIVES
- To be able to identify significant sentence forms
- To be able to analyse the impact of sentence forms

SPECIFICATION LINK
- 3.1.1 evaluation of a writer's choice of vocabulary, form and grammatical and structural features

STARTER ACTIVITY
- **Thinking about sentence forms; 10 minutes; page 72**
  Ask the student to read Source D: *One Hundred Years of Solitude* (page 20). Point out that this is a challenging text, in both its content and use of sentence forms. Assess awareness of sentence forms and their significance by focusing attention initially on question 1 only. Use the response to question 2 to assess confidence in analysing sentence forms.

MAIN ACTIVITIES
- **Identifying sentence forms; 20 minutes; page 73**
  Ask the student to complete the tasks, first identifying and eliminating the most apparent sentence forms, before moving on to the more challenging ones. Encourage them to choose sentences A, B or D to complete question 2. Ask them to consider how the newly structured sentence alters the original's emphasis and/or impact.
- **Sentence structure and effect; 15 minutes; page 74**
  Encourage the student to carefully explore the model response and discuss their analysis of their chosen sentence before committing it to writing.

PLENARY ACTIVITY
- **Review; 5 minutes**
  Ask the student to sum up their understanding of the ways in which sentences can be structured, and rate their confidence in analysing impact of structural choices.

HOMEWORK ACTIVITY
- **Writing sentence forms; 30 minutes; page 75**
  Discuss initial ideas, focusing on intention, and consider ways in which sentence forms could contribute to achieving intentions.

SUPPORT IDEAS
- **Identifying sentence forms** Model ways in which sentences can be re-structured, swapping clauses, repositioning adverbials, replacing conjunctions, etc.
- **Sentence structure and effect** Suggest that the student chooses the sentence that they feel most confident in analysing.

EXTENSION IDEAS
- **Identifying sentence forms** Ask the student to restructure two or more of the given sentences.
- **Sentence structure and effect** Challenge the student to analyse intention and impact as fully as possible.

PROGRESS AND OBSERVATIONS

ENGLISH
— Grades 5–9 —

AQA

Starter activity: Thinking about sentence forms

Timing: 10 mins

Learning objectives
- To be able to identify significant sentence forms
- To be able to analyse the impact of sentence forms

Equipment
- Source D: *One Hundred Years of Solitude*

Read Source D: *One Hundred Years of Solitude*.

1. Look at the source again. Underline two sentence structures that you feel have a significant impact. Think about whether they are single clause, multi-clause, compound or complex sentences.

2. Explain the impact of each of the sentence structures you have selected.

....

....

....

....

....

....

....

....

AQA ENGLISH — Grades 5-9

MAIN ACTIVITY: IDENTIFYING SENTENCE FORMS **TIMING: 20 MINS**

LEARNING OBJECTIVES
- To be able to identify significant sentence forms

EQUIPMENT
none

Look at these types of sentence form and examples from Source D: *One Hundred Years of Solitude*.

1. Long sentences
Multiple clauses suggest a sequence of connected events, pace of action, the range and variety of ideas or elements, etc.

2. Short sentences
These often add dramatic emphasis to an idea or suggest a tone of anger or impatience.

3. Balanced sentences
These feature two parts, both of equal importance (not necessarily of equal length), usually linked with coordinating conjunctions, e.g. 'but' or 'and', sometimes to link related ideas or to contrast them.

4. Fronted information
Significant information is positioned at the front of the sentence, for emphasis and/or to manipulate the reader's response to the rest of the sentence.

5. Delayed information
Significant information is positioned at the end of the sentence, as a kind of punchline or resolution to the tension built through the ideas that precede it.

A. For several months he worked hard to demonstrate the truth of his idea.

B. Melquíades, who was an honest man, warned him: "It won't work for that."

C. He went from house to house dragging two metal ingots and everybody was amazed to see pots, pans, tongs, and braziers tumble down from their places and beams creak from the desperation of nails and screws trying to emerge, and even objects that had been lost for a long time appeared from where they had been searched for most and went dragging along in turbulent confusion behind Melquíades' magical irons.

D. Úrsula Iguarán, his wife, who relied on those animals to increase their poor domestic holdings, was unable to dissuade him.

E. They placed a gypsy woman at one end of the village and set up the telescope at the entrance to the tent

1. Draw lines linking the definitions on the left with the sentences from the source on the right, to identify the sentence form the writer has used in each case.

2. Focus on one of these sentences from the source. Rewrite the sentence, keeping exactly the same meaning but changing the structure.

ENGLISH
Grades 5-9

AQA

| MAIN ACTIVITY: SENTENCE STRUCTURE AND EFFECT | TIMING: 15 MINS |

LEARNING OBJECTIVES
- To be able to analyse the impact of sentence forms
- To be able to identify sentence forms

EQUIPMENT
none

Look again at sentence C.

> He went from house to house dragging two metal ingots and everybody was amazed to see pots, pans, tongs, and braziers tumble down from their places and beams creak from the desperation of nails and screws trying to emerge, and even objects that had been lost for a long time appeared from where they had been searched for most and went dragging along in turbulent confusion behind Melquíades' magical irons.

Now look at one student's analysis of the writer's use of sentence form.

> The writer uses a long sentence and links clauses with the conjunction 'and' in order to emphasise the number of amazing things the 'magical irons' are capable of. This suggests why they so greatly impress the primitive people of Macondo. The writer lists the 'pots, pans, tongs and braziers', the 'nails and screws' and 'objects that had been lost', all contributing to the 'turbulent confusion' that demonstrates the incredible and impressive power of the magnets.

1. **Underline and label the key points in the analysis.**
    a) Underline where the student has highlighted how the writer has structured the sentence. Label it 'how'.
    b) Underline where they have explained why the writer has structured the sentence like this. Label it 'why'.
    c) Underline where they have explored the impact of the sentence structure. Label it 'impact'.

2. **Now choose another sentence from the previous activity.**
   Think about:
    - what is emphasised, highlighted or suggested by its form
    - how it contributes to the writer's intention.

3. **Write a short analysis of the writer's use of form in your chosen sentence. Use the elements you identified in the response above to help you.**

....

....

....

....

....

4. **Look again at your analysis. Underline and label where you have:**
    - highlighted how the writer has structured the sentence
    - analysed why the writer has structured it in this way
    - explored the impact of the writer's choice of sentence structure.

AQA ENGLISH — Grades 5-9

HOMEWORK ACTIVITY: WRITING SENTENCE FORMS   **TIMING: 30 MINS**

LEARNING OBJECTIVES
- To be able to analyse the impact of sentence forms

EQUIPMENT
none

You are going to write the opening to an imaginative writing task about the arrival of a visitor who has a significant impact on a group of people's lives. You will come across a similar question in Paper 1, Section B of the exam.

Your opening should:
- introduce the characters
- introduce the setting
- describe the visitor's arrival, and the impact it has.

1. Use the space below to note down some ideas about characters and setting.

Characters	Setting

2. On a separate piece of paper, write the first 100–150 words of your story.

3. Review your choice of sentence forms. Identify and revise any sentences that could have greater impact or make a more significant contribution to your intention.

4. Annotate each of the sentences you have structured for impact and effect.
   Think about:
   - how you have structured it
   - the impact and effect you intend it to have.

9 Answers

STARTER ACTIVITY: THINKING ABOUT SENTENCE FORMS
1. Student's own answers
2. Student's own answer. Ensure analysis focuses on impact.

MAIN ACTIVITY: IDENTIFYING SENTENCE FORMS
1. 1 C; 2 A, B; 3 E; 4 A; 5 D, B
2. Examples:
A: He worked hard for several months to demonstrate the truth of his idea. (The emphasis on the lengthy period of time is reduced.)
B: 'It won't work for that.' warned Melquíades who was an honest man. (The strength and impact of his warning are reduced.)
D: Úrsula Iguarán, his wife, was unable to dissuade him, even though she relied on those animals to increase their poor domestic holdings. (The dramatic emphasis on her husband's blind stubbornness is weakened.)

MAIN ACTIVITY: SENTENCE STRUCTURE AND EFFECT
1. Examples:
How: The writer uses a long sentence linking clauses with the conjunction 'and'.
Why: in order to emphasise the number of amazing things the 'magical irons' are capable of.
Impact: suggesting why they so greatly impress the primitive people of Macondo.
How: The writer lists the 'pots, pans, tongs and braziers', the 'nails and screws' and 'objects that had been lost'.
Why: all contributing to the 'turbulent confusion'.
Impact: that demonstrates the incredible and impressive power of the magnets.
2. Look for responses that identify the impact and its contribution to intention, e.g. an emphasis on the stubbornness and persistence of the character, suggesting his foolishness, naivety, etc.
3. Student's own answer
4. Student's own answer. Ensure they can show where they have highlighted sentence structure, analysed it and explored its impact.

HOMEWORK ACTIVITY: WRITING SENTENCE FORMS
1. Student's own answers
2. Student's own answer. Ensure they introduce the characters and setting, describe the visitor's arrival and explain the impact it has.
3. Student's own answer. Ensure response shows confidence in manipulating sentence structure for effect.
4. Student's own answer. Ensure annotations identify a range of sentence forms, crafted for impact.

Glossary

Single clause sentence
A sentence consisting of only one clause; also known as a simple sentence

Multi-clause sentence
A sentence consisting of two or more clauses; also known as a compound or complex sentence

Compound sentence
A sentence of two or more clauses of equal importance, linked by a co-ordinating conjunction, e.g. *and, but*

Complex sentence
A sentence of two or more clauses of differing importance (a main clause and at least one subordinate clause), linked by a subordinating conjunction, e.g. *because, although, if*, etc.

ENGLISH
Grades 5–9

10 READING: ANALYSING SENTENCE FORMS 2

LEARNING OBJECTIVES
- To be able to identify significant sentence forms
- To be able to analyse the impact of sentence forms

SPECIFICATION LINKS
- 3.1.1 evaluation of a writer's choice of vocabulary, form, grammatical and structural features

STARTER ACTIVITY
- **Refresher; 5 minutes; page 78**
Ask the student to complete the task, noting the kinds of sentence form used and their impact. Use the task to assess and highlight the student's growing awareness of sentence forms.

MAIN ACTIVITIES
- **Sentence types and repetition; 20 minutes; page 79**
Explain the difference between sentence form (its structure) and sentence type (its purpose). Point out that the question in the source ('What on earth...') is not marked with a question mark. Encourage the student to use the terms *repetition* (of single words or phrases) and *parallel structures* (repetition of grammatical constructions, e.g. 'To think that...').
- **Pace and tone; 20 minutes; page 80**
Clarify understanding of pace and tone, then ask the student to complete questions 1 and 2. Note the relationship between pace and tone (the hurried pace of the original version creates a tone of breathless excitement and enthusiasm). Ask the student to complete question 3. Note the use of 'Yet...' to signal the change of pace and tone.

PLENARY ACTIVITY
- **Review; 5 minutes**
Ask the student to compare the second sentence ('What on earth is this!') and the final sentence ('I wonder why only her anchors look small.') of Source B, noting the difference in pace, tone and impact. Note that sentence forms cannot be analysed by formula (e.g. short sentences do not necessarily create dramatic emphasis), and so content and context must also be taken into account.

HOMEWORK ACTIVITY
- **Write your response; 30 minutes; page 81**
Explain to the student that in the exam, this style of question will also ask for comment on words, phrases and language features (which are the focus of lessons 6–8), but in this task they need focus on sentence forms only.

SUPPORT IDEAS
- **Refresher** Use the prompts from the lesson 9 worksheet *Identifying sentence forms* to support identification and analysis.
- **Pace and tone** Read the extracts aloud with expression. Ask the student to note variations in tone and pace.

EXTENSION IDEA
- **Throughout** Challenge the student to consider the cumulative impact of sentence forms and the writer's choice of words, phrases and language features.

PROGRESS AND OBSERVATIONS

ENGLISH
— Grades 5-9 —

Starter activity: Refresher

Timing: 5 mins

Learning objectives
- To be able to identify significant sentence forms
- To be able to analyse the impact of sentence forms

Equipment
none

Read the first three sentences of Source B: *The Uncommercial Traveller*.

> Ding, Clash, Dong, BANG, Boom, Rattle, Clash, BANG, Clink, BANG, Dong, BANG, Clatter, BANG BANG BANG! What on earth is this! This is, or soon will be, the Achilles, iron armour-plated ship.

1. Annotate the extract, noting how the writer has used sentence forms.

AQA ENGLISH — Grades 5-9

MAIN ACTIVITY: SENTENCE TYPES AND REPETITION **TIMING: 20 MINS**

LEARNING OBJECTIVES
- To be able to identify significant sentence forms
- To be able to analyse the impact of sentence forms

EQUIPMENT
none

There are four types of sentence:
- **statement** – He is brave and daring.
- **question** – Do I dare?
- **exclamation** – How dare you!
- **command** – Be daring.

Statements are the most common sentence type. Commands, exclamations and questions are often used for effect.

Look again at the opening sentences of Source B: The *Uncommercial Traveller*.

> Ding, Clash, Dong, BANG, Boom, Rattle, Clash, BANG, Clink, BANG, Dong, BANG, Clatter, BANG BANG BANG! What on earth is this? This is, or soon will be, the Achilles, iron armour-plated ship.

1. How does this exclamatory question contribute to the writer's intended impact on the reader? Annotate the extract above, noting your ideas.

Read the end of the first paragraph of Source B.

> To think that this Achilles, monstrous compound of iron tank and oaken chest, can ever swim or roll! To think that any force of wind and wave could ever break her! To think that wherever I see a glowing red-hot iron point thrust out of her side from within – as I do now, there, and there, and there! – and two watching men on a stage without, with bared arms and sledge-hammers, strike at it fiercely, and repeat their blows until it is black and flat, I see a rivet being driven home, of which there are many in every iron plate, and thousands upon thousands in the ship!

2. How does this series of exclamations contribute to the writer's intended impact on the reader? Annotate the extract above, noting your ideas.
3. Circle any examples of repetition in the exclamations.
4. How does this repetition contribute to the writer's intended impact on the reader? Annotate the extract above, noting your ideas.
5. Write two sentences summarising how the writer uses exclamations, questions and repetition in Source B.

ENGLISH
Grades 5-9

| MAIN ACTIVITY: PACE AND TONE | TIMING: 20 MINS |

LEARNING OBJECTIVES
- To be able to identify significant sentence forms
- To be able to analyse the impact of sentence forms

EQUIPMENT
none

A writer's choice of sentence forms can have a significant impact on:
- **pace** – the speed at which ideas are presented or developed in the text
- **tone** – the 'voice' in which ideas are expressed.

Compare these two versions of the opening of Source B: *The Uncommercial Traveller.*

The original version

> Ding, Clash, Dong, BANG, Boom, Rattle, Clash, BANG, Clink, BANG, Dong, BANG, Clatter, BANG BANG BANG! What on earth is this! This is, or soon will be, the Achilles, iron armour-plated ship.

The rewritten version

> As I walked into the shipyard, I heard a great deal of noise and was, at first, not sure what I was looking at or where the noise was coming from. I later realised that I was witnessing the building of an armour-plated ship made of iron, named the Achilles.

1. How does the pace of the original version differ from the rewritten version? Annotate the original version, noting how the writer's use of sentence forms contributes to the text's pace.

2. How does the tone of the original version differ from the rewritten version? Annotate the original version, noting how the writer's use of sentence forms contributes to the text's tone.

Read another extract from Source B: *The Uncommercial Traveller.*

> Twelve hundred hammerers, measurers, caulkers, armourers, forgers, smiths, shipwrights; twelve hundred dingers, clashers, dongers, rattlers, clinkers, bangers bangers bangers! Yet all this stupendous uproar around the rising Achilles is as nothing to the reverberations with which the perfected Achilles shall resound upon the dreadful day when the full work is in hand for which this is but note of preparation – the day when the scuppers that are now fitting like great, dry, thirsty conduit-pipes, shall run red.

3. How do the pace and tone change in this extract? Annotate the text, noting how the writer's use of sentence forms contributes to the change of tone and pace.

ENGLISH
— Grades 5-9 —

HOMEWORK ACTIVITY: WRITE YOUR RESPONSE **TIMING: 30 MINS**

LEARNING OBJECTIVES
- To be able to identify significant sentence forms
- To be able to analyse the impact of sentence forms

EQUIPMENT
none

1. Write your response to this Paper 2, Section A exam-style question on a separate piece of paper.

> You now need to refer to Source B: *The Uncommercial Traveller*, from **lines 1 to 11**.
>
> How does Dickens use language to make you, the reader, feel as though you are in the shipyard, watching the building of the Achilles?
>
> [12 marks]

2. When you have written your response, check you have achieved all of the success criteria below.

   a) Tick the criteria you feel you have achieved.

   - ☐ focused on the writer's use of sentence forms
   - ☐ commented on the impact of the writer's use of sentence forms
   - ☐ explored how this impact supports the writer's intention
   - ☐ written in paragraphs
   - ☐ carefully checked for accurate spelling and punctuation, and clear written expression

   b) Look at any of the criteria you feel you have not achieved. Add to and improve your response so that you can tick all of them.

ENGLISH
Grades 5-9

10 Answers

STARTER ACTIVITY: REFRESHER

1. The lengthy list of onomatopoeic words and the short exclamation following them strongly suggest the noise of the shipyard and the writer's astonishment. The final short sentence form adds dramatic emphasis to the announcement of his subject matter.

MAIN ACTIVITY: SENTENCE TYPES AND REPETITION

1. The exclamatory question engages the reader and reflects the writer's surprise.
2. The exclamations suggest the writer's enthusiasm for the power of the ship.
3. 'To think that…'; 'there'
4. Repetition is used to add emphasis to the writer's enthusiasm, and to his vivid description of the quantity of rivets needed to build the ship.
5. Student's own answer

MAIN ACTIVITY: PACE AND TONE

1. The listing of the long sentence creates a frantic pace and a tone of frenzied excitement.
2. The short exclamatory question and final statement create the sense of a proud, declarative announcement.
3. The pace and tone change from a rapid series of enthusiastic exclamations of astonishment at the power of the ship, to one of calmer, quieter reflection on the deadly nature of that power. The change is signalled by the adverbial, 'Yet…'.

HOMEWORK ACTIVITY: WRITE YOUR RESPONSE

1.

Marks	Criteria
10–12 marks	• Clear and detailed analysis of the effect of the writer's language choices • A carefully selected range of relevant, focused textual evidence • A range of subject terminology to achieve clarity and precision
7–9 marks	• Clear comments on the effect of the writer's language choices • A range of relevant, focused textual evidence • A range of subject terminology to achieve clarity
4–6 marks	• Some comments on the effect of the writer's language choices • Relevant and focused textual evidence • Largely accurate subject terminology
1–3 marks	• Straightforward comments on the effect of the writer's language choices • Largely relevant textual evidence • Some use of subject terminology, with inconsistent accuracy
No marks	• No creditable response

2. Student's own answer. Ensure they have achieved all, or the majority of, the success criteria.

AQA ENGLISH — Grades 5–9

11 Reading: Developing language analysis

Learning objectives
- To be able to identify significant features of a text
- To be able to comment on the writer's choices of words, phrases, language features and sentence forms
- To be able to structure an effective analysis

Specification links
- 3.1.1 evaluation of a writer's choice of vocabulary, form, grammatical and structural features

Starter activity
- **Assessing an example; 10 minutes; page 84**
  Give the student five minutes to reread Source C: *Inside Facebook and Friends* (page 19), focusing on the first half of the text. As they complete the task, note where they select evidence that allows them to comment on the writer's use of both sentence forms and words, phrases and language features.

Main activities
- **Surveying the source; 20 minutes; page 85**
  Direct the student to select the richest features of the text, which allow the most detailed analysis.
- **Structuring your response; 15 minutes; page 86**
  Suggest that the student's final response should focus on at least three or four significant features of the source.

Plenary activity
- **Review; 5 minutes**
  Ask the student to review, evaluate and summarise their language analysis skills and their readiness to complete the homework task.

Homework activity
- **Write your response; 30 minutes; page 87**
  Remind the student of the importance of using key words from the question to focus their response, and paying close attention to the writer's intention in the text.

Support ideas
- **Surveying the source** Focus on each sentence in the extract in turn. What, if anything, is significant about that sentence's form? Prompt the student with examples of sentence forms explored in lessons 9 and 10.
- **Structuring your response** Prompt the student to identify patterns or similarities, e.g. both suggest the scale and recreational elements of the workplaces they describe.

Extension idea
- **Structuring your response** Challenge the student to identify and synthesise all the significant patterns in the writer's language.

Progress and observations

ENGLISH
— Grades 5–9 —

AQA

| STARTER ACTIVITY: ASSESSING AN EXAMPLE | TIMING: 10 MINS |

LEARNING OBJECTIVES
- To be able to comment on the writer's choice of words, phrases, language features and sentence forms

EQUIPMENT
- Source C: *Inside Facebook and Friends*

Read Source C: *Inside Facebook and Friends* and then look at this paragraph below from one student's response to the Paper 2, Section A exam-style question.

> You now need to refer only to Source C: *Inside Facebook and Friends* **from the beginning to line 20.**
>
> How does the writer use language to describe these workplaces?
>
> **[12 marks]**

> In opening sentence of the source, the writer presents an idyllic and surprising description of Samsung's headquarters: it has a "putting green" on the fifth floor which looks out over "a rolling horizon of sun-scorched mountains". This suggests a place of leisure and natural beauty, contrasting strongly with the word "headquarters", a contrast which is emphasised in the sentence form, delaying the reminder that "it's quite easy to forget you're at work" until the very end of the sentence. Immediately the writer creates the impression that these workplaces are not typical offices.

1. What has this student done well in their analysis? Annotate the paragraph.

ENGLISH
— Grades 5-9 —

MAIN ACTIVITY: SURVEYING THE SOURCE	**TIMING: 20 MINS**

LEARNING OBJECTIVES
- To be able to identify significant features of a text
- To be able to comment on the writer's choice of words, phrases, language features and sentence forms

EQUIPMENT
- Source C: *Inside Facebook and Friends*

In this lesson, you are going to focus on this exam-style question from Paper 2, Section A.

> You now need to refer only to Source C: *Inside Facebook and Friends* **from the beginning to line 20**.
>
> How does the writer use language to describe these workplaces?
>
> **[12 marks]**

When you are asked to analyse the writer's use of language, you need to think about the writer's choices of:
- words, phrases and language features
- sentence forms.

The most effective responses select quotations that allow comment on words and phrases, *and* sentence forms.

Read lines 1–20 from Source C: *Inside Facebook and Friends*.

1. **Identify any sentence forms that you feel make a significant contribution to the writer's description of the workplaces. Underline and annotate them.**

2. **Look at the sentences you have underlined. Identify any of the writer's choices of words or phrases that make a significant contribution to the description. Circle and annotate them.**

3. **Now look through the rest of the extract. Can you identify any other significance choices of words or phrases?**

4. **How might different readers respond to the sentences, words or phrases you have identified? Add your ideas to your annotations.**

ENGLISH
Grades 5–9

AQA

| MAIN ACTIVITY: STRUCTURING YOUR RESPONSE | TIMING: 15 MINS |

LEARNING OBJECTIVES
- To be able to structure an effective analysis

EQUIPMENT
- *Surveying the source* activity sheet
- Annotated Source C: *Inside Facebook and Friends*

1. Look again at your annotation of Source C. Can you identify any patterns or similarities in your notes? Draw lines or arrows to link related points.

2. Look again at your annotation. Do you have enough, too little or too much material to write an effective, detailed analysis in response to the exam-style question? Tick a box below and follow the instruction.

    ☐ Too little – return to the text. What other significant features of sentence form, word, phrase or language feature can you identify?
    ☐ Too much – which features will allow you to write the most detailed and perceptive analysis? Tick them.
    ☐ Enough – move on to question 3.

3. Note down three or four key points you will make in your analysis of the source.

    ....

    ....

    ....

    ....

4. Now you have gathered enough material, you need to sequence your ideas. Think about the most logical, effective order in which to put your ideas. Number your key points to show the order in which you will use them.

AQA ENGLISH
Grades 5–9

HOMEWORK ACTIVITY: WRITE YOUR RESPONSE

TIMING: 30 MINS

LEARNING OBJECTIVES
- To be able to comment on the writer's choices of words, phrases, language features and sentence forms
- To be able to structure an effective analysis

EQUIPMENT
- *Surveying the source* activity sheet
- *Structuring your response* activity sheet

Look at this Paper 2, Section A exam-style question.

> You now need to refer only to Source C: *Inside Facebook and Friends* **from the beginning to line 20.**
>
> How does the writer use language to describe these workplaces?
>
> **[12 marks]**

1. Write your response to the question on a separate sheet of paper, focusing on the writer's choices of words, phrases, language features and sentence forms.

2. When you have written your response, check you have achieved the success criteria below.

    a) Tick all the criteria you feel you have achieved.

    - ☐ commented on the writer's use of words, phrases or language features
    - ☐ commented on the writer's use of sentence form
    - ☐ explored how they support the writer's intention(s)
    - ☐ commented on the effect and impact of the writer's choices
    - ☐ written in paragraphs
    - ☐ carefully checked for accurate spelling and punctuation, and clear written expression

    b) Look at any of the criteria you feel you have not achieved. Add to and improve your response so that you can tick all of them.

ENGLISH
Grades 5-9
AQA

11 ANSWERS

STARTER ACTIVITY: ASSESSING AN EXAMPLE
1. The student should note: the writer's intention is identified; the use of embedded evidence; the detailed analysis of the cumulative impact of words, phrases and sentence forms.

MAIN ACTIVITY: SURVEYING THE SOURCE
1. Student's own answer. The selected sentences should focus on the description of the workplaces, and have forms that make a significant contribution to the description.
2. Student's own answer. The selected words and phrases should focus on the description of the workplaces, and make a significant contribution to the description.
3. Ensure responses focus on the relevant part of the text and feature an appropriate level of analysis.
4. Student's own answer. Likely to focus on positive and negative responses.

MAIN ACTIVITY: STRUCTURING YOUR RESPONSE
1. Student's own answer. May focus on scale, technology or recreation.
2. Student's own answer. Ensure they have judged correctly.
3. Examples: the vast scale of the workplaces; the focus on recreation; the surprising contrast of nature and technology (e.g. 'wireless-enabled wildflower meadows'); the limited references to work and the objects typically associated with workplaces.
4. Student's own answer. Ensure structure is logical and coherent.

HOMEWORK ACTIVITY: WRITE YOUR RESPONSE
1.

Marks	Criteria
10–12 marks	• Clear and detailed analysis of the effect of the writer's language choices • A carefully selected range of relevant, focused textual evidence • A range of subject terminology to achieve clarity and precision
7–9 marks	• Clear comments on the effect of the writer's language choices • A range of relevant, focused textual evidence • A range of subject terminology to achieve clarity
4–6 marks	• Some comments on the effect of the writer's language choices • Relevant and focused textual evidence • Largely accurate subject terminology
1–3 marks	• Straightforward comments on the effect of the writer's language choices • Largely relevant textual evidence • Some use of subject terminology, with inconsistent accuracy
No marks	• No creditable response

2. Student's own answer. Ensure the student has achieved all, or the majority of, the success criteria.

ENGLISH
Grades 5-9

12 READING: EXPLORING WHOLE TEXT STRUCTURE 1

LEARNING OBJECTIVES
- To be able to track the development of ideas through a text
- To be able to explore how the writer's ideas interact

SPECIFICATION LINKS
- 3.1.1 evaluation of a writer's choice of vocabulary, form, grammatical and structural features

STARTER ACTIVITY
- **First and last; 5 minutes; page 90**
Look at the format of the exam-style question and read through the subsequent task together. If the source is not familiar to the student from lesson 6, allow them a few minutes to read through it. Point out that although the first and final sentence may not be the beginning or ending of the complete text, they are still a useful way to begin exploring the source's structure.

MAIN ACTIVITIES
- **Tracking the elements; 20 minutes; page 91**
Encourage the student to note the key points as succinctly as possible.
- **How elements interact; 20 minutes; page 92**
Emphasise to the student that analysing whole text structure is not simply a question of exploring the order in which elements are sequenced. To be successful, they must also consider the selection and interaction of ideas and information. Ask them to complete the tasks, adding further circles/boxes if needed. Reflect on the outcome, highlighting the fact that every element in an effective text has a significant purpose that impacts on other elements.

PLENARY ACTIVITY
- **Review; 5 minutes**
Ask the student to review their understanding of the elements in the source and their interaction. How can these be used to respond to the exam-style question in the homework task?

HOMEWORK ACTIVITY
- **Plan your response; 30 minutes; page 93**
Emphasise that this is purely a planning task: the homework for next lesson will be a fully developed response. However, encourage the student to plan and develop their ideas as fully as possible, focusing closely on the key phrase in the question: 'to interest you as a reader'.

SUPPORT IDEA
- **How elements interact** Model an example using the key idea from the starter activity (the funeral prompting thoughts of the past).

EXTENSION IDEA
- **How elements interact** Challenge the student to explore the elements, their purposes and their connections fully.

PROGRESS AND OBSERVATIONS

ENGLISH
Grades 5-9

AQA

STARTER ACTIVITY: FIRST AND LAST

TIMING: 5 MINS

LEARNING OBJECTIVES
- To be able to explore how the writer's ideas interact

EQUIPMENT
- Source E: *The Ocean at the End of the Lane*

Read this Paper 2, Section A exam-style question.

> You now need to think about the **whole** of Source E: *The Ocean at the End of the Lane*.
>
> This text is from the opening of a novel.
>
> How has the writer structured the text to interest you as a reader?
>
> You could write about:
> - what the writer focuses your attention on at the beginning
> - how and why the writer changes this focus as the source develops
> - any other structural features that interest you.
>
> **[8 marks]**

Look at the first and last sentences of Source E: *The Ocean at the End of the Lane*.

> I wore a black suit and a white shirt, a black tie and black shoes, all polished and shiny: clothes that normally would make me feel uncomfortable, as if I were in a stolen uniform, or pretending to be an adult.

> That lane was how I remembered it, when nothing else was.

1. What is the focus of the first sentence?

....

....

2. What is the focus of the last sentence?

....

....

3. What connections can you make between the first and last sentences?

....

....

AQA ENGLISH — Grades 5-9

MAIN ACTIVITY: TRACKING THE ELEMENTS

TIMING: 20 MINS

LEARNING OBJECTIVES
- To be able to track the development of ideas through a text

EQUIPMENT
- Source E: *The Ocean at the End of the Lane*

Read Source E: *The Ocean at the End of the Lane*.

1. Use the space below to note down the key elements that the writer includes in Source E. Write them in the order they appear in the source.

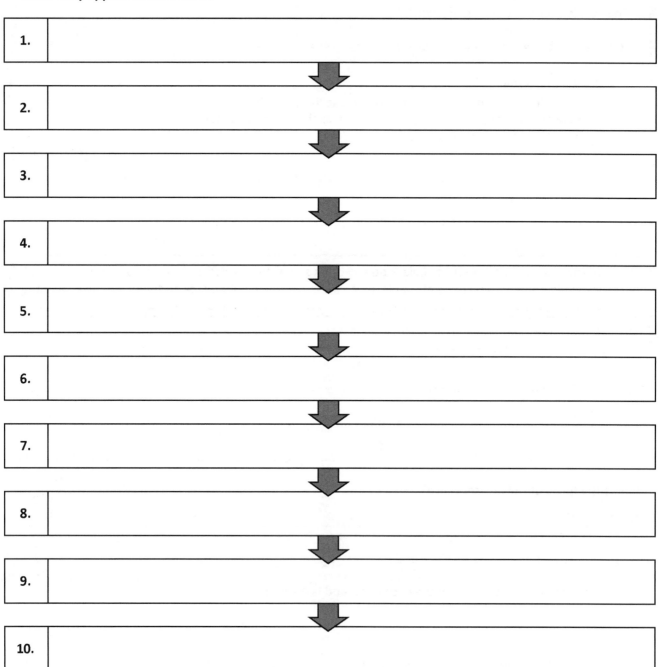

91

Main activity: How elements interact

Timing: 20 mins

Learning objectives

- To be able to explore how the writer's ideas interact

Equipment

- Source E: *The Ocean at the End of the Lane*

1. **Note one key idea or piece of information from Source E in each of the circles below. One has been done for you.**
2. **Use the boxes below the circles to note the purpose of each key idea or piece of information. What does it suggest or reveal about the narrator and the events that will unfold later in the story?**
3. **What connections can you make between the different elements in the source? Draw lines to connect the related elements and annotate them with explanations.**

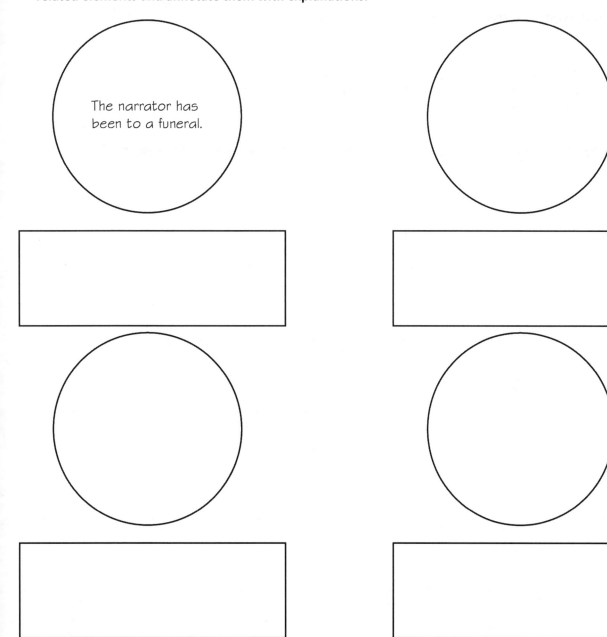

The narrator has been to a funeral.

AQA ENGLISH — Grades 5–9

HOMEWORK ACTIVITY: PLAN YOUR RESPONSE **TIMING: 30 MINS**

LEARNING OBJECTIVES
- To be able to explore how the writer's ideas interact

EQUIPMENT
- Source E: *The Ocean at the End of the Lane*

1. Plan your response to the Paper 1, Section A exam-style question below. Note at least four key points and add evidence to support them.

> You now need to think about the **whole** of Source E: *The Ocean at the End of the Lane*.
>
> This text is from the opening of a novel.
>
> How has the writer structured the text to interest you as a reader?
>
> You could write about:
> - what the writer focuses your attention on at the beginning
> - how and why the writer changes this focus as the source develops
> - any other structural features that interest you.
>
> [8 marks]

12 ANSWERS

STARTER ACTIVITY: FIRST AND LAST
1. The narrator's clothing; he is dressed for a funeral.
2. The narrator's past.
3. They suggest that the funeral has awakened thoughts of the past.

MAIN ACTIVITY: TRACKING THE ELEMENTS
1. Examples:
He drives aimlessly.
He thinks about the wake he will go to in an hour.
He is going somewhere where something happened in the past.
He is returning to his childhood home.
He thinks again about the wake he should be going to now.
He reveals details about his life: marriage, children and career.
He continues on his way.
He seems to have forgotten about the wake.
He is pursuing whatever it was that happened in the past.

MAIN ACTIVITY: HOW ELEMENTS INTERACT
1. to 3. Examples of ideas, explanations and links:
The funeral seems to prompt thoughts of the past.
The wake allows the writer to provide details of the narrator's life and, in forgetting all about it, show how absorbed he is in his thoughts of the past.
His aimless driving and subconscious decision to visit his childhood home suggest his emotional distress following the funeral and the overpowering nature of his thoughts of the past.
Details about the narrator's life suggest an emptiness that may be linked to his thoughts of the past and his desire to explore them.

HOMEWORK ACTIVITY: PLAN YOUR RESPONSE
1.

Marks	Criteria
7–8 marks	• Clear and detailed analysis of the effect of the writer's use of structural features • A carefully selected range of relevant, focused examples • A range of subject terminology to achieve clarity and precision
5–6 marks	• Clear comments on the effect of the writer's use of structural features • A range of relevant, focused examples • A range of subject terminology to achieve clarity
3–4 marks	• Some comments on the effect of the writer's use of structural features • Relevant and focused examples • Largely accurate use of subject terminology
1–2 marks	• Straightforward comments on the effect of the writer's use of structural features • Largely relevant examples • Some use of subject terminology, with inconsistent accuracy
No marks	• No creditable response

GLOSSARY

Chronological
The time order in which events happened

ENGLISH — Grades 5–9

13 READING: EXPLORING WHOLE TEXT STRUCTURE 2

LEARNING OBJECTIVES
- To be able to analyse the intention and impact of whole text structure

SPECIFICATION LINKS
- 3.1.1 evaluation of a writer's choice of vocabulary, form, grammatical and structural features

STARTER ACTIVITY
- **Opening intentions; 10 minutes; page 96**
Check understanding of 'intention' (the impact the writer wants the text to have on the reader). Point out that this is an abstract task in which the student will have to draw on their knowledge and experience of narrative and narrative writing. Encourage the student to note their ideas succinctly.

MAIN ACTIVITIES
- **Ingredients and intentions; 15 minutes; page 97**
Point out to the student that the ingredients and intentions form an effective (but not entirely exhaustive) list of how stories often begin, and why.
- **What is not said; 20 minutes; page 98**
Explain the idea that what is not said may be more important than what is said. For example, the writer might withhold information to prompt the reader to ask questions and seek answers. Ensure quotations are used as evidence of what is known.

PLENARY ACTIVITY
- **Review; 5 minutes**
Explain the homework task to the student (writing their response to the exam-style question, planned for homework following the last lesson). Ask them to review their plan and improve it to take into account their ideas from today's lesson.

HOMEWORK ACTIVITY
- **Write your response; 30 minutes; page 99**
Remind the student to focus on the key phrase from the question: 'to interest you as a reader'.

SUPPORT IDEA
- **Opening intentions** Focus the student on specific, familiar examples, e.g. set texts.

EXTENSION IDEAS
- **What is not said** Challenge the student to explore specifically how information is withheld and how questions are prompted.
- **Homework** Encourage the student to write about the opening of a novel of their own choosing.

PROGRESS AND OBSERVATIONS

ENGLISH
Grades 5-9

STARTER ACTIVITY: OPENING INTENTIONS   **TIMING: 10 MINS**

LEARNING OBJECTIVES
- To be able to analyse the intention and impact of whole text structure

EQUIPMENT
none

1. What different intentions might a writer have in the opening of any story or novel? How can they be achieved? Note your ideas below and draw lines to link the intentions with the different ways in which they could be achieved.

Intentions			

How?						

ENGLISH
— Grades 5-9 —

| MAIN ACTIVITY: INGREDIENTS AND INTENTIONS | TIMING: 15 MINS |

LEARNING OBJECTIVES
- To be able to analyse the intention and impact of whole text structure

EQUIPMENT
- Source E: *The Ocean at the End of the Lane*

The main purpose of any story opening is to engage the reader. Writers will have different ideas of how they want to do this, and will use a range of ingredients to achieve these intentions. For example:

Ingredients
characters
relationships
setting
events
dialogue

...can be used to...

Intentions
create drama
shock the reader
intrigue the reader

1. Can you think of any more ingredients or intentions? Add them to the lists above.
2. Which of the ingredients above does the writer of Source E: *The Ocean at the End of the Lane* use? Write them in the first column of the table below.
3. What are the writer's intentions in using them? Write them in the second column of the table below.
4. How does each ingredient help the writer achieve their intention? Write your explanations in the third column of the table below.

Ingredient	Intention	Explanation

ENGLISH
— Grades 5-9 —

MAIN ACTIVITY: WHAT IS NOT SAID	**TIMING: 20 MINS**

LEARNING OBJECTIVES
- To be able to analyse the intention and impact of whole text structure

EQUIPMENT
- Source E: *The Ocean at the End of the lane*

When you read a text, you may have questions that you expect the writer to answer. Fiction writers often deliberately withhold information, providing enough detail to prompt a question but not enough to answer it. This is intended to encourage the reader to continue reading in order to discover the answers.

1. Think about what you know, how you know it, and what you don't know by the end of Source E: *The Ocean at the End of the Lane*. Note your ideas in the table below.

What do you know about…	How do you know that?	What don't you know?
the funeral?		
the narrator's past?		
the narrator's house?		

2. What questions would you like to know the answers to? Write your top three below.

....

....

....

....

....

AQA ENGLISH
Grades 5-9

HOMEWORK ACTIVITY: WRITE YOUR RESPONSE **TIMING: 30 MINS**

LEARNING OBJECTIVES
- To be able to analyse the intention and impact of whole text structure

EQUIPMENT
- Source E: *The Ocean at the End of the Lane*

1. Write your response to this Paper 1, Section A exam-style question on a separate piece of paper.

> You now need to think about the **whole** of Source E: *The Ocean at the End of the Lane.*
>
> This text is from the opening of a novel.
>
> How has the writer structured the text to interest you as a reader?
>
> You could write about:
> - what the writer focuses your attention on at the beginning
> - how and why the writer changes this focus as the source develops
> - any other structural features that interest you.
>
> [8 marks]

2. When you have written your response, check you have achieved the success criteria below.

   a) Tick all the criteria you feel you have achieved.

   - ☐ commented on the writer's structural choices
   - ☐ explored how they support the writer's intentions
   - ☐ commented on the effect and impact of the writer's choices
   - ☐ written in paragraphs
   - ☐ carefully checked for accurate spelling and punctuation, and clear written expression

   b) Look at any of the criteria you feel you have not achieved. Add to and improve your response so that you can tick all of them.

13 ANSWERS

STARTER ACTIVITY: OPENING INTENTIONS
1. Examples: Intentions: to engage the reader; to introduce character; to prompt questions; to create drama; How: tension through use of description; dialogue; action; withholding information, etc. setting; relationships.

MAIN ACTIVITY: INGREDIENTS AND INTENTIONS
1. Example: to create a specific atmosphere.
2. to 4. Examples: characters: character of narrator is intriguing because his past holds secrets; setting: description of the house is intriguing, it suggests that it is the focus of these secrets; events: the funeral is intriguing, it seems to prompt the narrator's memories of the past.

MAIN ACTIVITY: WHAT IS NOT SAID
1. Examples:
The writer is upset by the funeral. / 'a hard day' / whose funeral it is
The narrator's past is troubled. / 'failed', 'frayed', 'broke' / what happened in the past
The narrator's old house has been demolished. / 'that house had been knocked down' / what happened at the house
2. Examples: Whose funeral is it, and how did they die?; Why is the narrator's past so troubled?; Why is the house so important to him, and what happened there?

HOMEWORK ACTIVITY: WRITE YOUR RESPONSE
1.

Marks	Criteria
7–8 marks	• Clear and detailed analysis of the effect of the writer's use of structural features • A carefully selected range of relevant, focused examples • A range of subject terminology to achieve clarity and precision
5–6 marks	• Clear comments on the effect of the writer's use of structural features • A range of relevant, focused examples • A range of subject terminology to achieve clarity
3–4 marks	• Some comments on the effect of the writer's use of structural features • Relevant and focused examples • Largely accurate use of subject terminology
1–2 marks	• Straightforward comments on the effect of the writer's use of structural features • Largely relevant examples • Some use of subject terminology, with inconsistent accuracy
No marks	• No creditable response

2. Student's own answer. Ensure student has achieved all, or the majority of, the success criteria.

AQA ENGLISH — Grades 5-9

14 READING: EXPLORING WHOLE TEXT STRUCTURE 3

LEARNING OBJECTIVES
- To be able to analyse the intention and impact of whole text structure
- To be able to write a critical response analysing text structure

SPECIFICATION LINKS
- 3.1.1 evaluation of a writer's choice of vocabulary, form, grammatical and structural forms

STARTER ACTIVITY
- **Assessing an example; 10 minutes; page 102**
  Give the student five minutes to reread Source D: *One Hundred Years of Solitude* (page 20). As they complete the task, draw their attention to where quotation and textual reference have been used as evidence.

MAIN ACTIVITIES
- **Surveying the source; 20 minutes; page 103**
  Direct the student to read through or 'track' the text, using the table to note and organise their ideas as they read. Clarify the definition of 'elements' (the ideas and information the writer has chosen to include) and 'ingredients' (the writer's focus on setting, character, events).
- **Structuring your response; 15 minutes; page 104**
  In response to question 1, encourage the student to identify as many connections as possible, and to connect each of the writer's structural choices to an intention.

PLENARY ACTIVITY
- **Review; 5 minutes**
  Ask the student to review, evaluate and summarise their structural analysis skills and their readiness to complete the homework task.

HOMEWORK ACTIVITY
- **Write your response; 30 minutes; page 105**
  Remind the student to use key words from the question to focus their response, and pay close attention to the writer's intentions in the text.

SUPPORT IDEAS
- **Surveying the source** Working with the student, track the text two or three times, focusing first on elements, then on ingredients.
- **Structuring your response** Guide the student to identify two or three key points and make detailed notes to support their analysis.

EXTENSION IDEA
- **Structuring your response** Challenge the student to identify and fully synthesise all significant connections.

PROGRESS AND OBSERVATIONS

ENGLISH
Grades 5-9
AQA

STARTER ACTIVITY: ASSESSING AN EXAMPLE **TIMING: 10 MINS**

LEARNING OBJECTIVES
- To be able to write a critical response analysing text structure

EQUIPMENT
- Source D: *One Hundred Years of Solitude*

Read Source D: *One Hundred Years of Solitude*, then look at the paragraph below from one student's response to a Paper 1, Section A exam-style question.

You now need to think about the **whole** of Source D: *One Hundred Years of Solitude*.

This text is from the opening of a novel.

How has the writer structured the text to interest you as a reader?

You could write about:
- what the writer focuses your attention on at the beginning
- how and why the writer changes this focus as the source develops
- any other structural features that interest you.

[8 marks]

The source begins with an intriguing sentence. Although the opening paragraphs of the novel focus on the past and mainly on the gullible naivety of Colonel Aureliano Buendía's father, the reader is immediately invited to question how and why the Colonel came to face 'the firing squad'. Even more intriguingly, neither the firing squad nor the Colonel are referred to again in the rest of the extract. The writer's intention is, perhaps, to suggest that the story will return to, and perhaps end with, dramatic events concluding in the execution of the Colonel.

---

1. What has this student done well in their analysis? Annotate the paragraph, thinking about the following points.

   - Have they analysed the effects of the writer's choice of structural features?
   - Have they used examples from the text?
   - Have they used the right terms to talk about structural features?

AQA ENGLISH — Grades 5–9

MAIN ACTIVITY: SURVEYING THE SOURCE **TIMING: 20 MINS**

LEARNING OBJECTIVES
- To be able to analyse the intention and impact of whole text structure

EQUIPMENT
- Source D: *One Hundred Years of Solitude*

In this lesson, you are going to focus on this Paper 1, Section A exam-style question.

> You now need to think about the **whole** of Source D: *One Hundred Years of Solitude.*
>
> This text is from the opening of a novel.
>
> How has the writer structured the text to interest you as a reader?
>
> You could write about:
> - what the writer focuses your attention on at the beginning
> - how and why the writer changes this focus as the source develops
> - any other structural features that interest you.
>
> **[8 marks]**

When you are asked to analyse the writer's use of structure, you need to think about:
- the different elements in the text – the ideas and information on which the writer focuses
- the ingredients the writer has chosen to use – for example, character and setting
- the writer's intention
- the questions that are prompted by the text.

1. Reread Source D: *One Hundred Years of Solitude* and note your ideas below.

Elements	Ingredients

Intentions	Questions

ENGLISH
Grades 5-9

MAIN ACTIVITY: STRUCTURING YOUR RESPONSE **TIMING: 15 MINS**

LEARNING OBJECTIVES
- To be able to analyse the intention and impact of whole text structure
- To be able to write a critical response analysing text structure

EQUIPMENT
- *Surveying the source* activity sheet

1. Look again at your notes from the last activity. Can you identify any connections or interactions between the ideas you gathered? Draw lines or arrows to link related ideas and add annotations to explain the connections.

2. Look again at your notes. Do you have enough, too little or too much material to write an effective, detailed analysis? Tick a box and follow the instructions.

    ☐ **Too little** – return to the text. What other significant structural features can you identify?
    ☐ **Too much** – which features will allow you to write the most detailed and perceptive analysis? Tick them.
    ☐ **Enough** – move on to question 3.

3. Note three or four key points you will make in your analysis of the source's structure.

------

4. Now you have gathered enough significant material for your response, you need to sequence your ideas. Think about the most logical, effective way to order your ideas. Number your key points.

AQA ENGLISH — Grades 5–9

| HOMEWORK ACTIVITY: WRITE YOUR RESPONSE | TIMING: 30 MINS |

LEARNING OBJECTIVES

- To be able to analyse the intention and impact of whole text structure
- To be able to write a critical response analysing text structure

EQUIPMENT

- *Surveying the source* activity sheet
- *Structuring your response* activity sheet
- Source D: *One Hundred Years of Solitude*

1. Write your response to this Paper 1, Section A exam-style question on a separate piece of paper.

> You now need to think about the **whole** of Source D: *One Hundred Years of Solitude*.
>
> This text is from the opening of a novel.
>
> How has the writer structured the text to interest you as a reader?
>
> You could write about:
> - what the writer focuses your attention on at the beginning
> - how and why the writer changes this focus as the source develops
> - any other structural features that interest you.
>
> **[8 marks]**

2. When you have written your response, check you have achieved the success criteria below.

   a) Tick all the criteria you feel you have achieved.

   - ☐ commented on the writer's structural choices
   - ☐ explored how they support the writer's intentions
   - ☐ commented on the effect and impact of the writer's choices
   - ☐ written in paragraphs
   - ☐ carefully checked for accurate spelling and punctuation, and clear written expression

   b) Look at any of the criteria you feel you have not achieved. Add to and improve your response so that you can tick all of them.

ENGLISH
— Grades 5-9 —

14 ANSWERS

STARTER ACTIVITY: ASSESSING AN EXAMPLE
1. The student should note: focuses closely on the opening; uses quotation and textual reference; explores the impact on the reader; identifies the writer's intention.

MAIN ACTIVITY: SURVEYING THE SOURCE
1. Examples:
Elements: execution; buying magnets; buying a magnifying glass
Ingredients: character (José); setting (Macondo)
Intentions: humour; character development; intriguing and engaging the reader
Questions: What is the relevance of the colonel's execution? What will his father do next and what impact will it have?

MAIN ACTIVITY: STRUCTURING YOUR RESPONSE
1. Student's own answer. Ensure appropriate links are identified and clearly explained.
2. Student's own answer. Ensure they have judged correctly.
3. Examples: execution in opening sentence; character development of José; connection between primitive setting and José's naïve gullibility; rapid sequence of two foolish investments suggests more will follow.
4. Student's own answer. Ensure points are sequenced logically and effectively.

HOMEWORK ACTIVITY: WRITE YOUR RESPONSE
1.

Marks	Criteria
7–8 marks	• Clear and detailed analysis of the effect of the writer's use of structural features • A carefully selected range of relevant, focused examples • A range of subject terminology to achieve clarity and precision
5–6 marks	• Clear comments on the effect of the writer's use of structural features • A range of relevant, focused examples • A range of subject terminology to achieve clarity
3–4 marks	• Some comments on the effect of the writer's use of structural features • Relevant and focused examples • Largely accurate use of subject terminology
1–2 marks	• Straightforward comments on the effect of the writer's use of structural features • Largely relevant examples • Some use of subject terminology, with inconsistent accuracy
No marks	• No creditable response

2. Student's own answer. Ensure student has achieved all, or the majority of, the success criteria.

ENGLISH
Grades 5-9

15 READING: BEGINNING AN EVALUATION

LEARNING OBJECTIVES
- To be able to identify the writer's intentions
- To be able to explore the success of the writer's intentions

SPECIFICATION LINKS
- 3.1.1 evaluation of a writer's choice of vocabulary, form, grammatical and structural features

STARTER ACTIVITY
- **Opinions; 10 minutes; page 108**
Explain to the student that the purpose of this lesson is to develop a personal response to a text and explore how successful the writer has been in producing that response. Lessons 16 and 17 will be more fully focused on developing a written response to a specific exam-style question. Use sample exam papers to ensure understanding of the question type.

MAIN ACTIVITIES
- **Different responses; 15 minutes; page 109**
Discuss the advantages of supporting and/or contradicting the opinion expressed in this question type. Highlight to the student the value of supporting the statement, while considering how other readers might respond to the text.
- **Evaluating different responses; 20 minutes; page 110**
Ensure the student stays focused on arguing for or against the response identified in the starter activity.

PLENARY ACTIVITY
- **Review; 5 minutes**
Review the starter activity. Ask the student to review their original response. How strongly do they agree or disagree? How effectively has the writer produced that response?

HOMEWORK ACTIVITY
- **More opinions; 30 minutes; page 111**
This task can be completed either with the opening of a novel of the student's own choosing (600–650 words long), or with a non-fiction text read in a previous lesson. Discuss the choice with the student. Note that in the exam, the evaluation question will focus on a fiction text, but that the skill is equally applicable to other text types. Encourage the student to tackle both parts of the task using the approach followed in the lesson.

SUPPORT IDEA
- **Opinions** Ask the student to focus on character or setting – do they respond to that character or setting negatively or positively? In what way? Prompt the student towards expressing a personal response to either or both.

EXTENSION IDEA
- **Different responses** Challenge the student to consider whether the writer may have intended to prompt differing or conflicting responses in the reader, and what their intention could have been in doing so.

PROGRESS AND OBSERVATIONS

ENGLISH
Grades 5-9

STARTER ACTIVITY: OPINIONS

TIMING: 10 MINS

LEARNING OBJECTIVES
- To be able to identify the writer's intentions

EQUIPMENT
- Source E: *The Ocean at the End of the Lane*

The evaluation question in Paper 1, Section A of your exam may look like this.

> Focus this part of your answer on Source E: *The Ocean at the End of the Lane*, **from lines _____ to _____** *(Use about half of the source.)*
>
> A student, having read this section of the text, said: '_____
> _____
> _____
> _____ ,'
>
> To what extent do you agree?
>
> **[20 marks]**

The opinion expressed in the question is likely to focus on:
- how character, setting or event is presented
- the mood or atmosphere created.

1. **Which part of the source do you find most effective? Tick one.**

   ☐ the first half of the source
   ☐ the second half of the source

2. **Note down two or three of the writer's possible intentions in your chosen half of the source.**

   ----

3. **Use one of your ideas to fill the gaps in the exam-style question above.**

108

AQA ENGLISH — Grades 5–9

MAIN ACTIVITY: DIFFERENT RESPONSES   **TIMING: 15 MINS**

LEARNING OBJECTIVES
- To be able to explore the success of the writer's intentions

EQUIPMENT
- *Opinions* activity sheet

Look again at the exam-style question you completed in the previous activity.

1. **Identify two or three pieces of evidence to support the opinion you expressed. Write them below in the 'for' column.**

2. **Identify two or three pieces of evidence you could use to support a different response arguing against the opinion. Write them in the 'against' column.**

For	Against
1.	1.
2.	2.
3.	3.

3. **Write three or four sentences, explaining each of your choices.**

ENGLISH
— Grades 5–9 —

| MAIN ACTIVITY: EVALUATING DIFFERENT RESPONSES | TIMING: 20 MINS |

LEARNING OBJECTIVES
- To be able to explore the success of the writer's intentions

EQUIPMENT
- *Opinions* activity sheet
- *Different responses* activity sheet

Look again at the previous activity.

1. **Which of your selected pieces of evidence most effectively supports the opinion you noted earlier? Tick it.**

2. **Now think about how this ticked piece of evidence supports your response to the text.**
   a) Which of the writer's choices has effectively created your response? Tick one.

   ☐ the idea or information the writer includes
   ☐ the position of that idea or information in the text's structure. For example, does it contradict or clarify an earlier idea or piece of information?
   ☐ the sentence form or vocabulary choice the writer has used to express it

   b) Write two or three sentences exploring the writer's choices in the quotation and evaluating their contribution to your response.

   ----

3. **Which of your chosen quotations most effectively argues against your opinion and supports a different response? Underline it.**

4. **Now think about how this quotation supports a different response to the text. Write two or three sentences exploring the writer's choices in the quotation and evaluating their contribution to that different response.**

AQA ENGLISH — Grades 5-9

HOMEWORK ACTIVITY: MORE OPINIONS

TIMING: 30 MINS

LEARNING OBJECTIVES
- To be able to identify the writer's intentions
- To be able to explore the success of the writer's intentions

EQUIPMENT
- your choice of source text

Use the source you have chosen to complete the activities below.

1. **Complete the gaps in this Paper 1, Section A exam-style question below.**

> Focus this part of your answer on Source: _____ ,
>
> from _____ to _____
>
> A student, having read this section of the text, said: '_____
>
> _____
>
> _____
>
> _____ ,'
>
> To what extent do you agree?
>
> [20 marks]

2. **Write 75–100 words in response to the exam-style question above.**

Make sure you:
- explore how effectively the writer creates the response you have noted
- use quotations to support your ideas.

111

15 ANSWERS

STARTER ACTIVITY: OPINIONS
1. Accept any valid response.
2. In the first half, answers might include: to engage the reader's interest in and sympathy for a narrator significantly affected by a death.
In the second half, answers might include: to intrigue the reader by revealing information about the narrator's past.
3. Student's own answer

MAIN ACTIVITY: DIFFERENT RESPONSES
1. Student's own answer. Ensure evidence is relevant and focused, supporting the student's judgement.
2. Student's own answer. Ensure evidence selected is relevant, focused and supports a distinctly different judgement.
3. Ensure clear justification and exploration of choices are given.

MAIN ACTIVITY: EVALUATING DIFFERENT RESPONSES
1. Student's own answer
2. a) Student's own answer; b) Ensure response is clearly explained and supported with evidence.
3. Student's own answer. Ensure the quotation supports a distinctly different judgement.
4. Ensure response is clearly explained and supported with evidence.

HOMEWORK ACTIVITY: MORE OPINIONS
1. Ensure a clear, evaluative judgement is expressed.
2.

Marks	Criteria
16–20 marks	• Clear and detailed analysis of the writer's choices • Clear and full evaluation of the effect on the reader • A carefully selected range of relevant, focused textual evidence • A developed and considered critical response to the statement
11–15 marks	• Clear comments on the writer's choices • Clear evaluation of the effect on the reader • A range of relevant, focused textual evidence • A relevant, focused response to the statement
6–10 marks	• Some comments on the writer's choices • Some evaluation of their effect on the reader • Relevant and focused textual evidence • A more developed response to the statement
1–5 marks	• Straightforward comments on the writer's choices • Straightforward evaluation of their effect on the reader • Largely relevant textual evidence • A straightforward response to the statement
No marks	• No creditable response

AQA ENGLISH — Grades 5-9

16 READING: WRITING AN EVALUATIVE RESPONSE

LEARNING OBJECTIVES
- To be able to develop critical engagement with, and evaluation of, a text
- To be able to structure an effective evaluation

SPECIFICATION LINKS
- 3.1.1 evaluation of a writer's choice of vocabulary, form, grammatical and structural features

STARTER ACTIVITY
- **Making a judgement; 10 minutes; page 114**
  Give the student two or three minutes to remind themselves of Source E: *The Ocean at the End of the Lane* (page 21). Ask the student to complete the task. Point out that the purpose of exploring a balanced response is to temper or qualify the primary statement, not simply to contradict it.

MAIN ACTIVITIES
- **Gathering your ideas; 15 minutes; page 115**
  Draw attention to the rubric of the exam-style question in the starter activity: it asks students to focus on the second half of the text only. Explain that not every key point needs a secondary point to balance or qualify it. In some cases, there may be only one that does. Make explicit the process of using all the evidence to develop a judgement, then refining the evidence that most effectively supports it.
- **Crafting your response; 20 minutes; page 116**
  Ask the student to complete the task, discussing how each sentence in the model paragraph contributes (or otherwise) to the evaluation. If time allows, ask them to write their own paragraph using the notes they compiled in the *Gathering your ideas* activity.

PLENARY ACTIVITY
- **Review; 5 minutes**
  Ask the student to summarise and evaluate their understanding of how to craft an evaluative response.

HOMEWORK ACTIVITY
- **Write your response; 30 minutes; page 117**
  Remind the student to refer to their work on the *Gathering your ideas* and *Crafting your response* worksheets.

SUPPORT IDEAS
- **Gathering your ideas** Focus the student on selecting and annotating evidence to support one or two key ideas.
- **Homework** Ask the student to write just one carefully crafted paragraph that meets all of the criteria.

EXTENSION IDEA
- **Gathering your ideas** Challenge the student to identify and explore patterns of language use that contribute cumulatively to their judgement.

PROGRESS AND OBSERVATIONS

ENGLISH
— Grades 5-9 —

STARTER ACTIVITY: MAKING A JUDGEMENT   **TIMING: 10 MINS**

LEARNING OBJECTIVES

- To be able to develop critical engagement with, and evaluation of, a text

EQUIPMENT

- Source E: *The Ocean at the End of the Lane*

You are going to develop your response to this Paper 1, Section A exam-style question.

> Focus this part of your answer on the second part of Source E: *The Ocean at the End of the Lane*, **from line 21 to the end**.
>
> A student, having read this section of the text, said: *'This part of the text shows the impact that past events have had on the narrator. It makes me wonder what memories the funeral has brought back.'*
>
> To what extent do you agree?
>
> In your response, you could:
> - consider your own impressions of the narrator and his past
> - evaluate how the writer creates these impressions
> - support your opinions with quotations from the text.
>
> [20 marks]

1. Circle a number on the scale below to show how strongly you agree or disagree with the student's judgement.

```
|    |    |    |    |    |    |    |    |    |    |
0    1    2    3    4    5    6    7    8    9    10
```
Strongly disagree   **Strongly agree**

2. Complete the sentences below, explaining your response.
I agree/disagree because …

....

....

....

....

However…

....

....

....

....

AQA ENGLISH — Grades 5-9

Main activity: Gathering your ideas

Timing: 15 mins

Learning objectives
- To be able to develop critical engagement with, and evaluation of, a text

Equipment
- Source E: *The Ocean at the End of the Lane*

You now need to start gathering and exploring the evidence in the source that supports your judgement.

1. Read the source, underlining any relevant evidence to support your judgement.

2. Review the evidence you have identified. What are the key points it could support? Use the table below to note the ideas that support and challenge your judgement.

Support	Challenge

3. Review your evidence again. Which pieces most effectively support your points above? Tick them.

4. Annotate the evidence you have ticked, noting how the writer's use of structure and choice of words, phrases, language features and/or sentence forms support your judgement.

115

ENGLISH
Grades 5-9

MAIN ACTIVITY: CRAFTING YOUR RESPONSE	TIMING: 20 MINS

LEARNING OBJECTIVES
- To be able to structure an effective evaluation

EQUIPMENT
- Source E: *The Ocean at the End of the Lane*
- *Making a judgement* activity sheet

A successful response to an evaluation question, like the question in the *Making a judgement* activity, needs to:
a) give a detailed critical evaluation of the effect on the reader
b) show clear analysis and evaluation of structure; sentence forms; words, phrases and language features
c) be supported with a range of evidence from the text
d) develop a convincing critical response to the statement in the question.

Look at the sentences below. They are taken from one student's response to the exam-style question from the *Making a judgement* activity.

1. Although it is suggested that some pieces of the narrator's past are highly significant, he draws attention to the idea that others are not.

2. It is strongly suggested that, following his marriage that 'failed… frayed…' and 'broke', he has lost faith in relationships: 'as they always seem to'.

3. The breakdown of his marriage appears to have had a significant effect on the narrator.

4. The demolition of his childhood home, 'knocked down' and 'lost for good', seems to have had little impact.

5. His potentially troublesome teenage years, featuring 'no good times, no bad times', seem uneventful and unimportant.

6. All details seem significant in light of the reference earlier in the text to 'leaving the past undisturbed'. The choice of 'undisturbed' strongly suggests that the past has been intentionally buried and forgotten.

1. Which of the above criteria do the sentences achieve? Label each sentence a, b, c or d.

2. Which sentences would you include in a paragraph responding to the exam-style question in the *Making a judgement* activity? Tick them.

3. In what order would you sequence your chosen sentences? Number them to show the order.

4. How would you link the sentences to form a cohesive paragraph? Write it out on a separate piece of paper.

AQA ENGLISH
Grades 5-9

HOMEWORK ACTIVITY: WRITE YOUR RESPONSE **TIMING: 30 MINS**

LEARNING OBJECTIVES
- To be able to structure an effective evaluation

EQUIPMENT
- Source E: *The Ocean at the End of the Lane*
- *Gathering your ideas* activity sheet
- *Crafting your response* activity sheet

Read this Paper 1, Section A exam-style question.

> Focus this part of your answer on the second part of Source D: *One Hundred Years of Solitude*, **from line 17 to the end**.
>
> A student, having read this section of the text, said: *'This part of the text shows how Jose Arcadio Buendia's ambitious and imaginative ideas end in failure. You feel excited but worried about what he will do next.'*
>
> To what extent do you agree?
>
> In your response, you could:
> - consider your own impressions of Jose Arcadio Buendia
> - evaluate how the writer creates these impressions
> - support your opinions with quotations from the text.
>
> [20 marks]

1. On a separate piece of paper, write a response of three or four paragraphs. Remember to write about the part of the text specified in the question, and not the whole of the text

2. When you have written your response, check you have achieved the success criteria below.

    a) Tick the criteria you feel you have achieved.

    - ☐ evaluated critically and in detail the effect on the reader.
    - ☐ showed clear analysis and evaluation of the writer's use of structure, sentence forms, words, phrases, language features
    - ☐ supported with a range of evidence synthesised from the text
    - ☐ developed a convincing and critical response to the statement in the question
    - ☐ written in paragraphs
    - ☐ carefully checked for accurate spelling and punctuation, and clear written expression

    b) Look at any of the criteria you feel you have not achieved. Add to and improve your response so that you can tick all of them.

16 ANSWERS

STARTER ACTIVITY: MAKING A JUDGEMENT

1. Accept any valid response.
2. Example: I agree because the narrator seems reluctant to go to the wake at his sister's house and talk about his past, suggesting its negative impact, but seems drawn to explore important places from his past without really explaining why. However it is suggested that the memories of the past are brought back by the places he travels through, not by the funeral.

MAIN ACTIVITY: GATHERING YOUR IDEAS

1. Ensure relevant evidence is underlined.
2. Ensure responses are valid and focused on the exam-style question. They could focus on: Those memories that are given significance, e.g. the narrator's failed marriage, the narrow lane, thoughts of 'the departed'; or those memories that appear less significant, e.g. the narrator's adolescence, the 'new' house.
3. Student's own response
4. Student's own response. Ensure relevance and focus on the exam-style question.

MAIN ACTIVITY: CRAFTING YOUR RESPONSE

1. 1. a; 2. b; 3. c; 4. b; 5. a; 6. d
2. Student's own answer. Ensure they choose appropriate sentences.
3. Student's own answer. Ensure a coherent order.
4. Ensure connectives are used to form a cohesive paragraph. Example: Although it is suggested that some pieces of the narrator's past are highly significant, he draws attention to the idea that others are not. It is strongly suggested that, following his marriage that 'failed', 'frayed' and 'broke', he has lost faith in relationships: 'as they always seem to'. The breakdown of this relationship appears to have had a significant effect on the narrator. In contrast, the demolition of his childhood home, 'knocked down' and 'lost for good', seems to have had little impact. Similarly, his potentially troublesome teenage years, featuring 'no good times, no bad times', seem uneventful and unimportant. However, all of these details seem significant in light of the reference earlier in the text to 'leaving the past undisturbed'. The choice of the word 'undisturbed' strongly suggests that the past has been intentionally buried and forgotten. This implies that the significance of the past will become clear as the narrator, prompted by a death and a funeral, finds that he is 'curious' about it and has been drawn back into the past, 'driven back in time.'

HOMEWORK ACTIVITY: WRITE YOUR RESPONSE

1.

Marks	Criteria	
16–20 marks	• Clear and detailed analysis of the writer's choices • Clear and full evaluation of the effect on the reader	• A carefully selected range of relevant, focused textual evidence • A developed and considered critical response to the statement
11–15 marks	• Clear comments on the writer's choices • Clear evaluation of the effect on the reader	• A range of relevant, focused textual evidence • A relevant, focused response to the statement
6–10 marks	• Some comments on the writer's choices • Some evaluation of their effect on the reader	• Relevant and focused textual evidence • A more developed response to the statement
1–5 marks	• Straightforward comments on the writer's choices • Straightforward evaluation of their effect on the reader	• Largely relevant textual evidence • A straightforward response to the statement
No marks	• No creditable response	

2. Student's own answer. Ensure student has achieved all, or the majority of, the success criteria.

GLOSSARY

Evaluation
Judging, as a reader, how successful a particular aspect of a text is, with an explanation

AQA ENGLISH — Grades 5-9

17 READING: DEVELOPING CRITICAL EVALUATION

LEARNING OBJECTIVES
- To be able to develop critical engagement with, and evaluation of, a text
- To be able to structure an effective evaluation

SPECIFICATION LINKS
- 3.1.1 evaluation of a writer's choice of vocabulary, form, grammatical and structural features

STARTER ACTIVITY
- **Moving up; 10 minutes; page 120**
  Give the student three to five minutes to reread Source D: *One Hundred Years of Solitude* (page 20). Ask them to complete the tasks, identifying where in the paragraph the assessment criteria have been achieved.

MAIN ACTIVITIES
- **Surveying the source; 20 minutes; page 121**
  Make explicit the process of clarifying and summarising the response, identifying relevant evidence to support it, establishing key points, and selecting the most relevant evidence to support them.
- **Structuring your response; 15 minutes; page 122**
  As the student completes question 1, encourage them to identify as many connections as possible in order to synthesise, rationalise and develop their ideas. As they complete question 2, draw attention again to the process of identifying key points and evidence, reviewing, synthesising and sequencing.

PLENARY ACTIVITY
- **Review; 5 minutes**
  Ask the student to review, evaluate and summarise their evaluation skills and their readiness to complete the homework task.

HOMEWORK ACTIVITY
- **Write your response; 30 minutes; page 123**
  Remind the student to focus their response using key words from the statement in the question.

SUPPORT IDEA
- **Structuring your response** Guide the student to identify only two or three key points and make detailed notes to support analysis and evaluation.

EXTENSION IDEA
- **Structuring your response** Challenge the student to identify and fully synthesise all significant connections.

PROGRESS AND OBSERVATIONS

ENGLISH
Grades 5–9

STARTER ACTIVITY: MOVING UP

TIMING: 10 MINS

LEARNING OBJECTIVES
- To be able to develop critical engagement with, and evaluation of, a text
- To be able to structure an effective evaluation

EQUIPMENT
- Source D: *One Hundred Years of Solitude*

Look at this Paper 1, Section A exam-style question and mark scheme.

> Focus this part of your answer on the second part of Source D: *One Hundred Years of Solitude*, **from line 17 to the end**.
>
> A student, having read this section of the text, said: *'This part of the text shows how Jose Arcadio Buendia's ambitious and imaginative ideas end in failure. You feel excited but worried about what he will do next.'*
>
> To what extent do you agree?
>
> In your response, you could:
> - consider your own impressions of Jose Arcadio Buendia
> - evaluate how the writer creates these impressions
> - support your opinions with quotations from the text.
>
> [20 marks]

An adequate response (11–15 marks) should:	A successful response (16–20 marks) should:
- evaluate the effect on the reader - show clear understanding of the writer's use of structure, sentence forms, words, phrases and language features - be supported with evidence from the text - make a clear and relevant response to the statement in the question.	- give a detailed and critical evaluation of the effect on the reader - show clear analysis and evaluation of the writer's use of structure, sentence forms, words, phrases and language features - be supported with a range of evidence synthesised from the text - develop a convincing critical response to the statement in the question.

Now read a paragraph from one student's response to the question.

> Although Buendia is very enthusiastic, it is humorous and worrying that he does not listen to anyone or seem to care about the consequences of his decisions. For example, Melquiades tells him quite clearly in a short simple sentence that the magnets cannot attract gold: 'It won't work for that.' However, Buendia does not believe him and spends a long time trying.

1. On a separate piece of paper, explain how you would assess this paragraph from one student's response to the exam-style question above.

2. On a separate piece of paper, explain how you would improve it.

AQA ENGLISH — Grades 5–9

MAIN ACTIVITY: SURVEYING THE SOURCE **TIMING: 20 MINS**

LEARNING OBJECTIVES
- To be able to develop critical engagement with, and evaluation of, a text

EQUIPMENT
- Source D: *One Hundred Years of Solitude*

In this lesson, you are going to focus on this Paper 1, Section A exam-style question.

> Focus this part of your answer on the second part of Source D: *One Hundred Years of Solitude*, **from line 17 to the end**.
>
> A student, having read this section of the text, said: *'This part of the text shows how Jose Arcadio Buendia's ambitious and imaginative ideas end in failure. You feel excited but worried about what he will do next.'*
>
> To what extent do you agree?
>
> In your response, you could:
> - consider your own impressions of Jose Arcadio Buendia
> - evaluate how the writer creates these impressions
> - support your opinions with quotations from the text.
>
> [20 marks]

1. Do you agree with the statement in the question? Why? Why not? Summarise your judgement in one sentence.

---

2. Survey the source, underlining any relevant evidence to support your judgement.
3. Review your evidence. What key points could it support? Use the table below to note points that support and challenge your argument.

Support	Challenge

4. Look again at the evidence you underlined in the source. Which quotations are the most relevant for supporting the ideas? Tick them.

ENGLISH
Grades 5–9

| MAIN ACTIVITY: STRUCTURING YOUR RESPONSE | TIMING: 15 MINS |

LEARNING OBJECTIVES
- To be able to structure an effective evaluation

EQUIPMENT
- Source D: *One Hundred Years of Solitude*
- *Surveying the source* activity sheet

1. Look again at your notes from the *Surveying the source* activity. Can you identify any connections or interactions between the ideas you have gathered? Draw lines to link the related ideas and annotate them.

2. Do you have enough, too little or too much material to write a successful, detailed evaluation in response to the exam-style question? Tick one and follow the instructions.

    ☐ **Too little** – Return to the text. What other significant ideas and evidence can you identify in support of your judgement?
    ☐ **Too much** – Which ideas will allow you to write the most detailed and perceptive evaluation? Tick them.
    ☐ **Enough** – Move on to question 3.

3. What three or four key points will you make in your evaluation? Write them below.

---

4. Now you have gathered enough significant material for your response, you need to sequence your ideas. Think about the most logical, effective order in which to put them. Number your key points.

AQA ENGLISH — Grades 5-9

| **HOMEWORK ACTIVITY: WRITE YOUR RESPONSE** | **TIMING: 30 MINS** |

LEARNING OBJECTIVES

- To be able to develop critical engagement with, and evaluation of, a text
- To be able to structure an effective evaluation

EQUIPMENT

- Source D: *One Hundred Years of Solitude*
- *Surveying the source* activity sheet
- *Structuring your response* activity sheet

Read this Paper 1, Section A exam-style question.

> Focus this part of your answer on the second part of Source D: *One Hundred Years of Solitude*, **from line 17 to the end**.
>
> A student, having read this section of the text, said: *'This part of the text shows how Jose Arcadio Buendia's ambitious and imaginative ideas end in failure. You feel excited but worried about what he will do next.'*
>
> To what extent do you agree?
>
> In your response, you could:
>
> - consider your own impressions of Jose Arcadio Buendia
> - evaluate how the writer creates these impressions
> - support your opinions with quotations from the text.
>
> [20 marks]

1. Write your response to this question on a separate piece of paper. You should write three to four paragraphs.

2. When you have written your response, check you have achieved the success criteria below.

   a) Tick the criteria you feel you have achieved.

   - ☐ given detailed critical evaluation of the effect on the reader
   - ☐ showed clear analysis and evaluation of the writer's use of structure, sentence forms, words, phrases and language features
   - ☐ supported your evaluation with a range of evidence synthesised from the text
   - ☐ developed a convincing and critical response to the statement in the question
   - ☐ written in paragraphs
   - ☐ carefully checked for accurate spelling and punctuation, and clear written expression

   b) Look at any of the criteria you feel you have not achieved. Add to and improve your response so that you can tick all of them.

17 ANSWERS

STARTER ACTIVITY: MOVING UP

1. The response achieves all of the criteria of an adequate response.
2. To achieve a successful response, the student could synthesise a broader range of evidence, and analyse and evaluate its effect on the reader in more detail. For example, they could explore Buendia's 'unbridled imagination', which presents his seemingly foolish behaviour as the result of a positive quality, suggesting that the writer may be encouraging the reader to enjoy or even admire his naïve enthusiasm.

MAIN ACTIVITY: SURVEYING THE SOURCE

1. Ensure judgement is closely focused on the statement in the question and adequately justified.
2. Ensure evidence is focused and supports the judgement made.
3. Key points may include: the presentation of Buendia's relentless enthusiasm and stubborn naivety; possible responses to Buendia's greed for gold and thirst for victory in war, in contrast to the more noble, scientific advantages of the magnet and magnifying glass that Melquiades draws attention to; the worrying, humorous and disturbing consequences of Buendia's wasteful and misguided projects, e.g. giving away his goats despite his family's need for them, unearthing a rusty suit of armour and a skeleton.
4. Student's own response. Ensure suitable, relevant quotations are chosen.

MAIN ACTIVITY: STRUCTURING YOUR RESPONSE

1. Ensure connections are valid and clearly explained.
2. Student's own answer. Ensure they have judged correctly.
3. Ensure key points are valid.
4. Ensure points are logically sequenced.

HOMEWORK ACTIVITY: WRITE YOUR RESPONSE

1.

Marks	Criteria
16–20 marks	• Clear and detailed analysis of the writer's choices • Clear and full evaluation of the effect on the reader • A carefully selected range of relevant, focused textual evidence • A developed and considered critical response to the statement
11–15 marks	• Clear comments on the writer's choices • Clear evaluation of the effect on the reader • A range of relevant, focused textual evidence • A relevant, focused response to the statement
6–10 marks	• Some comments on the writer's choices • Some evaluation of their effect on the reader • Relevant and focused textual evidence • A more developed response to the statement
1–5 marks	• Straightforward comments on the writer's choices • Straightforward evaluation of their effect on the reader • Largely relevant textual evidence • A straightforward response to the statement
No marks	• No creditable response

2. Student's own answer. Ensure the student has achieved all, or the majority of, the success criteria.

ENGLISH
Grades 5-9

18 READING: PLANNING A COMPARISON

LEARNING OBJECTIVES
- To be able to identify significant points of comparison in two texts
- To be able to compare the writer's choices in two texts

SPECIFICATION LINKS
- 3.1.1 comparing texts

STARTER ACTIVITY
- **Inferring ideas and attitudes; 10 minutes; page 126**
  Let the student know that the remaining lessons will focus on the skills needed for Paper 2 of the exam. Explain that they will begin by focusing on short extracts from source texts, but that the same skills are needed when referring to complete texts.

MAIN ACTIVITIES
- **Comparing ideas and attitudes; 20 minutes; page 127**
  Highlight that the most significant differences are those that are linked or related in some way.
- **Developing your comparison; 15 minutes; page 128**
  Explain that this is a preliminary activity to identify points of comparison in preparation for the homework task.

PLENARY ACTIVITY
- **Review; 5 minutes**
  Ask the student to summarise and evaluate their understanding of how to compare the writers' ideas and attitudes in two texts.

HOMEWORK ACTIVITY
- **Write your response; 30 minutes; page 129**
  Encourage the student to explore their points of comparison in detail and express their ideas with clarity and precision. Point out that although this task focuses on comparing the writers' use of language and sentence forms, a complete comparison should also explore the writers' structural choices.

SUPPORT IDEA
- **Comparing ideas and attitudes** Direct the student to focus on one paragraph of each text at a time, noting the writers' views and experiences of food.

EXTENSION IDEA
- **Developing your comparison** Challenge the student to explore how the writers' choices reflect and/or contribute to their intention.

PROGRESS AND OBSERVATIONS

ENGLISH
Grades 5-9

| STARTER ACTIVITY: INFERRING IDEAS AND ATTITUDES | TIMING: 10 MINS |

LEARNING OBJECTIVES
- To be able to identify significant points of comparison in two texts

EQUIPMENT
none

Look at these two extracts from the beginnings of Source A: *The Gastronomical Me* and Source F: *London Labour and the London Poor*.

Source A

The food writer, M F K Fisher, describes memories of her childhood.

The Gastronomical Me

The first thing I remember tasting and then wanting to taste again is the grayish-pink fuzz my grandmother skimmed from a spitting kettle of strawberry jam. I suppose I was about four.

Source F

From the 1840s to the 1860s, Henry Mayhew studied and recorded how working people in London lived. He published his findings in *London Labour and the London Poor*.

London Labour and the London Poor

First, as to the number of stalls in the streets of London, I caused personal observations to be made; and in a walk of 46 miles, 632 stalls were counted, which is at the rate of very nearly 14 to the mile. This, too, was in bad weather, was not on a Saturday night, and at a season when the fruit-sellers all declare that "things is dull".

---

1. What can you infer from these openings about:
   a) the two writers' intentions?

   ....
   ....
   ....
   ....

   b) the two writers' views and experiences of food?

   ....
   ....
   ....
   ....

126

ENGLISH
Grades 5-9

MAIN ACTIVITY: COMPARING IDEAS AND ATTITUDES	TIMING: 20 MINS

LEARNING OBJECTIVES
- To be able to identify significant points of comparison in two texts

EQUIPMENT
- Source A: *The Gastronomical Me*
- Source F: *London Labour and the London Poor*

Read this Paper 2, Section A exam-style question.

> For this question, you need to refer to the **whole** of Source F: *London Labour and the London Poor* together with the **whole** of source A: *The Gastronomical Me*.
>
> Compare how the writers have conveyed their different views and experiences of food.
>
> In your answer, you could:
> - compare their different views and experiences
> - compare the methods used to convey those views and experiences
> - support your ideas with quotations from both texts.
>
> **[16 marks]**

One way to begin tackling this kind of question is to identify the writer's ideas and attitudes in one of the texts, then look for points of comparison in the other.

1. Reread Source A: *The Gastronomical Me*. As you read, note down three pieces of relevant evidence and what they reveal about the writer's views and experiences of food.

	Source A: *The Gastronomical Me*	Source F: *London Labour and the London Poor*
Evidence		
Views/ experiences		

2. Now reread Source F: *London Labour and the London Poor*. Does the evidence suggest that the writer has similar or different views and experiences of food to the writer of Source A? Note three pieces of evidence and what they reveal.

ENGLISH
Grades 5-9

MAIN ACTIVITY: DEVELOPING YOUR COMPARISON	**TIMING: 15 MINS**

LEARNING OBJECTIVES
- To be able to compare the writer's choices in two texts

EQUIPMENT
none

Look closely at these two short extracts from Source A: *The Gastronomical Me* and Source F: *London Labour and the London Poor*.

> In spite of any Late Victorian asceticism, though, the hot kitchen sent out tantalizing clouds, and the fruit on the porch lay rotting in its crates, or readied for the pots and the wooden spoons, in fair glowing piles upon the juice-stained tables. Grandmother, saving always, stood like a sacrificial priestess in the steam, "skimming" into a thick white saucer, and I, sometimes permitted and more often not, put my finger into the cooling froth and licked it. Warm and sweet and odorous. I loved it, then.

> Most of the fruit-stalls are, in the winter time, fitted up with an apparatus for roasting apples and chestnuts; this generally consists of an old saucepan with a fire inside; and the woman who vends them, huddled up in her old faded shawl or cloak, often presents a picturesque appearance, in the early evening, or in a fog, with the gleam of the fire lighting up her half somnolent figure.

1. What does each extract suggest about the writer's views and experiences of food? Write your ideas below.

Source A

....

....

Source F

....

....

2. Now look again at the extracts above.
    a) Circle any words or phrases that help to convey the views and experiences you identified.
    b) Underline any sentence forms that help to convey the views and experiences you identified.

3. Look carefully at the words, phrases and sentences you identified. Write one or two sentences summarising the similarities or differences in the ways in which the two writers convey their views and experiences.

....

....

....

....

....

ENGLISH
— Grades 5-9 —

| HOMEWORK ACTIVITY: **WRITE YOUR RESPONSE** | TIMING: **30** MINS |

LEARNING OBJECTIVES
- To be able to identify significant points of comparison in two texts
- To be able to compare the writer's choices in two texts

EQUIPMENT
none

1. On a separate piece of paper write two paragraphs in response to the Paper 2, Section A exam-style question below, focusing on the two short extracts.

> For this question, you need to refer to the **whole** of Source F: *London Labour and the London Poor* together with the **whole** of source A: *The Gastronomical Me*.
>
> Compare how the writers have conveyed their different views and experiences of food.
>
> In your answer, you could:
> - compare their different views and experiences
> - compare the methods used to convey those views and experiences
> - support your ideas with quotations from both texts.
>
> **[16 marks]**

2. When you have written your response, check you have achieved the success criteria below.
   a) Tick the criteria you feel you have achieved.

   ☐ identified and compared the writers' views and experiences of food in detail
   ☐ supported with relevant, focused evidence from the text
   ☐ analysed and compared how the writers use sentence forms, words, phrases and language features to convey their views and experiences
   ☐ written in paragraphs
   ☐ carefully checked for accurate spelling and punctuation, and clear written expression

   b) Look at any of the criteria you feel you have not achieved. Add to and improve your response so that you can tick all of them.

ENGLISH
Grades 5-9

18 ANSWERS

STARTER ACTIVITY: INFERRING IDEAS AND ATTITUDES

1. a) Example: The opening of Source A suggests the text will explore the origins of the writer's interest in food. Source F's opening suggests a statistical survey and description of the stalls of London.
b) Example: Source A's opening suggests enthusiasm for the pleasures of food; Source F's opening suggests that the writer is more interested in surveying the way food is sold on the streets of London than in the food itself.

MAIN ACTIVITY: COMPARING IDEAS AND ATTITUDES

1. Examples: 'The first thing I remember… wanting to taste again' – the writer's enthusiasm for food began at an early age; 'opulent fragrance… a beautiful smelly task', 'glowing piles upon the juice-stained table', 'a whole battery of enamel pots' – the writer appreciates the smells, sights and equipment of cooking; 'I longed to' – the writer is keen to help with the cooking.
2. Examples: '632 stalls were counted' – the writer appears fascinated by the number of stalls; 'peas-soup, pickled whelks, sweetmeats' – the writer is interested in the variety of food available; 'an old saucepan', 'tin oval pots' – the writer appreciates the cooking equipment; 'The woman who vends them, huddled up in her old faded shawl or cloak, often presents a picturesque appearance.' – the writer appreciates the appearance of the sellers; However, he shows little interest in the smell or taste of the food.

MAIN ACTIVITY: DEVELOPING YOUR COMPARISON

1. Example: Source A: The writer of *The Gastronomical Me's* description of her grandmother suggests an almost religious devotion to cooking. She effuses about the sights, smells and tastes of cooking.
Source F: The writer of *London Labour and the London Poor* enjoys the romantic, 'picturesque' sight of the chestnut seller.
2. a) Examples: Source A: 'tantalising clouds'; 'juice-stained tables'; Source F: 'apparatus'; 'gleam', 'faded shawl'.
b) Student's own answers
3. Examples: The writer of *The Gastronomical Me* uses vividly descriptive language choices, focused on the senses. The writer of *London Labour and the London Poor* uses more purely factual descriptions of 'apparatus', although his description of the 'gleam' of the fire and the chestnut seller's 'faded shawl' create a striking visual impression. This even, factual tone is reflected in the use of a lengthy sentence form, whereas the writer of *The Gastronomical Me* uses, for example, two short sentences in succession to emphasise her passion for jam ('Warm and sweet and odorous. I loved it, then.')

HOMEWORK ACTIVITY: WRITE YOUR RESPONSE

1.

Marks	Criteria
13–16 marks	• Clear and detailed analysis of the writers' choices • A carefully selected range of relevant, focused textual evidence from both texts • A developed and considered understanding of the different ideas and perspectives in both texts
9–12 marks	• Clear explanation on the writer's choices • A range of relevant, focused textual evidence from both texts • A clear understanding of the different ideas and perspectives in both texts
5–8 marks	• Some comments on the writer's choices • Relevant and focused textual evidence from one or both texts • Awareness of range of different ideas and perspectives
1–4 marks	• Straightforward comments on the writer's choices • Largely relevant textual evidence • Some awareness of ideas and or perspectives
No marks	• No creditable response

2. Student's own answer. Ensure student has achieved all, or the majority of, the success criteria.

ENGLISH
Grades 5-9

19 Reading: Developing a comparison

Learning objectives	Specification links
• To be able to analyse and compare pace and tone in two texts • To be able to craft a cohesive comparison of two texts	• 3.1.1 comparing texts

Starter activity

- **Thinking about pace and tone; 5 minutes; page 132**
  Review the student's understanding of pace and tone (see Glossary). Fold the sheet in half and then ask the student to complete the task. Unfold the sheet and ask the student to compare their response to the prompts. Are any of the prompts more precise or appropriate than the student's response?

Main activities

- **Comparing tone and pace; 20 minutes; page 133**
  This task is complex and challenging. Ensure the student has a clear understanding of it before they begin. Allow time for them to review and revise their writing choices, reflecting on the pace and tone created. Provide support with this review process.

- **Structuring a comparison; 20 minutes; page 134**
  Carefully read through the sentences together and explore ways in which the paragraph could be structured. A simple approach would focus first on one text, then on the other, whereas a more sophisticated construction would consider similar or contrasting features in turn. Suggest the use of conjunctions (*although, whereas*) and non-finite verbs (*using, focusing*) to link sentences, and adverbials (*both, however, similarly*) to link ideas and signal comparison.

Plenary activity

- **Review; 5 minutes**
  Ask the student to summarise and evaluate their skills in comparing two writers' ideas and attitudes, and in writing a well-structured comparison.

Homework activity

- **Write your response; 30 minutes; page 135**
  Emphasise the opportunity to explore the pace and tone achieved in the two short extracts, and the importance of carefully sequencing and linking their ideas in a cohesive paragraph.

Support idea

- **Thinking about pace and tone** Ask the student to select an initial response from the prompts in the activity.

Extension idea

- **Comparing tone and pace** Ask the student to reverse the process by rewriting the extract from Source F: *London Labour and the London Poor* (page 22) to create the tone and pace of Source A: *The Gastronomical Me* (page 17).

Progress and observations

ENGLISH
Grades 5-9
AQA

| STARTER ACTIVITY: THINKING ABOUT PACE AND TONE | TIMING: 5 MINS |

LEARNING OBJECTIVES
- To be able to analyse and compare pace and tone in two texts

EQUIPMENT
none

1. Think of two or three words to describe the pace and tone of these extracts from Source A and Source F. Write them in the table below.

> In spite of any Late Victorian asceticism, though, the hot kitchen sent out tantalizing clouds, and the fruit on the porch lay rotting in its crates, or readied for the pots and the wooden spoons, in fair glowing piles upon the juice-stained tables. Grandmother, saving always, stood like a sacrificial priestess in the steam, "skimming" into a thick white saucer, and I, sometimes permitted and more often not, put my finger into the cooling froth and licked it. Warm and sweet and odorous. I loved it, then.

> Most of the fruit-stalls are, in the winter time, fitted up with an apparatus for roasting apples and chestnuts; this generally consists of an old saucepan with a fire inside; and the woman who vends them, huddled up in her old faded shawl or cloak, often presents a picturesque appearance, in the early evening, or in a fog, with the gleam of the fire lighting up her half somnolent figure.

Source A: *The Gastronomical Me*	Source F: *London Labour and the London Poor*

---------- fold ----------

urgent · enthusiastic · calm · sentimental

quiet · relaxed · flat · factual

excited · reverential · surprised

aggressive · emotional · emotive

slow · measured · hurried

132

AQA ENGLISH — Grades 5-9

Main activity: Comparing tone and pace

Timing: 20 mins

Learning objectives
- To be able to analyse and compare pace and tone in two texts

Equipment
none

Look again at your responses in the previous activity.

1. Which words and sentence forms make a significant contribution to the pace and tone of the extracts? Underline them.

2. Look at the pace and tone you identified in Source F: *London Labour and the London Poor*, and the words and sentence forms that contribute to them. Use them to help you rewrite the extract from Source A: *The Gastronomical Me* with a similar tone and pace.
   Make sure you:
   - reuse the key points of information in the extract
   - use sentence forms and vocabulary choice to change its tone.

   ----

3. Review your rewritten version of the extract from Source A. Which sentence forms and vocabulary choices make a significant contribution to its new tone and pace? Underline them.

ENGLISH
Grades 5-9

MAIN ACTIVITY: STRUCTURING A COMPARISON	**TIMING: 20 MINS**

LEARNING OBJECTIVES
- To be able to craft a cohesive comparison of two texts

EQUIPMENT
none

Look at these sentences exploring the writers' views and experiences of food in Source F: *London Labour and the London Poor*, and Source A: *The Gastronomical Me*.

- The writer of Source F: *London Labour and the London Poor* initially creates a measured, factual tone.
- The writer of Source A uses a long sentence to build up cumulative detail.
- The writer initially focuses on specific, factual details of the time of year and cooking equipment: 'in the wintertime…' the stalls are 'fitted up with… an old saucepan with a fire inside…'.
- The writer of Source A: *The Gastronomical Me* creates a tone of excited anticipation.
- The writer of Source F uses a long sentence to build up cumulative detail.
- The writer focuses on the impact of the food on her senses: 'tantalizing clouds… juice-stained tables.'

1. Sequence and link these sentences to create a fluent, cohesive paragraph. Write your paragraph below.

AQA ENGLISH
Grades 5-9

| **Homework activity: Write your response** | **Timing: 30 mins** |

Learning objectives	**Equipment**
• To be able to analyse and compare pace and tone in two texts • To be able to craft a cohesive comparison of two texts	none

1. On a separate piece of paper, write a paragraph about the extracts in response to the Paper 2, Section A exam-style question.

> For this question, you need to refer to the **whole** of Source F: *London Labour and the London Poor* together with the **whole** of source A: *The Gastronomical Me*.
>
> Compare how the writers have conveyed their different views and experiences of food.
>
> In your answer, you could:
> - compare their different views and experiences
> - compare the methods used to convey those views and experiences
> - support your ideas with quotations from both texts.
>
> **[16 marks]**

2. When you have written your response, check you have achieved the success criteria below.
   a) Tick the criteria you feel you have achieved.

   ☐ identified and compared the writers' views and experiences of food in detail
   ☐ supported with relevant, focused evidence from the text
   ☐ compared how the writers use sentence forms, words, phrases and language features to convey their views and experiences
   ☐ carefully sequenced and linked your ideas
   ☐ carefully checked for accurate spelling and punctuation, and clear written expression

   b) Look at any of the criteria you feel you have not achieved. Add to and improve your response so that you can tick all of them.

ENGLISH
Grades 5-9
AQA

19 ANSWERS

STARTER ACTIVITY: THINKING ABOUT PACE AND TONE
1. Examples: Source A: enthusiastic, excited, emotional, reverential; Source F: factual, calm, measured.

MAIN ACTIVITY: COMPARING TONE AND PACE
1. Examples: Source F: dispassionate detail, e.g. 'winter time', 'apparatus', and longer sentence forms.
Source A: emotive vocabulary, e.g. 'tantalizing', 'loved', 'sacrificial priestess', and short sentence forms.
2. Examples: Clouds of steam emerged from the kitchen, while the fruit was on the porch in crates, or readied for the pots upon the juice-stained tables. Grandmother, always saving, stood in the steam, 'skimming' into a thick white saucer, and I, sometimes permitted and more often not, put my finger into the froth and licked it, which I enjoyed greatly.
3. Responses should show awareness of less emotive, more neutral vocabulary choices and longer sentence forms.

MAIN ACTIVITY: STRUCTURING A COMPARISON
1. Examples: <u>Both</u> writers use a long sentence to build up cumulative detail, <u>however</u> the writer of Source F: *London Labour and the London Poor* initially creates a measured, factual tone, <u>whereas</u> the writer of Source A: *The Gastronomical Me* creates a tone of excited anticipation. The writer of Source F initially focuses on specific, factual details of the time of year and cooking equipment: 'in the wintertime' the stalls are 'fitted up with… an old saucepan with a fire inside' <u>while</u> the writer of Source A focuses on the impact of the food on her senses: 'tantalizing clouds', 'juice-stained tables.'

HOMEWORK ACTIVITY: WRITE YOUR RESPONSE
1. Points covered might include: Source F: the factual tone created through the use of formal language choice, e.g. 'observation', and statistics; the more engaging use of first person and direct quotation.
Source A: the casual, intimate tone of first person, informal language choice, e.g. 'I suppose' and the second, short, conversational sentence; vivid descriptive language, e.g. 'greyish-pink fuzz', 'spitting kettle'.
2. Student's own answer. Ensure student has achieved all, or the majority of, the success criteria.

GLOSSARY

Pace
The speed at which ideas are presented or developed in the text

Tone
The voice in which ideas are expressed in the text

ENGLISH
Grades 5-9

20 READING: WRITING A COMPARISON

LEARNING OBJECTIVES
- To be able to analyse and compare ideas and perspectives in two texts
- To be able to plan and structure a comparison of two texts

SPECIFICATION LINKS
- 3.1.1 comparing texts

STARTER ACTIVITY
- **Assessing an example; 10 minutes; page 138**
  Give the student five minutes to reread Source B: *The Uncommercial Traveller* (page 18) and Source C: *Inside Facebook and Friends* (page 19). Ask the student to complete the task, identifying the successful features of this paragraph.

MAIN ACTIVITIES
- **Surveying the sources; 20 minutes; page 139**
  Suggest that the student numbers each significant view and experience, and then annotates the relevant evidence in the source with the same number. Make explicit the process of clarifying and summarising the writers' intentions, ideas and perspectives, and then identifying relevant supporting evidence.
- **Structuring your response; 15 minutes; page 140**
  Before the student begins question 1, remind them to look for any clear similarities and parallels that reveal significant differences. In question 2, draw attention to the process of identifying key points and evidence, reviewing, synthesising and sequencing.

PLENARY ACTIVITY
- **Review; 5 minutes**
  Ask the student to evaluate and summarise their comparison skills and their readiness to complete the homework task.

HOMEWORK ACTIVITY
- **Write your response; 30 minutes; page 141**
  Remind the student to focus their response on the point of comparison in the question – views and experiences of workplaces.

SUPPORT IDEA
- **Surveying the sources** Prompt the student to identify key points in one text, and then consider whether the second text features similar or different views and experiences.

EXTENSION IDEA
- **Surveying the sources; Structuring your response** Challenge the student to identify and fully synthesise all significant views and experiences, and points of comparison.

PROGRESS AND OBSERVATIONS

ENGLISH
Grades 5-9
AQA

STARTER ACTIVITY: ASSESSING AN EXAMPLE

TIMING: 10 MINS

LEARNING OBJECTIVES
- To be able to analyse and compare ideas and perspectives in two texts
- To be able to plan and structure a comparison of two texts

EQUIPMENT
- Source B: *The Uncommercial Traveller*
- Source C: *Inside Facebook and Friends*

Read Source B: *The Uncommercial Traveller* and Source C: *Inside Facebook and Friends*. Then look at the paragraph below from one student's response to the Paper 2, Section A exam-style question.

For this question, you need to refer to the **whole** of Source B: *The Uncommercial Traveller* and the **whole** of source C: *Inside Facebook and Friends*.

Compare how the writers have conveyed their different views and experiences of the workplaces they visit.

In your response, you could:
- compare their different views and experiences
- compare the methods they use to convey those views and experiences
- support your ideas with quotations from both texts.

[16 marks]

The openings of both texts immediately engage the reader with surprising and vivid descriptions. In The Uncommercial Traveller, the writer begins with a deafeningly onomatopoeic and repetitive list of sounds, some capitalised for even greater impact, before revealing their source: the building of an 'iron armour-plated ship'. The writer suggests his own shock as though he has come across this noise by mistake: 'What on earth is this!' Similarly, the writer of Inside Facebook and Friends focuses initially on a 'fifth floor putting green' before revealing that he is visiting 'Samsung's Silicon Valley headquarters', and going on to list 'a cactus garden... a robotic massage chair... a volleyball match... nap pods...' and more. Both sources effectively conjure a clear impression of the workplace they are describing: the noise and clamour of one, the extraordinary and luxurious facilities at the other.

---

1. **What has this student done well in their analysis? Annotate the paragraph, thinking about the following points.**

   - Has the student compared ideas and perspectives in a perceptive way?
   - Have they analysed how writers' methods are used?
   - Have they used examples from the text?
   - Have they shown an understanding of the different ideas and perspectives in both texts?

AQA ENGLISH
Grades 5-9

MAIN ACTIVITY: SURVEYING THE SOURCES **TIMING: 20 MINS**

LEARNING OBJECTIVES
- To be able to analyse and compare ideas and perspectives in two texts
- To be able to plan and structure a comparison of two texts

EQUIPMENT
- Source B: *The Uncommercial Traveller*
- Source C: *Inside Facebook and Friends*

In this lesson, you are going to focus on the Paper 2, Section A exam-style question from the Starter activity.

> For this question, you need to refer to the **whole** of Source B: *The Uncommercial Traveller* and the **whole** of source C: *Inside Facebook and Friends*.
>
> Compare how the writers have conveyed their different views and experiences of the workplaces they visit.
>
> In your response, you could:
> - compare their different views and experiences
> - compare the methods they use to convey those views and experiences
> - support your ideas with quotations from both texts.
>
> [16 marks]

1. What are the writers' intentions in each source? Write a sentence summarising them in the table below.
2. Survey Source B: *The Uncommercial Traveller*. Note the writer's views and experiences in the table below and underline any relevant evidence in the source.
3. Survey Source C: *Inside Facebook and Friends*. Note the writer's views and experiences in the table below and underline any relevant evidence in the source.

	Source B: *The Uncommercial Traveller*	Source C: *Inside Facebook and Friends*
Intention		
Views/experiences		

4. Review the evidence you have identified in each text. How do the writers' choices convey their views and experiences? Annotate the evidence.

ENGLISH
— Grades 5-9 —

| MAIN ACTIVITY: STRUCTURING YOUR RESPONSE | TIMING: 15 MINS |

LEARNING OBJECTIVES
- To be able to plan and structure a comparison of two texts

EQUIPMENT
- Source B: *The Uncommercial Traveller*
- Source C: *Inside Facebook and Friends*
- *Surveying the sources* activity sheet

1. Review your notes from the previous activity. What points of comparison can you find? Draw lines to link any significant similarities or differences.

2. Look again at your notes. Do you have enough, too little or too much material to write a successful, detailed comparison in response to the exam-style question? Tick one box and follow the instructions.

    ☐ **Too little** – return to the sources. What other significant views, experiences and evidence can you identify?
    ☐ **Too much** – which are the most significant points that will allow you to write the most detailed and perceptive comparison? Tick them.
    ☐ **Enough** – Move on to question 3.

3. What three or four key points will you make in your comparison? Write them below.

----

4. Now you have gathered enough significant material for your response, you need to sequence your ideas. Think about the most logical, effective order in which to use your ideas. Number your key points.

AQA ENGLISH
Grades 5-9

HOMEWORK ACTIVITY: WRITE YOUR RESPONSE   **TIMING: 30 MINS**

LEARNING OBJECTIVES
- To be able to analyse and compare ideas and perspectives in two texts
- To be able to plan and structure a comparison of two texts

EQUIPMENT
- Source B: *The Uncommercial Traveller*
- Source C: *Inside Facebook and Friends*
- *Surveying the sources* activity sheet
- *Structuring your response* activity sheet

Read this Paper 2, Section A exam-style question.

> For this question, you need to refer to the **whole** of Source B: *The Uncommercial Traveller* and the **whole** of source C: *Inside Facebook and Friends*.
>
> Compare how the writers have conveyed their different views and experiences of the workplaces they visit.
>
> In your response, you could:
> - compare their different views and experiences
> - compare the methods they use to convey those views and experiences
> - support your ideas with quotations from both texts.
>
> **[16 marks]**

1. Write your response to this question on a separate piece of paper.

2. When you have written your response, check you have achieved the success criteria below.

    a) Tick the criteria you feel you have achieved.

    - ☐ identified and compared the writers' views and experiences
    - ☐ supported with relevant, focused evidence from the text
    - ☐ analysed and compared how the writers use structure, sentence forms, words, phrases and language features to convey their views and experiences
    - ☐ carefully sequenced and linked your ideas
    - ☐ written in paragraphs
    - ☐ carefully checked for accurate spelling and punctuation, and clear written expression

    b) Look at any of the criteria you feel you have not achieved. Add to and improve your response so that you can tick all of them.

20 ANSWERS

STARTER ACTIVITY: ASSESSING AN EXAMPLE

1. Annotations may identify: focuses on structural feature (the opening); identifies impact on the reader (immediate engagement); comments on language (onomatopoeia) and sentence forms (repetitive listing); comments on effect ('conjure a clear impression'); provides a range of supporting evidence; cohesive features ('both texts', 'similarly')

MAIN ACTIVITY: SURVEYING THE SOURCES

1. Source B: to convey the scale of, and labour needed to build, the ship; Source C: to convey the scale and facilities of technology companies' workplaces.
2. Examples:
The writer represents the work as physically challenging ('busy figures', 'smoke and fire', 'bared arms and sledge-hammers').
The environment is loud and chaotic (Boom, Rattle, Clash, BANG).
The writer is awed by the scale of the workplace ('twelve hundred men working on stages over her sides, over her bows, over her stern, under her keel').
He is concerned by the boat's purpose (the dreadful day... when the scuppers... shall run red).
3. Examples:
The writer represents the work as surprisingly relaxed ('spinning class', 'grilled cheese bar').
The environment is filled with the sounds of play ('Raucous shrieks of table football').
The writer is impressed by the size of the workspace ('Stretching across 40,000 square metres').
He is concerned by the contrasting poverty outside ('the tents of a homeless encampment').
4. Ensure appropriate focus on writers' choices of sentence form and vocabulary.

MAIN ACTIVITY: STRUCTURING YOUR RESPONSE

1. Ensure the student makes appropriate links.
2. Student's own answer. Ensure they have judged correctly.
3. Ensure they choose valid points that can be supported by evidence.
4. Ensure the points are logically sequenced.

HOMEWORK ACTIVITY: WRITE YOUR RESPONSE

1.

Marks	Criteria
13–16 marks	<ul><li>Clear and detailed analysis of the writers' choices</li><li>A carefully selected range of relevant, focused textual evidence from both texts</li><li>A developed and considered understanding of the different ideas and perspectives in both texts</li></ul>
9–12 marks	<ul><li>Clear explanation on the writer's choices</li><li>A range of relevant, focused textual evidence from both texts</li><li>A clear understanding of the different ideas and perspectives in both texts</li></ul>
5–8 marks	<ul><li>Some comments on the writer's choices</li><li>Relevant and focused textual evidence from one or both texts</li><li>Awareness of range of different ideas and perspectives</li></ul>
1–4 marks	<ul><li>Straightforward comments on the writer's choices</li><li>Largely relevant textual evidence</li><li>Some awareness of ideas and or perspectives</li></ul>
No marks	<ul><li>No creditable response</li></ul>

2. Student's own answer. Ensure student has achieved all, or the majority of, the success criteria.

ENGLISH
Grades 5-9

21 Descriptive and narrative writing: Gathering ideas

LEARNING OBJECTIVES	SPECIFICATION LINKS
• To be able to gather ideas for a descriptive writing task • To be able to gather ideas for a narrative writing task	• 3.1.2 writing for impact

STARTER ACTIVITY

- **Perspective and intention; 10 minutes; page 144**
  Ask the student to complete the task. Discuss each perspective and intention, establishing clear connections between them. Which perspective is most likely to achieve each possible intention?

MAIN ACTIVITIES

- **Gathering descriptive ideas; 15 minutes; page 145**
  Give the student a time limit of five to seven minutes to complete questions 1 and 2, encouraging them to note as many ideas as possible, whether good or bad, in the time available. Prompt them to discuss their decisions as they complete question 3.
- **Gathering narrative ideas; 20 minutes; page 146**
  Remind the student of Source E: *The Ocean at the End of the Lane* (page 21) as a stimulus to the task. Emphasise that the narrative can be entirely fictional – and the narrator entirely unlike the writer. Explain that identifying the intention of the writing can be a source of inspiration. Direct the student to consider events, settings and characters that will make a contribution to their intention.

PLENARY ACTIVITY

- **Review; 5 minutes**
  Explain to the student that they will focus on structuring their ideas in the next lesson. Ask them to review the ideas they have gathered in this lesson. Do they have enough ideas to move on to structuring them? Emphasise that lack of raw material is a significant factor in less successful writing responses.

HOMEWORK ACTIVITY

- **Gathering practice; 30 minutes; page 147**
  Remind the student of Source D: *One Hundred Years of Solitude* (page 20) as a stimulus to the task. Note the similarity to the tasks completed in the lesson and explain that the more generous time allowance should produce a fuller, more considered response.

SUPPORT IDEA

- **Perspective and intention** Begin by focusing on just one perspective and the intentions it would support.

EXTENSION IDEA

- **Perspective and intention** Challenge the student to develop as many ideas as possible and add as many different adjectives as they can.

PROGRESS AND OBSERVATIONS

ENGLISH
Grades 5-9

STARTER ACTIVITY: PERSPECTIVE AND INTENTION	TIMING: 10 MINS

LEARNING OBJECTIVES
- To be able to gather ideas for a descriptive writing task

EQUIPMENT
none

Look at this Paper 1, Section B exam-style writing task.

Write a description suggested by this picture.

[40 marks]

Think about the **perspective** from which you could write. Ask yourself:

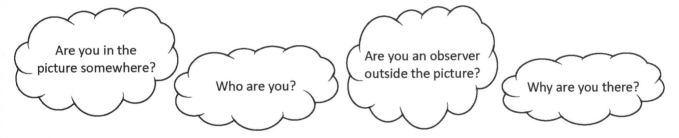

- Are you in the picture somewhere?
- Who are you?
- Are you an observer outside the picture?
- Why are you there?

1. On a separate piece of paper, write down as many different possibilities as you can.
2. To begin developing your ideas, add at least one adjective to each of your ideas.
3. Now think about your intention. What impact do you want your description to have on the reader? Do you want to create:

- sympathy?
- tension?
- humour?
- mystery?
- something else?

4. On a separate piece of paper, write down all the possible intentions you might have.

144

ENGLISH
Grades 5-9

| MAIN ACTIVITY: GATHERING DESCRIPTIVE IDEAS | TIMING: 15 MINS |

LEARNING OBJECTIVES
- To be able to gather ideas for a descriptive writing task

EQUIPMENT
- *Perspective and intention* activity sheet

1. Look again at your responses to the previous activity. From which perspective will you write? Which intention will you aim to achieve? Tick them.

2. Use the questions below to note down and develop as many ideas as you can.

What period of time will your description cover? Seconds, minutes or hours? What will happen in that time?	
What thoughts and feelings will your narrator experience and describe?	Think about the narrator's five senses. What will they see, hear, smell, taste or touch?

3. Look at the ideas you have gathered. Which might you use in your response to the writing task? Tick them.

ENGLISH
— Grades 5-9 —

Main activity: Gathering narrative ideas

Timing: 20 mins

Learning objectives
- To be able to gather ideas for a narrative writing task

Equipment
none

Look at this Paper 1, Section B exam-style writing task.

> Describe an occasion when a place or an event sparked a memory of your childhood.
> **[40 marks]**

1. **Think about the main focus of your writing. What event or place will you write about? What memory will it spark?**
   a) Write down three ideas.

   ----

   b) Choose **one** of your ideas. Tick it.

2. **Think about the intention or intentions you could aim to achieve in your writing.**
   a) Note your intention(s) in the space below.
   b) How will you use events, characters and settings to help you achieve them? Use the spaces below to develop your ideas.

Intention(s)	
Events / action	
Characters	**Settings**

146

ENGLISH
— Grades 5–9 —

HOMEWORK ACTIVITY: GATHERING PRACTICE   **TIMING: 30 MINS**

LEARNING OBJECTIVES
- To be able to gather ideas for a narrative writing task

EQUIPMENT
none

Look at this Paper 1, Section B exam-style writing task.

> Describe an occasion when you bought something and regretted it.
> **[40 marks]**

1. **Think about the main focus of your writing. What did you buy? Why did you regret it?**
   a) Write down three ideas.

   ----

   b) Choose one of your ideas. Tick it.

2. **Think about the intention or intentions you could aim to achieve in your writing.**
   a) Note your intention(s) in the space below.
   b) How will you use events, characters and settings to help you achieve them? Use the spaces below to develop your ideas.

Intention(s)	
Events / action	
Characters	**Settings**

147

21 ANSWERS

STARTER ACTIVITY: PERSPECTIVE AND INTENTION
1. Examples: a driver or passenger; a child in the back of the car.
2. Examples: a lost, late or frustrated driver or passenger; a bored, anxious or irritating child in the back of the car.
3. All suggestions given are valid; other intentions could include creating a sense of danger, frustration or isolation.
4. Student's own answers

MAIN ACTIVITY: GATHERING DESCRIPTIVE IDEAS
1. Student's own answer
2. Student's own answers. Ensure as wide a range of focused, relevant responses as possible. Ensure each idea contributes to the identified intention.
3. Student's own answer. Ensure the chosen ideas are appropriate and focused.

MAIN ACTIVITY: GATHERING NARRATIVE IDEAS
1. Student's own answers
2. Student's own answers. Ensure as wide a range of focused, relevant responses as possible. Ensure each idea contributes to the identified intention.

HOMEWORK ACTIVITY: GATHERING PRACTICE
1. Student's own answer
2. Student's own answers. Ensure as wide a range of focused, relevant responses as possible. Ensure each idea contributes to the identified intention.

GLOSSARY
Perspective
The writer or narrator's viewpoint

ENGLISH
Grades 5-9

22 DESCRIPTIVE AND NARRATIVE WRITING: STRUCTURING IDEAS

LEARNING OBJECTIVES
- To be able to structure and sequence ideas for impact

SPECIFICATION LINKS
- 3.1.2 writing for impact

STARTER ACTIVITY
- **Story structure; 5 minutes; page 150**
  Begin by explaining the difference between descriptive and narrative writing, and that the student will have a choice between them in Paper 1, Section B of the exam. This activity focuses on the same exam-style writing task as the homework from lesson 21. Ask the student to respond to the questions, using the ideas gathered in the homework task to clarify and structure their ideas.

MAIN ACTIVITIES
- **Structuring description; 20 minutes; page 151**
  Focus the student's attention on ways in which ideas could be selected and shaped for impact. For example, could the spider's progress become a metaphor for the driver's progress? Emphasise that ideas that do not make a significant contribution to the text should be cut.
- **Structuring narrative writing; 20 minutes; page 152**
  Draw attention to the similarity between this task and the previous activity – both involve reviewing, selecting and shaping ideas. Suggest that the student reviews the plan in light of the story structure explored in the starter activity. Remind them that the strongest planning is likely to focus on dramatic impact and character, avoiding unnecessary detail or distraction.

PLENARY ACTIVITY
- **Review; 5 minutes**
  Ask the student to summarise and evaluate their skills in structuring narrative and descriptive writing.

HOMEWORK ACTIVITY
- **Plan your response; 30 minutes; page 153**
  This narrative task featured in lesson 21. You may wish to direct the student towards or away from it, depending on their confidence in gathering and structuring ideas.

SUPPORT IDEA
- **Structuring description; Structuring narrative writing** Focus on sequencing ideas logically before considering revisions to achieve impact.

EXTENSION IDEAS
- **Story structure** If time allows, ask the student to complete the task twice, exploring different ideas and ways of structuring them.
- **Structuring description; Structuring narrative writing** Challenge the student to develop and explore as many possibilities, and their impact, as time allows.

PROGRESS AND OBSERVATIONS

ENGLISH
Grades 5-9

STARTER ACTIVITY: STORY STRUCTURE   **TIMING: 5 MINS**

LEARNING OBJECTIVES
- To be able to structure and sequence ideas for impact

EQUIPMENT
none

Look at this Paper 1, Section B exam-style writing task.

> Describe an occasion when you bought something and regretted it.
> [40 marks]

Often stories follow this pattern:

Exposition — the setting and situation are explained → **Conflict** — a problem is introduced → **Climax** — the problem becomes more serious → **Resolution** — the problem is resolved, either happily or unhappily

1. Complete the table below to structure a story in response to the exam-style writing task at the top of the page.

What does the reader need to know at the beginning of this story?	
What problem will the character(s) have to face?	
How do things become more serious?	
How is the situation resolved?	

150

AQA ENGLISH — Grades 5-9

MAIN ACTIVITY: STRUCTURING DESCRIPTION **TIMING: 20 MINS**

LEARNING OBJECTIVES
- To be able to structure and sequence ideas for impact

EQUIPMENT
none

Look at one student's ideas, gathered in response to the Paper 1, Section B exam-style writing task below.

Write a description suggested by this picture.

[40 marks]

Writers often withhold information from the reader. When they reveal that information, it can change the whole perspective of the text and the reader's response to it. For example, they could withhold:
- who the narrator is
- where they are going
- who they are with

1. Which of these ideas would you advise the student to use in their description? Tick them.

2. Which ideas would you advise the student to withhold? Add your ideas to the student's notes on the right.

3. How would you sequence the ideas you have ticked and added to the notes on the right? Number them.

- ☐ I'm driving somewhere
- ☐ Boredom and frustration
- ☐ What other drivers are doing – laughing, yawning, singing
- ☐ Sunny weather – car getting hotter and hotter
- ☐ Hot, sweating, sticking to the car seat
- ☐ Counting the cars I can see, counting white lines on the road
- ☐ Wondering what's in the truck
- ☐ Increasingly angry
- ☐ Moving forward a metre... and another... and another every 5 minutes.
- ☐ Eating sweets, running out of water
- ☐ Car making strange noises
- ☐ Spider walking across dashboard of my car
- ☐ Drivers getting out and talking to each other
- ☐
- ☐
- ☐
- ☐
- ☐
- ☐

ENGLISH
Grades 5-9

AQA

MAIN ACTIVITY: STRUCTURING NARRATIVE WRITING   **TIMING: 20 MINS**

LEARNING OBJECTIVES
- To be able to structure and sequence for impact

EQUIPMENT
none

Read this Paper 1, Section B exam-style writing task.

> Describe an occasion when you bought something and regretted it.
> **[40 marks]**

Now look at one student's ideas, gathered in response to this task.

- ☐ Going to a Halloween party
- ☐ Everyone was going to be there – including Alex
- ☐ Alex is in my history lessons – really quiet but really clever...
- ☐ My friend told me Alex would be there. I didn't believe my friend. We had an argument about it and didn't speak to each other for ages.
- ☐ Couldn't decide what to go to the party as... had lots of ideas...
- ☐ Decided to go as Frankenstein's monster
- ☐ Spent hours planning costume – and bought face paint, bolts to go through my neck...
- ☐ The day of the party. My sister helped me get ready.
- ☐ My sister's really good at make up because she goes to our local drama club and has been in lots of plays and done the make-up.
- ☐ Got to the party. Saw Alex standing alone in the corner.
- ☐ Alex took one look and left the party

1. **Which of these ideas would you advise this student to use in their narrative writing? Tick them.**
   Remember: to craft the best possible piece of descriptive writing, you need to be ruthless in your selection of ideas!

2. **Review the ideas you have selected. How could this story be improved? Add your ideas to the notes above.**
   You could think about:
   - changing or adding to some of the ideas for the story
   - withholding information to create a surprise or twist in the story.

3. **How would you sequence the ideas you have ticked and added to the notes above? Number them.**
   Remember: you need to sequence and shape your ideas to create maximum impact on the reader.

AQA ENGLISH
Grades 5–9

HOMEWORK ACTIVITY: PLAN YOUR RESPONSE	TIMING: 30 MINS

LEARNING OBJECTIVES
- To be able to structure and sequence ideas for impact

EQUIPMENT
none

1. **Plan your response to one of these tasks on a separate piece of paper.**
   Make sure you:
   - gather a range of ideas
   - select, shape and sequence them.

Write a description suggested by this picture.

[40 marks]

Describe an occasion when a place or an event sparked a memory of your childhood.
[40 marks]

22 ANSWERS

STARTER ACTIVITY: STORY STRUCTURE
1. Student's own answers

MAIN ACTIVITY: STRUCTURING DESCRIPTION
1. All are potentially valid.
2. Ensure suggestions create a significant impact, e.g. to build tension; to create a surprise; to alter the reader's perspective.
3. Ensure sequence follows a logical progression, with appropriate attention to its impact.

MAIN ACTIVITY: STRUCTURING NARRATIVE WRITING
1. The relevance or likely impact of some suggestions is questionable, e.g. the argument with a friend, the sister's make-up skills.
2. The resolution lacks impact and significance in the light of the preceding ideas. Why might Alex have left in such a hurry?
3. Ensure sequence follows a logical progression, with appropriate attention to its impact.

HOMEWORK ACTIVITY: PLAN YOUR RESPONSE
1. See exam-style mark scheme on pages 251–253.

GLOSSARY

Exposition
The beginning of a story, when the setting and situation are introduced

Conflict
A complication in the plot

Climax
The building of tension, which creates a sense of expectation in the reader

Resolution
The ending, when the action is resolved

AQA ENGLISH — Grades 5-9

23 DESCRIPTIVE AND NARRATIVE WRITING: BEGINNINGS AND ENDINGS

LEARNING OBJECTIVES	SPECIFICATION LINKS
• To be able to plan effective openings • To be able to plan effective endings	• 3.1.2 writing for impact

STARTER ACTIVITY

- **Top and tail; 5 minutes; page 156**
  Discuss genre with the student. Do these story plans fit a specific genre? How could it guide their responses? How could they avoid the stereotypes of the genre? Review responses to question 2, aiming for as complete a response as possible.

MAIN ACTIVITIES

- **Openings; 20 minutes; page 157**
  Remind the student that they planned a response to this exam-style writing task for homework in lesson 21 and/or 22, and that they can develop those ideas here. Review the advantages of each possible opening: what impact would each have on the reader?

- **Endings; 20 minutes; page 158**
  Ask the student to identify effective endings to stories and films they have read or seen. What made them effective? What impact did they have? Refer the student to ideas they gathered in the starter activity, which they may want to adapt or revise for question 2.

PLENARY ACTIVITY

- **Gathering some ideas; 5 minutes**
  Ask the student to look at the homework task and suggest two or three possible beginnings and endings. Point out that they may want to refer to or adapt the plans they made for homework in lesson 21.

HOMEWORK ACTIVITY

- **From start to finish; 30 minutes; page 159**
  Highlight the details of the task: planning two or three possible openings and endings, and writing one opening.

SUPPORT IDEAS

- **Top and tail** Prompt the student to consider the conventions of each genre.
- **Openings; Endings** Concentrate on two possible openings and endings, focusing closely on the impact of each.

EXTENSION IDEA

- **Openings; Endings** Challenge the student to generate original ideas that go beyond, or subvert, the conventions of genre.

PROGRESS AND OBSERVATIONS

ENGLISH
Grades 5-9

AQA

| STARTER ACTIVITY: TOP AND TAIL | TIMING: 5 MINS |

LEARNING OBJECTIVES
- To be able to plan effective openings
- To be able to plan effective endings

EQUIPMENT
none

Look at these incomplete story plans.

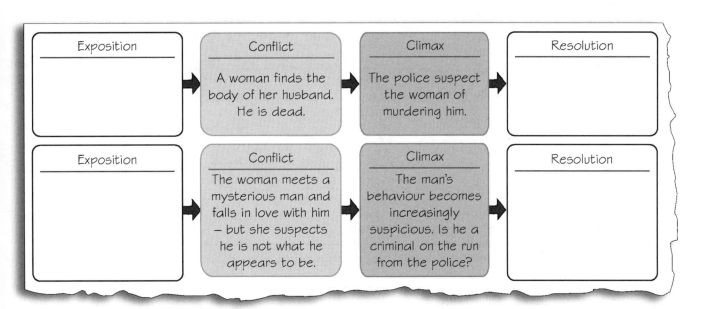

1. How could they begin? How might they end? Fill in the gaps in the plans.

2. Complete the sentences below.

   a) An effective story opening should…

   ....

   ....

   ....

   b) An effective story ending should…

   ....

   ....

   ....

AQA ENGLISH — Grades 5-9

MAIN ACTIVITY: OPENINGS **TIMING: 20 MINS**

LEARNING OBJECTIVES
- To be able to plan effective openings

EQUIPMENT
- *Top and tail* activity sheet

1. Look again at your responses to the *Top and tail* activity.
    a) Which of these suggestions would you choose as the opening focus of the story? Tick it.

   | Expoisition: A woman finds her husband's body. | Conflict: A man is out walking. He suspects someone is following him... | Climax: A happy couple eat breakfast together. The husband decides to go for a walk... |

   Write a sentence explaining your choice.

   _____

   _____

   _____

2. Look at this Paper 1, Section B exam-style writing task.

   > Describe an occasion when a place or an event sparked a memory of your childhood.
   > **[40 marks]**

   a) Plan three different openings to your response, each with a different focus. Examples of occasions might be listening to a certain song, going on holiday somewhere, or eating a special meal.

1.	2.	3.

   b) Which of your ideas would be most effective? Write a sentence explaining your choice.

   _____

   _____

   _____

ENGLISH
— Grades 5-9 —

MAIN ACTIVITY: ENDINGS **TIMING: 20 MINS**

LEARNING OBJECTIVES
- To be able to plan effective endings

EQUIPMENT
none

A story ending can have a range of different impacts on the reader. For example, it could:
- shock
- surprise
- amuse
- satisfy expectations.

1. **Look at these four different kinds of ending. Label each one with the different impacts it might have on the reader. Use the ideas above and add some of your own.**

A happy ending	A twist	An unhappy ending	A cliffhanger
The conflict in the story is successfully resolved.	The conflict is resolved in an unexpected way.	The conflict is resolved – but not happily.	The conflict is not resolved.

Look at this incomplete story plan.

> **Expoisition:** A woman has lived alone for years. Will she ever find love?
>
> **Conflict:** The woman meets a mysterious man and falls in love with him – but she suspects he is not what he appears to be.
>
> **Climax:** The man's behaviour becomes increasingly suspicious. Is he a criminal on the run from the police?

2. **Plan four different possible endings to this story.**

A happy ending	A twist	An unhappy ending	A cliffhanger

3. **Which of your endings do you find most effective? Tick it. Write a sentence or two explaining your choice.**

158

AQA ENGLISH
Grades 5-9

HOMEWORK ACTIVITY: FROM START TO FINISH   TIMING: 30 MINS

LEARNING OBJECTIVES
- To be able to plan effective openings
- To be able to plan effective endings

EQUIPMENT
none

Look at this Paper 1, Section B exam-style writing task.

> Describe an occasion when you bought something and regretted it.
> [40 marks]

1. Plan three different possible openings to this story on a separate piece of paper.

2. Choose one of your openings. Write the opening paragraph of your response to the task on a separate piece of paper.

3. What impact do you want this opening paragraph to have on the reader? Write three or four sentences explaining how you have tried to achieve it.

----

4. How could you end your story? Plan three different possible endings on a separate piece of paper.

5. What different impacts might these ending have on the reader? Write three or four sentences summarising their impact and how you might achieve it.

ENGLISH
Grades 5-9

23 ANSWERS

STARTER ACTIVITY: TOP AND TAIL
1. Student's own answers
2. a) An effective opening should immediately engage the reader.
b) An effective ending should resolve the conflict of the story and in some way justify the reader's engagement in it.

MAIN ACTIVITY: OPENINGS
1. a) All are valid responses
b) Examples: Action can launch the reader into immediate engagement; description can create mood or atmosphere; character can engage the reader's empathy.
2. a) Student's own answers
b) Student's own answers

MAIN ACTIVITY: ENDINGS
1. A happy ending: satisfy expectations; A twist: shock, surprise; An unhappy ending: shock, surprise, satisfy expectations; A cliffhanger: engage the reader's curiosity and imagination, or disappointment!
2. Examples:
A happy ending: The man is behaving suspiciously because he is buying her a surprise present.
A twist: The man is a policeman. He has been on a highly secret case that he has now successfully solved.
An unhappy ending: He is a criminal. She wakes up one morning and finds he has stolen all her money and valuables.
A cliffhanger: She becomes even more suspicious when he asks her about her jewellery.
3. Student's own answer

HOMEWORK ACTIVITY: FROM START TO FINISH
1. Student's own answers
2. Student's own answer
3. Student's own answer. Ensure response focuses on the impact of the opening on the reader.
4. Student's own answers
5. Student's own answer. Ensure response focuses on the impact of the ending on the reader.

GLOSSARY
Genre
A type of story or other text (e.g. romance, crime, supernatural) often characterised by typical features of character, plot, etc.

ENGLISH
Grades 5-9

24 Descriptive and narrative writing: Structuring paragraphs for effect

Learning objectives
- To be able to structure paragraphs for effect

Specification links
- 3.1.2 writing for impact

Starter activity
- **Thinking about paragraphs; 5 minutes; page 162**
  Ensure the student is confident in the 'rules' of paragraphing: new topic, new time, new setting, new speaker. Give them two or three minutes to consider and note their response to the prompt questions. Discuss. Explain that this lesson will explore ways in which the 'rules' can be ignored, and the impact that carefully sequenced sentences within paragraphs can have.

Main activities
- **Exploring paragraphs; 20 minutes; page 163**
  Read the exemplar paragraph aloud, emphasising key points of drama. As the student completes the task, note the positioning of the key points, drawing attention to the techniques of delaying them and isolating them in their own, short paragraph.
- **Structuring paragraphs; 20 minutes; page 164**
  Ask the student to cut out the sentences and complete the task, leaving a double space to indicate a change of paragraph. Encourage the student to experiment with alternative choices to test their impact, before making a final decision.

Plenary activity
- **Review; 5 minutes**
  Ask the student to summarise and evaluate their paragraphing skills. Ask the student to consider the homework task: how confident do they feel in applying their paragraphing skills to it?

Homework activity
- **Focus on paragraphing; 30 minutes; page 165**
  Suggest that the student focuses their writing on a moment of tension or revelation, selected from their planning for this task in previous lessons.

Support idea
- **Structuring paragraphs** Direct the student to focus on five or six of the sentences that would be effective structured in one longer and one shorter paragraph.

Extension idea
- **Homework** Challenge the student to produce two versions of their response, using different paragraphing choices. Which version is more effective? Why?

Progress and observations

ENGLISH
Grades 5–9

STARTER ACTIVITY: THINKING ABOUT PARAGRAPHS **TIMING: 5 MINS**

LEARNING OBJECTIVES
- To be able to structure paragraphs for effect

EQUIPMENT
none

1. List three reasons why writers use paragraphs.

....

....

....

2. How long should a paragraph be?

....

....

....

ENGLISH
Grades 5-9

| MAIN ACTIVITY: EXPLORING PARAGRAPHS | TIMING: 20 MINS |

LEARNING OBJECTIVES
- To be able to structure paragraphs for effect

EQUIPMENT
none

Read this extract from one student's response to the Paper 1, Section B exam-style writing task below.

Write a description suggested by this picture.

[40 marks]

I could feel the sun burning, blistering, cooking the back of my neck, and the hot sand searing the soles of my feet through my thick boots. My legs wanted me to fall to the ground and crawl. Only the thought of the hot sand on the soft, bare palms of my hands stopped me. If I fell, I would not get up again.

I peered helplessly towards the horizon, knowing I would see nothing but sand. But there in the distance, I saw a shape or shadow of a something.

I walked faster, legs aching, heart racing, until the shape become a cluster of shapes. The cluster became little white boxes sheltering in the shadow of lush green trees. It was a huddle of buildings. It was the village.

I had arrived.

1. Where are the key points of emphasis and drama in this extract? Identify and label them.

2. How has the student used paragraph structure to achieve this emphasis? Write two or three sentences explaining your ideas on a separate piece of paper.

ENGLISH
Grades 5-9

MAIN ACTIVITY: STRUCTURING PARAGRAPHS   **TIMING: 20 MINS**

LEARNING OBJECTIVES
- To be able to structure paragraphs for effect

EQUIPMENT
- scissors
- glue

Look at the sentences from one student's response to the Paper 1, Section B exam-style question below.

1. **Cut out the sentences and arrange them into paragraphs to achieve the greatest impact.**

2. **When you are happy with your paragraph(s), glue the sentences to a piece of paper and annotate your choices, identifying the impact you have tried to achieve with your structure.**

Write a description suggested by this picture.

[40 marks]

The air conditioning spluttered and wheezed, and the icy cold air quickly turned warm, then warmer, then hot.

Sweat gathered on my forehead, dripped into my eyebrows and ran down my face.

Panicking, I opened all the windows and the warm blast of city air choking in exhaust fumes and factory smoke hit me.

I looked at the clock, watching the minutes ticking away, racing towards midday.

Time was running out.

In less than an hour, it would be too late.

I sensed movement up ahead.
My heart leapt and I grabbed the wheel, my foot hovering over the accelerator.
One by one, the cars in front were edging forward, first one, then the next, and the next and, finally, me.

We edged another thirty centimetres forward and ground to a halt again.

My teeth and fists clenched tight, I ground my head into the steering wheel and tried to breathe.

Boredom turned to irritation. Irritation became frustration. Frustration became anger. Anger turned to fury. Fury became panic.

AQA ENGLISH — Grades 5-9

HOMEWORK ACTIVITY: FOCUS ON PARAGRAPHING   **TIMING: 30 MINS**

LEARNING OBJECTIVES
- To be able to structure paragraphs for effect

EQUIPMENT
none

1. Write a short section of your response to the Paper 1, Section B exam-style writing task below.
   Make sure you:
   - write 150–200 words
   - carefully structure your paragraphs for impact.

   > Describe an occasion when you bought something and regretted it.
   > [40 marks]

2. Annotate your writing, noting the paragraphing choices you have made and the impact you have tried to achieve.

24 Answers

Starter activity: Thinking about paragraphs
1. To make a text look more approachable; to signal a change of focus and to clarify meaning.
2. The minimum length of a paragraph is one sentence. A sentence can consist of a single word. There is no maximum length.

Main activity: Exploring paragraphs
1. Annotations should highlight the building tension and final revelation.
2. Responses should show awareness of: the tension built through longer sentences in the body of the longer paragraphs, culminating in the revelation of the final clause or sentence; the impact of the short paragraph.

Main activity: Structuring paragraphs
1. Example:
The air conditioning spluttered and wheezed and the icy cold air quickly turned warm, then warmer, then hot. Sweat gathered on my forehead, dripped into my eyebrows and ran down my face. Panicking, I opened all the windows and the warm blast of city air choking in exhaust fumes and factory smoke hit me.

I sensed movement up ahead.

My heart leapt and I grabbed the wheel, my foot hovering over the accelerator. One by one, the cars in front were edging forward, first one, then the next, and the next and, finally, me.

We edged another thirty centimetres forward and ground to a halt again.

I looked at the clock, watching the minutes ticking away, racing towards midday. Time was running out. My teeth and fists clenched tight, I ground my head into the steering wheel and tried to breathe. Boredom turned to irritation. Irritation became frustration. Frustration became anger. Anger turned to fury. Fury became panic.

In less than an hour, it would be too late.
2. Student's own answers

Homework activity: Focus on paragraphing
1. See exam-style mark scheme on pages 251–253.
2. Student's own answer. Ensure response is annotated, clearly identifying the choices made and their impact.

AQA ENGLISH — Grades 5-9

25 DESCRIPTIVE AND NARRATIVE WRITING: STRUCTURING SENTENCES

LEARNING OBJECTIVES

- To be able to structure sentences in a variety of ways

SPECIFICATION LINKS

- 3.1.2 producing clear and coherent text

STARTER ACTIVITY

- **Thinking about sentences; 10 minutes; page 168**
  Give the student two or three minutes to consider and note their response to the first question. Discuss the importance of punctuation and clear expression. Ask them to respond to questions 2 and 3 and then discuss their answers.

MAIN ACTIVITIES

- **Building up sentences; 20 minutes; page 169**
  This activity gives an opportunity to focus on how information can be linked within sentences. Focus on the ways in which sentences can be linked and the variety of possibilities, rather than parsing the sentences and memorising the terminology. Point out that every method is not necessarily possible in every case.
- **Structuring sentences; 15 minutes; page 170**
  Emphasise that in this activity, the student is practising a variety of sentence structures, but that variety is not the ultimate goal. The activity is preparation for the next lesson, where they will explore the impact of different sentence structures.

PLENARY ACTIVITY

- **Review; 5 minutes**
  Ask the student to summarise and evaluate their skill in structuring sentences.

HOMEWORK ACTIVITY

- **Crafting sentences; 30 minutes; page 171**
  Discourage the student from using one of each sentence type explored in the lesson for variety. Guide them to focus on achieving clarity and impact instead.

SUPPORT IDEA

- **Structuring sentences** Focus on the first five sentences. If time allows, then move on to the remaining sentences.

EXTENSION IDEA

- **Building up sentences** Explore how different structures clarify the relationship between the two pieces of information (e.g. the conjunction 'when' indicates time) and/or change the emphasis of the sentence.

PROGRESS AND OBSERVATIONS

ENGLISH
Grades 5-9

| STARTER ACTIVITY: THINKING ABOUT SENTENCES | TIMING: 10 MINS |

LEARNING OBJECTIVES
- To be able to structure sentences in a variety of ways

EQUIPMENT
none

Compare these two story openings.

> as i walked the sky darkening and the rain starting to fall and run down the back of my neck i saw something familiar from the corner of my eye i recognised the black railings the low wall the gate i had walked along that wall and through that gate every day for six years it was my primary school i stopped and stood in the rain and looked across the playground

> I walked and the sky darkened and the rain started to fall and run down the back of my neck and I saw something familiar from the corner of my eye and I recognised the black railings, the low wall and the gate because I had walked along and through them every day for six years and it was my primary school so I stopped and stood in the rain and looked across the playground.

1. What is missing from each one?

2. Give two ways in which sentences can improve our writing.

3. How long should a sentence be?

ENGLISH
Grades 5–9

MAIN ACTIVITY: BUILDING UP SENTENCES

TIMING: 20 MINS

LEARNING OBJECTIVES
- To be able to structure sentences in a variety of ways

EQUIPMENT
none

The sentences below all link the following two pieces of information:

> I was walking along the pavement. **+** I realised the sky had begun to darken.

Look carefully at the different ways in which the sentences link the information.

A. I was walking along the pavement and I realised the sky had begun to darken.

B. I was walking along the pavement when I realised the sky had begun to darken.

C. Walking along the pavement, I realised the sky had begun to darken.

D. I was walking along the pavement and looking at the sky, which was beginning to darken.

E. I walked along the pavement beneath the darkening sky.

1. Which word indicates the link between the two pieces of information in each sentence? Underline it.

2. In how many different ways can you link these two pieces of information? Write them out below.

> I stopped. **+** I looked across the empty playground.

ENGLISH — Grades 5-9 — AQA

MAIN ACTIVITY: STRUCTURING SENTENCES   **TIMING: 15 MINS**

LEARNING OBJECTIVES
- To be able to structure sentences in a variety of ways

EQUIPMENT
none

These sentences are all taken from a paragraph of one student's response to the Paper 1, Section B exam-style writing task below.

> Describe an occasion when a place or an event sparked a memory of your childhood.
> **[40 marks]**

- I walked.
- The sky darkened.
- Rain started to fall.
- It ran down the back of my neck.
- I saw something familiar from the corner of my eye.
- I recognised the black railings, the low wall, the gate.
- It was my primary school.
- I stopped.
- I stood in the rain.
- I looked across the playground.
- I had walked along that wall and through that gate every day for six years.

1. **Rewrite the sentences using different structures.**
   You could:
   - leave some pieces of information as short, simple sentences
   - link two, three or more pieces of information to form multiclause sentences.

   ....
   ....
   ....
   ....

2. **Use the checklist below to review your sentences.**
   - ☐ your meaning is clear
   - ☐ you have used a variety of different sentence structures.

3. **If you haven't ticked both boxes, revise your sentences.**

AQA ENGLISH — Grades 5-9

HOMEWORK ACTIVITY: CRAFTING SENTENCES   **TIMING: 30 MINS**

LEARNING OBJECTIVES
- To be able to structure sentences in a variety of ways

EQUIPMENT
none

1. Write one paragraph in response to the Paper 1, Section B exam-style writing task below.

   > Describe an occasion when a place or an event sparked a memory of your childhood.
   > **[40 marks]**

2. **Review your sentence structures.**
   Make sure that:
   - your meaning is clear
   - you have used a variety of different sentence structures.

3. **Rewrite your paragraph using a variety of different sentence structures.**
   You could:
   - change the ways you have linked information in multiclause sentences
   - break some sentences down into shorter sentences
   - build up shorter sentences by linking them.

4. **Which version of your paragraph do you prefer? Write a sentence or two explaining your choice.**

ENGLISH
Grades 5-9

25 ANSWERS

STARTER ACTIVITY: THINKING ABOUT SENTENCES
1. The first is missing all punctuation; the second lacks variety and is one long, unmanageable, repetitive sentence.
2. Examples: to make meaning clearer; to create an effect such as suspense.
3. There is no minimum or maximum length.

MAIN ACTIVITY: BUILDING UP SENTENCES
1. A: I was walking along the pavement and I realised the sky had begun to darken.
B: I was walking along the pavement when I realised the sky had begun to darken.
C: Walking along the pavement, I realised the sky had begun to darken.
D: I was walking along the pavement and looking at the sky, which was beginning to darken.
E: I walked along the pavement beneath the darkening sky.
2. Examples:
I stopped <u>and</u> looked across the empty playground.
<u>As</u> I stopped, I looked across the empty playground.
<u>Stopping</u>, I looked across the empty playground.
I stopped <u>and</u> looked across the playground <u>which</u> was empty.

MAIN ACTIVITY: STRUCTURING SENTENCES
1. Student's own answer. Example: As I walked, the sky darkening and the rain starting to fall and run down the back of my neck, I saw something familiar from the corner of my eye. I recognised the black railings, the low wall, the gate because I had walked along that wall and through those gates every day for six years. It was my primary school. I stopped and stood in the rain and looked across the playground.
2. Ensure both criteria are met.
3. Student's own answers

HOMEWORK ACTIVITY: CRAFTING SENTENCES
1. See exam-style mark scheme on pages 251–253.
2. Ensure both criteria are met.
3. Student's own answer. Ensure clarity of meaning and a variety of sentence structures.
4. Student's own answer

GLOSSARY

Coordinating conjunction
A word linking two coordinate clauses, such as *and*, *but*, *or*. For example: I ate dinner <u>and</u> went to bed

Subordinating conjunction
A word linking a subordinate clause to a main clause, such as *when*, *if*, *although*. For example: I ate dinner <u>because</u> I was hungry

Adverbial phrase
A phrase that modifies a verb, an adjective or another adverbial. For example: He hid <u>under the table</u>

Non-finite verb
A verb form that can be a present participle (*walking*), a past participle (*walked*) or an infinitive (*to walk*)

Relative clause
Modifies a noun phrase, linked with a relative pronoun, such as *that*, *who*, *which*. For example: The man <u>who lives next door</u> is noisy

ENGLISH
— Grades 5-9 —

26 DESCRIPTIVE AND NARRATIVE WRITING: STRUCTURING SENTENCES FOR EFFECT

LEARNING OBJECTIVES	SPECIFICATION LINKS
• To be able to manipulate sentence structure for effect	• 3.1.2 writing for impact

STARTER ACTIVITY

- **Sentence length; 5 minutes; page 174**
  Read the extract carefully. Focus the student's attention on the use of longer sentences to convey descriptive detail and shorter sentences to achieve dramatic impact. Note the use of minor sentences for still greater emphasis.

MAIN ACTIVITIES

- **Comparing sentence structures; 20 minutes; page 175**
  Ask the student to focus firstly on the differences between the two extracts and then on the impact of those differences. Point out that, when producing their own writing, their decisions about sentence structure are likely to be instinctive rather than academic. The aim of this activity is simply to acknowledge that there are numerous ways to express the same ideas, some of which are more effective than others.

- **Building sentences for impact; 20 minutes; page 176**
  Explain to the student that using the ideas provided will allow them to focus on crafting effective sentences. However, they can edit or add to them if they wish. Suggest that they consider using a minor sentence (with the caveat that these should be used sparingly!)

PLENARY ACTIVITY

- **Review; 5 minutes**
  Ask the student to review their two responses from the previous activity. Which version do they prefer? Why? Focus attention on clarity of expression, and the ways in which sentence form alters the emphasis and impact of their writing.

HOMEWORK ACTIVITY

- **Crafting sentences for impact; 30 minutes; page 177**
  Ask the student to write an extract of 100–150 words. Emphasise the importance of completing the task twice, experimenting with different sentence structures in each version. You may want to ask the student to produce a final draft, compiling the most effective elements of each version.

SUPPORT IDEA

- **Comparing sentence structures** Focus only on the sentence structures whose impact is immediately apparent to the student.

EXTENSION IDEA

- **Comparing sentence structures** Ask the student to compile a final draft of the extract, taking the most successful elements of each version. Explore their decisions and the impact they create.

PROGRESS AND OBSERVATIONS

ENGLISH
Grades 5–9

| STARTER ACTIVITY: SENTENCE LENGTH | TIMING: 5 MINS |

LEARNING OBJECTIVES
- To be able to manipulate sentence structure for effect

EQUIPMENT
none

Look at this extract from one student's response to the Paper 1, Section B exam-style writing task below.

> Describe an occasion when a place or an event sparked a memory of your childhood.
> **[40 marks]**

> As I peered through the school railings, a cold wind blew up, sending a crisp packet bounding and flapping and turning somersaults across the playground.
>
> 'Come back here!' shouted a voice in my memory.
>
> It was me, aged seven, shouting at the backs of the biggest, scariest boys in the school as they ran off with my packed lunch.
>
> 'Please!'
>
> I can still feel the tears now, and the frustration, and the rage. I can remember running after them, my arms flailing. But I can't remember what happened next. None of it. Nothing.

1. **Look closely at the length of the sentences. How does the student use sentences of different lengths to achieve their intention and create a significant impact on the reader? Annotate the extract.**

ENGLISH
— Grades 5–9 —

MAIN ACTIVITY: COMPARING SENTENCE STRUCTURES   **TIMING: 20 MINS**

LEARNING OBJECTIVES
- To be able to manipulate sentence structure for effect

EQUIPMENT
none

Look at two different versions of the same sentences, taken from one student's response to the Paper 1, Section B exam-style writing task below.

> Describe an occasion when a place or an event sparked a memory of your childhood.
> **[40 marks]**

As I peered through the school railings, a cold wind blew up, sending a crisp packet bounding and flapping and turning somersaults across the playground.

'Come back here!' shouted a voice in my memory.

It was me, aged seven, shouting at the backs of the biggest, scariest boys in the school as they ran off with my packed lunch.

'Please!'

A crisp packet, blown by the cold wind, bounded and flapped and turned somersaults across the playground as I peered through the school railings.

'Come back here! Please!' shouted a voice in my memory.

It was me, aged seven. The biggest, scariest boys in the school had run off with my packed lunch. I was shouting at their backs.

---

1. What differences can you see in the sentence forms the writer has chosen to use in each version? Annotate them.

2. How does each of these differences alter the emphasis of the sentences? Annotate them.

3. How does each of these differences contribute to the writer's intention? Annotate them.

ENGLISH
— Grades 5-9 —

MAIN ACTIVITY: BUILDING SENTENCES FOR IMPACT　　　　**TIMING: 20 MINS**

LEARNING OBJECTIVES
- To be able to manipulate sentence structure for effect

EQUIPMENT
none

Look at these ideas from one student's plan, written in response to the Paper 1, Section B exam-style writing task below.

> Describe an occasion when a place or an event sparked a memory of your childhood.
> [40 marks]

- busy school canteen
- hubbub of voices, clatter of plates, shouting, laughing
- crash of dropped plate
- shocked silence
- sudden eruption of cheers and laughter
- reminded me of that disastrous Christmas all those years ago…

1. Use the student's ideas to write four or five sentences.

2. Review the structure and impact of your sentences, then redraft them using different sentence forms and structures.
   Think about:
   - how you have linked information in sentences
   - the order in which you have linked information in sentences
   - the length of your sentences.

ENGLISH
— Grades 5-9 —

HOMEWORK ACTIVITY: CRAFTING SENTENCES FOR IMPACT   TIMING: **30** MINS

LEARNING OBJECTIVES
- To be able to manipulate sentence structure for effect

EQUIPMENT
none

1. On a separate piece of paper, write the opening of your response to the Paper 1, Section B exam-style writing task below.

Write a description suggested by this picture.

[40 marks]

2. Rewrite the opening of your response, revising your use of sentence forms for greater impact.
   Think about:
   - how you have linked information in sentences
   - the order in which you have linked information in sentences
   - the length of your sentences.

3. Which draft do you prefer? Annotate your preferred draft, noting the impact of each chosen sentence form.

26 ANSWERS

STARTER ACTIVITY: SENTENCE LENGTH

1. Longer sentences convey descriptive detail; shorter sentences create dramatic impact; minor sentences create still greater emphasis.

MAIN ACTIVITY: COMPARING SENTENCE STRUCTURES

1. Examples: Paragraph 1: The subordinate clause 'As I peered' is in a different position.
Paragraph 2: 'Please' is in a different position.
Paragraph 3: Shorter sentences, and the two clauses focusing on 'the biggest, scariest boys' and the narrator 'shouting at their backs' are reversed.
2. Paragraph 1: The sentence's initial emphasis is focused either on the narrator 'As I peered…' or 'A crisp packet…'.
Paragraph 2: Positioning 'Please' later allows each shorter piece of dialogue greater emphasis.
Paragraph 3: The more staccato short sentences arguably suggest the narrator's anger.
3. Paragraph 1: Arguably, the focus on the crisp packet draws the reader's focus away from the narrator, weakening cohesion with the next paragraph.
Paragraph 2: Positioning 'Please' here effectively suggests the narrator's increasing desperation.
Paragraph 3: The longer, more fluid, single-sentence version does not draw attention so markedly from the dialogue.

MAIN ACTIVITY: BUILDING SENTENCES FOR IMPACT

1. Student's own answer
2. Student's own answer. Ensure significant revision to sentence forms.

HOMEWORK ACTIVITY: CRAFTING SENTENCES FOR IMPACT

1. See exam-style mark scheme on pages 251–253.
2. Student's own answer. Ensure significant revision to sentence forms.
3. Student's own answer. Ensure response is fully annotated, clearly identifying intended impact.

GLOSSARY

Minor sentence
Also known as a sentence fragment; a sentence containing no finite verb

AQA ENGLISH — Grades 5-9

27 Descriptive and narrative writing: Vocabulary for impact

LEARNING OBJECTIVES	SPECIFICATION LINKS
• To be able to select vocabulary for clarity, precision and impact	• 3.1.2 writing for impact

STARTER ACTIVITY

- **Reviewing vocabulary choice; 5 minutes; page 180**
  Ask the student to focus on over-use of descriptive vocabulary and inappropriate or ineffective vocabulary choice.

MAIN ACTIVITIES

- **Clarity, precision and intention; 20 minutes; page 181**
  Read through the activity, ensuring the student understands why some of the vocabulary choices have been highlighted.
- **Review and revise; 15 minutes; page 182**
  Make explicit the process of highlighting weak vocabulary choices, gathering possible replacements, and then making a final selection.

PLENARY ACTIVITY

- **Review; 10 minutes**
  Summarise and evaluate criteria for reviewing and revising vocabulary choices. Look for responses that recognise the need to: look out for intensifiers that could be replaced (e.g. *really, quite, slightly, very*); avoid stacking multiple adjectives; replace *adjective + noun* or *verb + adverb* constructions with more carefully chosen and precise noun or verb choices; select vocabulary that supports intention and tone.

HOMEWORK ACTIVITY

- **Crafting vocabulary; 30 minutes; page 183**
  Ask the student to write one or two paragraphs in response to the exam-style task. Emphasise the importance of reviewing and clearly revising vocabulary choices.

SUPPORT IDEA

- **Clarity, precision and intention; Review and revise** Ask the student to select the three weakest sentences or vocabulary choices in order to ensure a complete cycle of review and revision.

EXTENSION IDEA

- **Clarity, precision and intention; Review and revise** Challenge the student to share their thought processes and question them as they select vocabulary choices for revision, gather alternatives and make their final choices.

PROGRESS AND OBSERVATIONS

ENGLISH
Grades 5-9

AQA

| STARTER ACTIVITY: REVIEWING VOCABULARY CHOICE | TIMING: 5 MINS |

LEARNING OBJECTIVES
- To be able to select vocabulary for clarity, precision and impact

EQUIPMENT
none

Read this paragraph, written by a student in response to the Paper 1, Section B exam-style writing task below.

Write a description suggested by this picture.

[40 marks]

The desert wind wafts across the sand, smashing hundreds and thousands and millions and billions of harsh, hard grains into my red, swollen, sore, blistering face. I am really, really boiling hot.

Look closely at the student's vocabulary choices.

1. **Which are effective? Tick them.**

2. **Which could be improved? Underline them.**

AQA ENGLISH — Grades 5–9

Main activity: Clarity, precision and intention   Timing: 20 mins

Learning objectives
- To be able to select vocabulary for clarity, precision and impact

Equipment
none

Look at these sentences from a student's response to the writing task from the previous activity. Some of the student's vocabulary choices have been highlighted and annotated with suggestions for improvements.

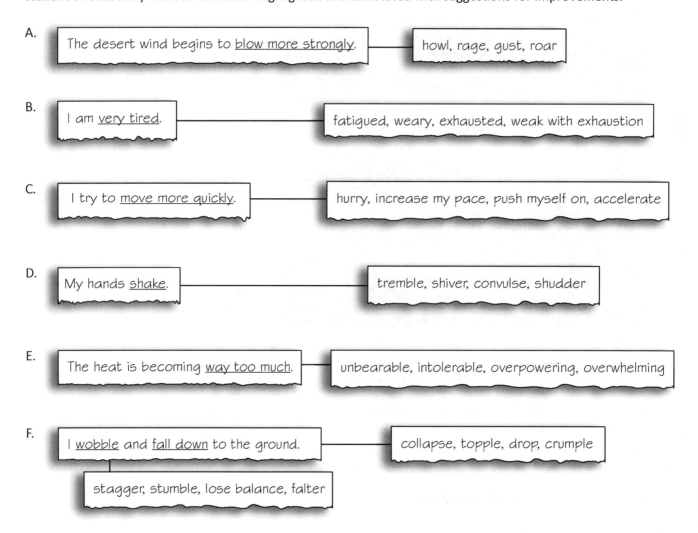

1. **Label each of the highlighted vocabulary choices to indicate whether they would benefit from revision.**
   - Label as 'precision' the choices that use two or more words when a single, more precise choice would be more effective.
   - Label as 'intention' the choices that do not support the writer's intention and/or are not in keeping with the mood suggested by the subject matter.

2. **Look at the suggested replacements for each of the highlighted vocabulary choices. Which one would you choose? Tick it.**

3. **Review your choices. Could they be made more effective in any way? Annotate them.**

ENGLISH
Grades 5-9

MAIN ACTIVITY: REVIEW AND REVISE **TIMING: 15 MINS**

LEARNING OBJECTIVES
- To be able to select vocabulary for clarity, precision and impact

EQUIPMENT
none

Look at these sentences, taken from the same student's response to the Paper 1, Section B exam-style writing task.

Write a description suggested by this picture.

[40 marks]

Mumbling and grumbling, I pulled myself up onto my hands and knees and began to move forwards on all fours. My head felt as though it would pop.

Look carefully at the writer's vocabulary choices in these sentences.
Think about:
- **concision and precision** – have they chosen vocabulary that expresses their ideas as clearly, precisely and succinctly as possible?
- **intention** – have they chosen vocabulary that supports the intention and tone or mood of their writing?

1. **Which vocabulary choices would benefit from revision? Underline them.**

2. **Annotate each word or phrase you have underlined with three or four possible alternative vocabulary choices.**

3. **Review your annotations. Which words or phrases are the most concise and precise, and make the most significant contribution to the writer's intention? Tick them.**

AQA ENGLISH — Grades 5-9

Homework activity: Crafting vocabulary

Timing: 30 mins

Learning objectives
- To be able to select vocabulary for clarity, precision and impact

Equipment
none

1. Write the opening of your response to the Paper 1, Section B exam-style writing task below.

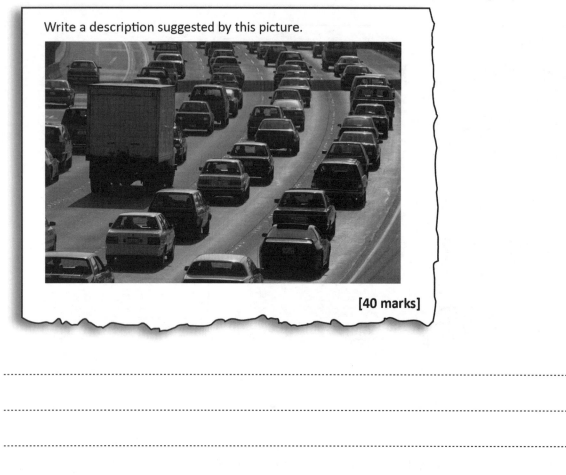

Write a description suggested by this picture.

[40 marks]

----

2. Review and revise your vocabulary choices. Remember to clearly show all the alternative vocabulary choices you consider, and all the choices you make as you review and revise your writing.

27 ANSWERS

STARTER ACTIVITY: REVIEWING VOCABULARY CHOICE
1. Examples: 'wafts'; 'harsh, hard grains'.
2. Examples: 'hundreds and thousands and millions and billions'; 'red, swollen, sore, blistering'; 'really, really boiling hot'.

MAIN ACTIVITY: CLARITY, PRECISION AND INTENTION
1. Precision: a, b, c, e, f; Intention: d, e, f
2. Arguably the most effective/appropriate suggested replacements are: a) roar; b) exhausted; c) push myself on; d) tremble; e) overwhelming, unbearable; f) stumble; topple.
3. Student's own answers

MAIN ACTIVITY: REVIEW AND REVISE
1. Examples: mumbling and grumbling; pull; move forwards on all fours; pop.
2. Examples: mumbling and grumbling: groaning, muttering, moaning; pull: heave, drag; move forwards on all fours: crawl, scramble, plod; pop: explode, burst, crack open.
3. Student's own answers

HOMEWORK ACTIVITY: CRAFTING VOCABULARY
1. See exam-style mark scheme on pages 251–253.
2. Student's own answer. Ensure clear evidence of review and revision is shown.

GLOSSARY

Modification
The use of words, phrases or clauses, that function as adjectives or adverbs, to modify the meaning of nouns and verbs

ENGLISH
Grades 5-9

28 Descriptive and Narrative Writing: Consolidation

Learning Objectives
- To be able to plan and write an effective piece of descriptive or narrative writing

Specification Links
- 3.1.2 producing clear and coherent text
- 3.1.2 writing for impact

Starter Activity
- **The map; 5 minutes; page 186**
  Explain to the student that this lesson will consolidate all their learning on descriptive and narrative writing. Emphasise that this activity will form the 'map' they will follow as they craft their response to the writing task.

Main Activities
- **Planning; 15 minutes; page 187**
  Reiterate the importance of planning over the need to 'just get on with the writing'.
- **Beginning writing; 20 minutes; page 188**
  If the previous activity goes over time, focus this activity on the opening sentence or two of the response. Explain to the student that pausing, reviewing and revising during writing plays an important part in crafting a successful response. Direct them to recall the techniques and choices they have explored in the last seven lessons regarding structure, paragraphing, sentence forms and vocabulary choice.

Plenary Activity
- **Review; 10 minutes**
  Work with the student to review the impact of their response. Encourage experimentation with possible revisions to paragraphing, sentence structures and vocabulary choices.

Homework Activity
- **Complete your response; 30 minutes; page 189**
  Emphasise the importance of following the 'map' established in the starter activity.

Support Idea
- **Planning** Encourage the student to verbalise their thinking. Prompt where necessary.

Extension Idea
- **Planning; Beginning writing** Challenge the student to constantly review and revise throughout the planning and writing process, focusing on how effectively their response will achieve their identified intention.

Progress and Observations

ENGLISH
— Grades 5–9 —

STARTER ACTIVITY: THE MAP

TIMING: 5 MINS

LEARNING OBJECTIVES

- To be able to plan and write an effective piece of descriptive or narrative writing

EQUIPMENT

none

You are going to write your response to this Paper 1, Section B exam-style writing task.

> Describe an occasion when you could not believe your eyes. Focus on the thoughts and feelings you had at that time.
> **[40 marks]**

Now look at this list of tasks you will need to complete to craft an effective response to the task above. At what stage and in what order will you complete them?

1. **Tick to show whether you will complete each task before, during or after writing.**

2. **Number the tasks 1–10 to show the order in which you will complete them.**

No.		Before	During	After
☐	Gather a range of ideas.	☐	☐	☐
☐	Check your spelling, punctuation and grammar.	☐	☐	☐
☐	Think about how you will use paragraph structure in your writing.	☐	☐	☐
☐	Structure your sentences for clarity and impact.	☐	☐	☐
☐	Identify the central idea on which you will focus.	☐	☐	☐
☐	Select precise vocabulary for impact.	☐	☐	☐
☐	Review, select, structure and sequence your ideas.	☐	☐	☐
☐	Review and revise your choices of paragraph and sentence structure, and vocabulary.	☐	☐	☐
☐	Identify your intention.	☐	☐	☐
☐	Think carefully about the beginning and ending of your writing.	☐	☐	☐

ENGLISH
— Grades 5-9 —

| MAIN ACTIVITY: PLANNING | TIMING: 15 MINS |

LEARNING OBJECTIVES
- To be able to plan and write an effective piece of descriptive or narrative writing

EQUIPMENT
none

You are going to plan your response to the Paper 1, Section B exam-style writing task below.

> Describe an occasion when you could not believe your eyes.
> Focus on the thoughts and feelings you had at that time.
> **[40 marks]**

1. **The central idea** – think of two different ideas, and then choose the strongest.

   ....

   ....

   ....

   ....

2. **The intention** – what impact do you want your writing to have on the reader? How do you want your reader to respond to it?

   ....

   ....

   ....

   ....

3. **The details** – note down the ideas, events and details you will include.

   ....

   ....

   ....

   ....

4. **Review and select** – discard any ideas that do not support your intention or will not engage the reader.

5. **Sequence and shape** – number the ideas you have selected to show the order in which you will write about them, thinking particularly about how your response will begin and end.

ENGLISH
— Grades 5-9 —

| MAIN ACTIVITY: BEGINNING WRITING | TIMING: 20 MINS |

LEARNING OBJECTIVES
- To be able to plan and write an effective piece of descriptive or narrative writing

EQUIPMENT
none

1. Write the opening of your response to the Paper 1, Section B exam-style question below.

   > Describe an occasion when you could not believe your eyes. Focus on the thoughts and feelings you had at that time.
   > **[40 marks]**

   ---

2. Pause to review and revise your writing so far.

   You should think about:
   - **Structure** – Will your opening effectively engage and interest the reader?
   - **Paragraphs** – Could any of your paragraphs be restructured to add impact?
   - **Sentence structure** – Could any of your sentences be restructured to add impact?
   - **Vocabulary** – Could any of your vocabulary choices be more concise or precise, or have more effective connotations?

AQA ENGLISH — Grades 5-9

HOMEWORK ACTIVITY: COMPLETE YOUR RESPONSE   **TIMING: 30 MINS**

LEARNING OBJECTIVES
- To be able to plan and write an effective piece of descriptive or narrative writing

EQUIPMENT
none

1. On a separate piece of paper, complete your response to the Paper 1, Section B exam-style writing task below.

   > Describe an occasion when you could not believe your eyes.
   > Focus on the thoughts and feelings you had at that time.
   > **[40 marks]**

2. **When you have completed your response, review and revise it.**
   Think about your choices of:
   - whole text structure
   - paragraph structure
   - sentence structure
   - vocabulary.

28 ANSWERS

STARTER ACTIVITY: THE MAP
1–2. Before writing:
1. Identify the central idea on which you will focus.
2. Identify your intention.
3. Gather a range of ideas.
4. Review select, structure and sequence your ideas.
5. Think carefully about the beginning and ending of your writing.

During writing:
6. Think about how you will use paragraph structure in your writing.
7. Structure your sentences for clarity and impact.
8. Select precise vocabulary for impact.

During and after writing:
9. Review and revise your choices of paragraph and sentence structure, and vocabulary.
10. Check your spelling, punctuation and grammar.

MAIN ACTIVITY: PLANNING
1. Student's own answer. Ensure two suitable ideas are suggested.
2. Student's own answer. Ensure a relevant intention is identified.
3. Student's own answer. Ensure enough material is gathered.
4. Student's own answer. Ensure the most relevant material is selected.
5. Student's own answer. Ensure the material is structured effectively.

MAIN ACTIVITY: BEGINNING WRITING
1. See exam-style mark scheme on pages 251–253.
2. Student's own answer. Ensure revision of paragraph, sentence and vocabulary choices is thorough and carefully considered.

HOMEWORK ACTIVITY: COMPLETE YOUR RESPONSE
1. See exam-style mark scheme on pages 251–253.
2. Student's own answer. Ensure revision of whole text, paragraph, sentence and vocabulary choices is thorough and carefully considered.

AQA ENGLISH — Grades 5-9

29 Writing to present a viewpoint: Gathering ideas

Learning objectives
- To be able to identify the appropriate form, purpose and audience for a writing task
- To be able to gather ideas to present a viewpoint

Specification links
- 3.1.2 producing clear and coherent text
- 3.1.2 writing for impact

Starter activity
- **Key words; 5 minutes; page 192**
  Ensure the student notes answers that are not explicitly stated in the task, e.g. the purpose, audience and register. Note that, although the apparent key purpose of the task is to 'explain', it is also an opportunity to argue a viewpoint.

Main activities
- **Intention and methods; 20 minutes; page 193**
  Make explicit the process of refining an initial response to the task, then considering ways to achieve the key intention of influencing the reader's viewpoint. Note that other approaches/methods are possible, and the ones here are simply prompts for generating ideas.
- **Policies; 20 minutes; page 194**
  Explain to the student that this is another activity to help generate and develop ideas, and that they may reuse some from the previous activity. Suggest that one approach to effectively expressing a viewpoint is to think of it as a 'goal' that must be supported with clear policies in order to convince the reader that it is valid and achievable.

Plenary activity
- **Select and reject; 5 minutes**
  Ask the student to review all the ideas gathered in the previous task. Which ideas are the strongest? Which will form the basis of a powerful response to the writing task, which might be combined to form a more developed argument, and which should be rejected?

Homework activity
- **Gathering ideas; 30 minutes; page 195**
  Ensure that the student understands the importance of following the sequence of tasks used in the lesson to gather a range of relevant ideas, and is able to repeat it independently. Explain that they will only have 45 minutes to answer this question in the exam, so should only spend around five minutes planning their answer.

Support idea
- **Intention and methods** Direct the student to focus on problems and solutions.

Extension idea
- **Intention and methods; Policies** Challenge the student to gather the widest possible range of ideas, explaining that a process of selection and rejection will follow.

Progress and observations

ENGLISH
Grades 5-9

STARTER ACTIVITY: KEY WORDS　　　　　　　　**TIMING: 5 MINS**

LEARNING OBJECTIVES

- To be able to identify the appropriate form, purpose and audience for a writing task

EQUIPMENT

none

Look at this Paper 2, Section B-style writing task.

> 'Schools and colleges need to do more to make learning fun. It would help students learn, and encourage them to want to learn.'
>
> Write a letter to your local newspaper in which you explain your point of view on this statement.
>
> [40 marks]

1. **For each of the questions below:**
   - **underline the relevant word or phrase in the task that tells you the answer**
   - **label the relevant word or phrase**
   - **write your answer beneath the question.**

   a) **Audience**
      Who are you being asked to write for?

   ---

   b) **Purpose**
      What does your text need to achieve?

   ---

   c) **Form**
      What kind of text are you being asked to write?

   ---

   d) **Register**
      How formal should your writing be?

   ---

   e) **Central idea**
      What are you being asked to write about?

AQA ENGLISH — Grades 5-9

MAIN ACTIVITY: INTENTION AND METHODS **TIMING: 20 MINS**

LEARNING OBJECTIVES
- To be able to gather ideas to present a viewpoint

EQUIPMENT
none

Look at the Paper 2, Section B exam-style writing task below.

> 'Schools and colleges need to do more to make learning fun. It would help students learn, and encourage them to want to learn.'
>
> Write a letter to your local newspaper in which you explain your point of view on this statement.
>
> [40 marks]

1. **Before you begin gathering ideas, you first need to identify your viewpoint.**
   Do you:
   ☐ agree?   ☐ partly agree?   ☐ disagree?

2. **Write a sentence summing up your viewpoint.**

   ....

   ....

   ....

Your **intention** is to encourage the reader to share your viewpoint by the time they have finished reading. Below are some examples of how you could achieve this.

Problems Explain the problems that need to be overcome.	**Solutions** Explain the benefits of your ideas.
Fear Explain the potential risks of ignoring your ideas.	**Humour** Use humour to engage the reader.

3. **Which methods will you use in your response?**
4. **Note down some ideas about how you could use the methods you have selected in your writing.**

ENGLISH
Grades 5-9

| **MAIN ACTIVITY: POLICIES** | **TIMING: 20 MINS** |

LEARNING OBJECTIVES
- To be able to gather ideas to present a viewpoint

EQUIPMENT
none

Now you have identified your viewpoint, you can think about your policies. These are the actions you will take to make learning more fun.

Ask yourself:
- what must be done?
- what needs to change?

1. Note three policy ideas below.

For each one, ask yourself:
- Why would this make things better?
- How could it be achieved?

Policy	Why?	How?

ENGLISH
— Grades 5-9 —

Homework activity: Gathering ideas

Timing: 30 mins

Learning objectives
- To be able to identify the appropriate form, purpose and audience for a writing task
- To be able to gather ideas to present a viewpoint

Equipment
none

You are going to gather a range of ideas in response to this Paper 2, Section B exam-style writing task.

> 'We need to think more about the food we put in our bodies and the effect it has on our lives. You are what you eat.'
>
> Write an article for a broadsheet newspaper in which you explain your point of view on this statement.
>
> **[40 marks]**

1. Annotate the task, identifying the form, purpose, audience, register and central idea.

2. Write a sentence summing up your viewpoint in response to the statement in the task.

----

3. Note down all the ideas you could include in your response.
   Remember to think about:
   - problems
   - solutions
   - fear
   - humour
   - policies.

4. Review your ideas. Which will you use in your response to the task above? Tick them.

29 ANSWERS

STARTER ACTIVITY: KEY WORDS

1. a) Audience: editor/readers of a local newspaper
b) Purpose: explain your viewpoint/argue
c) Form: letter
d) Register: formal
e) Idea: Schools and colleges need to do more to make learning fun

MAIN ACTIVITY: INTENTION AND METHODS

1. Student's own answer
2. Student's own answer. Ensure they have engaged with the viewpoint and come up with a relevant response.
3. Student's own answer
4. Student's own answer. Ensure a range of relevant ideas is gathered.

MAIN ACTIVITY: POLICIES

1. Student's own answer. Ensure at least two key ideas are identified and supported with consideration of how they might be achieved and why they would bring benefits.

HOMEWORK ACTIVITY: GATHERING IDEAS

1. Form: a broadsheet newspaper article; Purpose: to persuade; Audience: adult newspaper readers; Register: formal; Central idea: that diet has a significant effect on our quality of life.
2. Student's own answer. Ensure they have engaged with the viewpoint and come up with a relevant response.
3. Student's own answers. Ensure a range of ideas is noted.
4. Student's own answer. Ensure an appropriate number of key ideas is selected.

AQA ENGLISH — Grades 5–9

30 Writing to Present a Viewpoint: Structure and Shape

Learning Objectives
- To be able to structure and shape an argument text

Specification Links
- 3.1.2 producing clear and coherent text
- 3.1.2 writing for impact

Starter Activity
- **Structure; 5 minutes; page 198**
  Ask the student to assess their familiarity with 'typical' formulaic structures. This will provide a baseline from which to develop more sophisticated structures.

Main Activities
- **Review, select or reject; 20 minutes; page 199**
  Explain to the student they are going to structure and shape the ideas they gathered for homework in lesson 29. To do this, they must identify the strongest ideas; rationalise and consolidate related ideas; and reject ideas that, no matter how strong, seem out of place.
- **Shaping for impact; 20 minutes; page 200**
  Explain to the student that this activity is intended to take them beyond the typical, formulaic structure of an argument. The process of sequencing focuses on the impact on the reader; on how best to exploit the strongest and most controversial ideas.

Plenary Activity
- **Review; 5 minutes**
  Ask the student to review and evaluate their learning, and their confidence in completing the homework task.

Homework Activity
- **Shape your ideas; 30 minutes; page 201**
  Explain to the student that they can use the ideas gathered during lesson 29, adding to or developing them as necessary. Emphasise the importance of producing a clear, carefully structured and shaped plan. Suggest that they experiment with a variety of sequences before settling on their final plan.

Support Idea
- **Shaping for impact** Ask the student to cut the ideas into strips and physically sequence them.

Extension Idea
- **Shaping for impact** Challenge the student to track the reader's likely response to each idea, in sequence, as they progress through the planned text.

Progress and Observations

ENGLISH
Grades 5-9

STARTER ACTIVITY: STRUCTURE　　　　　　　　**TIMING: 5 MINS**

LEARNING OBJECTIVES
- To be able to structure and shape an argument text

EQUIPMENT
none

Look at all the different elements you might expect to find in a typical response to the Paper 2, Section B exam-style writing task below.

> 'We need to think more about the food we put in our bodies and the effect it has on our lives. You are what you eat.'
>
> Write an article for a broadsheet newspaper in which you explain your point of view on this statement.
>
> **[40 marks]**

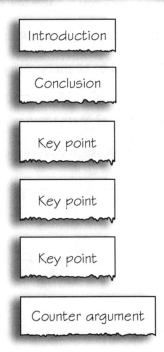

1. Number the elements from 1 to 6 to show how you would sequence them.

ENGLISH
— Grades 5-9 —

MAIN ACTIVITY: REVIEW, SELECT OR REJECT   **TIMING: 20 MINS**

LEARNING OBJECTIVES
- To be able to structure and shape an argument text

EQUIPMENT
- *Gathering ideas* homework activity (lesson 29)

Look at the ideas you gathered in response to the Paper 2, Section B exam-style writing task below.

> 'We need to think more about the food we put in our bodies and the effect it has on our lives. You are what you eat.'
>
> Write an article for a broadsheet newspaper in which you explain your point of view on this statement.
>
> **[40 marks]**

Your aim is to identify three or four strong key points you can use to express your viewpoint.

1. Which are your strongest, most influential ideas? Mark them with an asterisk *.

2. Are any of your ideas linked or related? Could they be merged to form a single idea? Link them with an arrow.

3. Do any of your ideas not really fit with the others? Mark them with a cross.

4. Note the three or four strong key points you will use in your response.

....

....

....

....

....

....

ENGLISH
Grades 5-9

MAIN ACTIVITY: SHAPING FOR IMPACT **TIMING: 20 MINS**

LEARNING OBJECTIVES
- To be able to structure and shape an argument text

EQUIPMENT
- scissors

Look at the ideas that one student selected for their response to the Paper 2, Section B exam-style writing task below.

> 'We need to think more about the food we put in our bodies and the effect it has on our lives. You are what you eat.'
>
> Write an article for a broadsheet newspaper in which you explain your point of view on this statement.
>
> **[40 marks]**

A. Fast food restaurants are everywhere – and people lead busy lives so grab food in a hurry. Microwave meals are quick and easy – people are busy and need food fast. Fast food is so nice because it's full of salt and sugar – so it tastes delicious. Tempting!

B. Some unhealthy food is OK – but too much is a problem. A balanced diet, with not too much of any one type of food + physical exercise is the answer.

C. Counter argument
The media and social media are full of people telling us to give up fat or sugar or meat or wheat or processed food... or all of them. Maybe we would all be happier and healthy if we did – but it's not possible for people with no time or no money. The reason these people can afford to live that way is because they're making a fortune out of telling us to live that way!

D. People are living longer, putting pressure on hospitals and collecting their pensions for longer. It's costing us a fortune so maybe everyone being healthy isn't a good thing!

E. We need to be taught how to cook. I've got no idea how to make a meal out of ingredients. No wonder people eat unhealthy fast food or get stuff out of packets and jars.

The aim of structuring your response is to...	To achieve this, you need...
engage the reader's interest	→ a strong, engaging opening
make your viewpoint clear	→ a logical sequence of ideas with a convincing conclusion
encourage the reader to agree with your viewpoint	→ ideas to make the reader re-think their viewpoint

1. Which is the strongest idea in the plan above? Label it 'strong'.
2. Which is the most shocking, surprising or controversial idea in the plan? Label it 'shock'.
3. How would you order the ideas to achieve a logical sequence? Number them.
4. Review your sequence. Does it provide a strong, engaging opening? If not, try a different sequence.
5. Review your sequence, thinking carefully about where you have positioned the idea labelled 'shock'. How could you change the sequence to hold the reader's interest?
6. Give your sequence one final review. Does it achieve all the criteria above? If not, keep trying different sequences until you are happy with it.

AQA ENGLISH — Grades 5-9

HOMEWORK ACTIVITY: SHAPE YOUR IDEAS **TIMING: 30 MINS**

LEARNING OBJECTIVES
- To be able to structure and shape an argument text

EQUIPMENT
none

1. On a separate piece of paper, plan and shape your response to the Paper 2, Section B exam-style writing task below.

   > 'We need to think more about the food we put in our bodies and the effect it has on our lives. You are what you eat.'
   >
   > Write an article for a broadsheet newspaper in which you explain your point of view on this statement.
   >
   > [40 marks]

2. Review your planning.
   a) Tick all the criteria you feel you have achieved.

   - ☐ Engages the reader's interest with a strong opening
   - ☐ Gives a clear viewpoint with a logical progression of ideas
   - ☐ Holds the reader's interest and encourages them to re-think their viewpoint

   b) If there are any criteria you feel you have not achieved, review and improve your planning so that you can tick all of them.

ENGLISH
Grades 5-9

30 ANSWERS

STARTER ACTIVITY: STRUCTURE
1. Examples: introduction, key point, key point, key point, counter argument, conclusion.

MAIN ACTIVITY: REVIEW, SELECT OR REJECT
1. Student's own answers. Ensure the strongest points are identified.
2. Student's own answers. Ensure clear links are made.
3. Student's own answers. Ensure student shows discernment.
4. Student's own answers. Ensure the chosen points have been carefully selected through a process of review, consolidation and/or rejection.

MAIN ACTIVITY: SHAPING FOR IMPACT
1. Student's own answer. Ensure a suitable point is identified.
2. Student's own answer. Ensure a suitable point is identified.
3. Student's own answer. Ensure a clear and coherent structure.
4. Student's own answer. Ensure a clear and coherent structure.
5. Student's own answer
6. Student's own answer. Ensure a clear and coherent structure.

HOMEWORK ACTIVITY: SHAPE YOUR IDEAS
1. See exam-style mark scheme on pages 251–253.
2. Student's own answers. Ensure response achieves all, or the majority of, the criteria.

GLOSSARY

Counter argument
An argument that opposes the writer's point of view; a counter argument is often included in an argument text in order to highlight its failings and therefore reinforce the strength of the writer's point of view

ENGLISH
Grades 5-9

31 Writing to Present a Viewpoint: Introductions and Conclusions

Learning Objectives
- To be able to craft an effective introduction
- To be able to craft an effective conclusion

Specification Links
- 3.1.2 producing clear and coherent text
- 3.1.2 writing for impact

Starter Activity
- **First and last; 5 minutes; page 204**
  Use the activity as an opportunity to discuss and clarify the purpose of an introduction (to introduce the topic and engage the reader) and a conclusion (to sum up and drive home the writer's viewpoint).

Main Activities
- **Introductions; 20 minutes; page 205**
  Explain that effectively introducing an argument is very different from simply stating the purpose of the text (e.g. In this essay I am going to...), which contributes little to impact. Ensure understanding of *anecdote*, and emphasise that the anecdote does not need to be true: it can be imagined and tailored to the task. Finally, review the sequenced introduction. Does it achieve the suggested criteria?
- **Conclusions; 20 minutes; page 206**
  Emphasise the importance of planning conclusions: it is important to know the final destination of a text before setting out to write it. Point out that repeating the key points is not an effective method of summarising them. Review the sequenced conclusion. Does it achieve the suggested criteria?

Plenary Activity
- **Review; 5 minutes**
  Ask the student to summarise and evaluate their understanding of how to craft effective introductions and conclusions, and their confidence in successfully tackling the homework task.

Homework Activity
- **Introduction and conclusion; 30 minutes; page 207**
  Ask the student to refer to the ideas they gathered for this task in lesson 30 before writing their introduction and conclusion.

Support Idea
- **Introductions; Conclusions** Focus attention on those approaches that the student finds the most immediately accessible and achievable. Model those that are not.

Extension Idea
- **Introductions; Conclusions** Challenge the student to develop a range of possible ideas for each approach and select the most powerful and relevant to form an effective, coherent introduction or conclusion.

Progress and Observations

ENGLISH
Grades 5-9

Starter activity: First and last

Timing: 5 mins

Learning objectives
- To be able to craft an effective introduction
- To be able to craft an effective conclusion

Equipment
none

Read the first and last sentences from one student's response to the Paper 2, Section B exam-style writing task below.

> 'We need to think more about the food we put in our bodies and the effect it has on our lives. You are what you eat.'
>
> Write an article for a broadsheet newspaper in which you explain your point of view on this statement.
>
> **[40 marks]**

> The food we choose to eat affects our lives more than anything else: it can be the reason we lead happy, healthy lives, or a miserable existence of sickness and discomfort.

> The big question we must ask ourselves is: if we do nothing, where will it all end?

1. **Are these sentences effective? Why?**

....

....

....

....

....

....

ENGLISH
— Grades 5-9 —

MAIN ACTIVITY: INTRODUCTIONS   **TIMING: 20 MINS**

LEARNING OBJECTIVES
- To be able to craft an effective introduction

EQUIPMENT
none

You are going to craft an introduction to the Paper 2, Section B exam-style writing task below.

> 'We need to think more about the food we put in our bodies and the effect it has on our lives. You are what you eat.'
>
> Write an article for a broadsheet newspaper in which you explain your point of view on this statement.
>
> **[40 marks]**

An effective introduction should:
  a) orientate the reader
  b) engage the reader
  c) introduce your point of view.

1. Which of the approaches below would achieve which of the criteria? Label each one a, b and/or c.

i) An explanation of the problem or situation you are concerned about
ii) An example showing the problem or situation you are concerned about
iii) An anecdote from your own experience, relevant to the topic and your viewpoint
iv) A rhetorical question summing up the issue you are concerned about
v) A shocking or surprising fact relevant to the topic and your viewpoint

2. In the spaces above, write an example of each of the approaches that you could include in your introduction to the exam-style writing task above.

3. Look at the sentences you have written. Which would you include in your introduction? Tick them.

4. In what order would you sequence the sentences in your introduction? Number them.

ENGLISH
Grades 5-9

MAIN ACTIVITY: CONCLUSIONS   **TIMING: 20 MINS**

LEARNING OBJECTIVES
- To be able to craft an effective conclusion

EQUIPMENT
none

You are going to craft a conclusion to the Paper 2, Section B exam-style writing task below.

> 'We need to think more about the food we put in our bodies and the effect it has on our lives. You are what you eat.'
>
> Write an article for a broadsheet newspaper in which you explain your point of view on this statement.
>
> **[40 marks]**

An effective conclusion should:
    a) summarise (but not repeat) your ideas
    b) drive home your viewpoint
    c) convince the reader to agree with your viewpoint.

1. Which of the approaches below would achieve which of the criteria above? Label each one a, b and/or c.

i) A final statement summarising your viewpoint
ii) A rhetorical question to direct the reader towards agreeing with your viewpoint
iii) A positive consequence of accepting or acting upon your ideas
iv) A negative consequence of ignoring or failing to act upon your ideas

2. In the spaces above, write an example of each of the approaches that you could include in your conclusion to the writing task above.

3. Look at the sentences you have written. Which would you include in your conclusion? Tick them.

4. In what order would you sequence the sentences in your conclusion? Number them.

AQA ENGLISH — Grades 5-9

HOMEWORK ACTIVITY: INTRODUCTION AND CONCLUSION **TIMING: 30 MINS**

LEARNING OBJECTIVES
- To be able to craft an effective introduction
- To be able to craft an effective conclusion

EQUIPMENT
none

1. Write the introduction and conclusion of your response to this Paper 2, Section B exam-style writing task.

   > 'We need to think more about the food we put in our bodies and the effect it has on our lives. You are what you eat.'
   >
   > Write an article for a broadsheet newspaper in which you explain your point of view on this statement.
   >
   > [40 marks]

2. Annotate your introduction, identifying where you have:
   - orientated the reader
   - engaged the reader
   - introduced your point of view.

3. Annotate your conclusion, identifying where you have:
   - summarised (but not repeated) your ideas
   - driven home your viewpoint
   - convinced the reader to agree with your viewpoint.

31 ANSWERS

STARTER ACTIVITY: FIRST AND LAST
1. The opening sentence clearly orientates the reader and powerfully conveys the writer's viewpoint. The final sentence is far less effective. It neither sums up nor drives home the writer's viewpoint; the rhetorical question is effectively meaningless.

MAIN ACTIVITY: INTRODUCTIONS
1. i) a and c; ii) a and c; iii) b and c; iv) b and c; v) b and c.
2. Student's own answers. Ensure they have understood and engaged with each of the approaches.
3. Student's own answers
4. Student's own answers. Ensure a coherent structure is chosen.

MAIN ACTIVITY: CONCLUSIONS
1. i) a and b; ii) a, b and c; iii) c; iv) c
2. Student's own answers. Ensure they have understood and engaged with each of the approaches.
3. Student's own answers
4. Student's own answers. Ensure a coherent structure is chosen.

HOMEWORK ACTIVITY: INTRODUCTION AND CONCLUSION
1. See exam-style mark scheme on pages 251–253.
2. Student's own answers. Ensure all, or the majority of, criteria have been achieved and annotated.
3. Student's own answers. Ensure all, or the majority of, criteria have been achieved and annotated.

ENGLISH
Grades 5-9

32 Writing to present a viewpoint: Building a paragraph

Learning objectives
- To be able to structure a paragraph to present a viewpoint with clarity and impact

Specification links
- 3.1.2 producing clear and coherent text
- 3.1.2 writing for impact

Starter activity
- **The building blocks; 5 minutes; page 210**
  Explain that this lesson will explore the ways in which paragraphs can be structured to achieve both clarity and the greatest impact on the reader. As the student completes the task, discuss the role that each building block plays in a paragraph written to present a viewpoint.

Main activities
- **Exploring structure; 20 minutes; page 211**
  Ask the student to complete question 1. Note that the paragraph does not follow the typical formula of point-evidence-explain, but clearly expresses the writer's viewpoint with impact. Ask the student to complete question 2, focusing on the elements individually, without considering how they might be structured.
- **Experimenting with structure; 20 minutes; page 212**
  Ask the student to complete question 1, emphasising that there is no one correct answer or formula to follow. Instead, direct their attention to achieving impact on the reader. Afterwards, discuss their choices and the impact they have created.

Plenary activity
- **Review; 5 minutes**
  Ask the student to summarise and evaluate their understanding of paragraph structure when writing to express a viewpoint.

Homework activity
- **Crafting paragraphs; 30 minutes; page 213**
  The student should complete two paragraphs, following on from the introduction they wrote for homework in lesson 31. Remind them to make use of the plan they completed for homework in lesson 30. Emphasise the importance of reviewing and revising their weakest paragraph and evaluating its impact.

Support idea
- **Exploring structure** Prompt the student to recall (or imagine) a personal anecdote as evidence and note how it supports or explains the key point being made.

Extension idea
- **Experimenting with structure** Challenge the student to experiment with a range of possible sequences and explicitly identify the changes in impact.

Progress and observations

ENGLISH
Grades 5-9

STARTER ACTIVITY: THE BUILDING BLOCKS **TIMING: 5 MINS**

LEARNING OBJECTIVES

- To be able to structure a paragraph to present a viewpoint with clarity and impact

EQUIPMENT

none

1. Which of these elements are likely to appear in a typical paragraph, written in response to a Paper 2, Section B exam-style writing task like the one below? Tick them.

> 'We need to think more about the food we put in our bodies and the effect it has on our lives. You are what you eat.'
>
> Write an article for a broadsheet newspaper in which you explain your point of view on this statement.
>
> **[40 marks]**

- ☐ evidence supporting the writer's viewpoint
- ☐ a clear statement of the writer's viewpoint in response to the statement in the task
- ☐ an anecdote from the writer's experience
- ☐ a fact or statistic
- ☐ analysis and explanation of the writer's viewpoint
- ☐ rhetorical devices such as a rhetorical question

AQA ENGLISH — Grades 5–9

MAIN ACTIVITY: EXPLORING STRUCTURE **TIMING: 20 MINS**

LEARNING OBJECTIVES
- To be able to structure a paragraph to present a viewpoint with clarity and impact

EQUIPMENT
none

Look at this paragraph taken from one student's response to the Paper 2, Section B exam-style writing task below.

1. **Underline the key elements of the paragraph and draw lines linking them to the annotations.**

> 'We need to think more about the food we put in our bodies and the effect it has on our lives. You are what you eat.'
>
> Write an article for a broadsheet newspaper in which you explain your point of view on this statement.
>
> **[40 marks]**

> Evidence supporting the writer's viewpoint.

> In under two hours, my grandmother can create a roast dinner for ten people. I can barely work the toaster. A generation of cooks is getting older and soon they will be gone. There will be no one left who actually knows how to turn a cupboard full of ingredients into something delicious, leaving the rest of us completely reliant on ready meals in plastic trays and microwaves. Parents, grandparents and schools need to spend more time teaching us how to cook or we're going to microwave ourselves to an early, unhealthy death.

> A clear statement of the writer's viewpoint in response to the statement in the task.

> Analysis and explanation of the writer's viewpoint.

2. **On a separate piece of paper, write the three key elements (evidence, a clear statement and analysis) of your own paragraph in response to the exam-style writing task above. You could use one of the ideas below, or one from your own planning.**

A.
> Fast food restaurants are everywhere – and people lead busy lives so grab food in a hurry.
> Microwave meals are quick and easy – people are busy and need food fast.
> Fast food is so nice because it's full of salt and sugar – so it tastes delicious. Tempting!

B.
> Some unhealthy food is OK – but too much is a problem. A balanced diet, with not too much of any one type of food + physical exercise is the answer.

	ENGLISH	AQA
TUTORS GUILD	Grades 5-9	

MAIN ACTIVITY: EXPERIMENTING WITH STRUCTURE	TIMING: 20 MINS
LEARNING OBJECTIVES	**EQUIPMENT**
• To be able to structure a paragraph to present a viewpoint with clarity and impact	• *Exploring structure* worksheet

Look again at the five sentences below, taken from a paragraph of one student's response to a Paper 2, Section B exam-style writing task.

A. In under two hours, my grandmother can create a roast dinner for ten people.

B. I can barely work the toaster.

C. A generation of cooks is getting older and soon they will be gone.

D. There will be no one left who actually knows how to turn a cupboard full of ingredients into something delicious, leaving the rest of us completely reliant on microwaves and ready meals in plastic trays.

E. Parents, grandparents and schools need to spend more time teaching us how to cook, or we're going to microwave ourselves to an early, unhealthy death.

1. **In what order would you sequence them? Number them.**

2. **Write one or two sentences explaining your choices.**

....

....

....

....

3. **Look again at the sentences you wrote in the previous activity. In what order would you sequence them to express your viewpoint with clarity and impact? Number them.**

212

ENGLISH
Grades 5-9

AQA

| HOMEWORK ACTIVITY: CRAFTING PARAGRAPHS | TIMING: 30 MINS |

LEARNING OBJECTIVES
- To be able to structure a paragraph to present a viewpoint with clarity and impact

EQUIPMENT
none

1. On a separate piece of paper, write two carefully structured paragraphs in response to the Paper 2, Section B exam-style writing task below.

   > 'Schools and colleges need to do more to make learning fun. It would help students learn, and encourage them to want to learn.'
   >
   > Write a letter to your local newspaper in which you explain your point of view on this statement.
   >
   > [40 marks]

2. Which is the stronger of your two paragraphs? Which is the weaker? Label them.

Look carefully at each element and sentence in your **weaker** paragraph.
Ask yourself:
- am I missing any key elements?
- can I restructure my paragraph to achieve greater clarity or impact?

3. On a separate piece of paper, rewrite your weaker paragraph to give it greater clarity and impact.

4. Write one or two sentences explaining the changes you have made and the impact of those changes.

ENGLISH
Grades 5-9

32 ANSWERS

STARTER ACTIVITY: THE BUILDING BLOCKS

1. Evidence supporting the writer's viewpoint; a clear statement of the writer's viewpoint in response to the statement in the task; analysis and explanation of the writer's viewpoint. The rest are common features, but not key structural elements.

MAIN ACTIVITY: EXPLORING STRUCTURE

1. Evidence: In under two hours, my grandmother can create a roast dinner for ten people. I can barely work the toaster.
Analysis: A generation of cooks is getting older and soon they will be gone. There will be no one left who actually knows how to turn a cupboard full of ingredients into something delicious, leaving the rest of us completely reliant on ready meals in plastic trays and microwaves.
Statement: Parents, grandparents and schools need to spend more time teaching us how to cook or we're going to microwave ourselves to an early, unhealthy death.
2. Student's own answers

MAIN ACTIVITY: EXPERIMENTING WITH STRUCTURE

1. Student's own answer. Ensure responses structure ideas with clarity.
2. Student's own answer. Ensure impact is confidently evaluated.
3. Student's own answer. Ensure responses structure ideas with clarity.

HOMEWORK ACTIVITY: CRAFTING PARAGRAPHS

1. See exam-style mark scheme on pages 251–253.
2. Student's own answers
3. Student's own answer. Ensure revisions show confident ability in manipulating paragraph structure.
4. Student's own answer. Ensure impact of changes is evaluated.

ENGLISH — Grades 5–9

33 Writing to present a viewpoint: Paragraph and sentence forms for impact

Learning objectives
- To be able to structure paragraphs for impact
- To be able to structure sentences for impact

Specification links
- 3.1.2 producing clear and coherent text
- 3.1.2 writing for impact

Starter activity
- **Playing with sentences; 5 minutes; page 216**
  Explain that this lesson builds on lessons 24–26, looking at paragraph and sentence structure in descriptive and narrative writing. Emphasise that there are three distinct elements to this sentence that can be repositioned without changing its meaning.

Main activities
- **Spot the difference; 20 minutes; page 217**
  Ask the student to complete question 1 independently. For question 2, discuss each difference, explicitly considering its construction and its impact, before asking the student to note their key findings.
- **Experimenting; 20 minutes; page 218**
  As the student begins to structure their sentences, draw attention to the need for pronouns (*it*, *them*, *their*) and synonyms to avoid repetition of key nouns such as 'vegetables', 'children'.

Plenary activity
- **Review; 5 minutes**
  Review the two paragraphs written in the previous activity. Which achieves the greatest clarity, and why? Which achieves the greatest impact, and why? Avoid deducing hard and fast rules for paragraph and sentence construction; instead, emphasise that structural choices should be judged in the context of each specific writing task.

Homework activity
- **Crafting for impact; 30 minutes; page 219**
  If the student has completed the homework for lesson 32, they can redraft those paragraphs, focusing on revisions to sentence and paragraph structure for effect.

Support idea
- **Spot the difference; Experimenting** Focus the student's attention on a limited range of differences/sentences.

Extension idea
- **Playing with sentences** Ask the student to consider how different structures change the sentence's emphasis, impact and clarity.

Progress and observations

ENGLISH
Grades 5-9

STARTER ACTIVITY: PLAYING WITH SENTENCES **TIMING: 5 MINS**

LEARNING OBJECTIVES
- To be able to structure sentences for impact

EQUIPMENT
none

Look at this sentence, taken from a student's response to the Paper 2, Section B exam-style writing task below.

> 'We need to think more about the food we put in our bodies and the effect it has on our lives. You are what you eat.'
>
> Write an article for a broadsheet newspaper in which you explain your point of view on this statement.
>
> **[40 marks]**

> In the last few years, as our time and attention-span have got shorter and shorter, sales of fast food have rocketed.

1. **In how many different ways can you structure the student's sentence without changing its meaning?**

216

ENGLISH
Grades 5–9

MAIN ACTIVITY: SPOT THE DIFFERENCE   **TIMING: 20 MINS**

LEARNING OBJECTIVES
- To be able to structure paragraphs for impact
- To be able to structure sentences for impact

EQUIPMENT
none

Read these three different versions of a paragraph from one student's response to a Paper 2, Section B exam-style writing task.

A.
> Fast food is delicious. It is crammed with salt, sugar and fat. Fast food contains precisely the ingredients that human beings crave. Sadly, they are also the ingredients that kill us, slowly but surely leading us to obesity, diabetes, a heart attack, or a stroke. Fast food is delicious and deadly.

B.
> Fast food is delicious because it is crammed with salt, sugar and fat which are precisely the ingredients that human beings crave. They are also, sadly, the ingredients that kill us. They lead us, slowly but surely, to obesity, diabetes, a heart attack or a stroke. Fast food is delicious. And deadly.

C.
> Fast food is delicious. Crammed with salt, sugar and fat, fast food contains precisely the ingredients that human beings crave and also the ingredients that kill us, sadly. Slowly but surely they lead us to obesity, diabetes, a heart attack, or a stroke.
>
> Fast food is delicious. And deadly.

1. **How many differences can you spot? Label them.**
2. **How does each difference alter the clarity, emphasis and impact of the paragraph? Write your ideas below.**

217

ENGLISH
Grades 5-9

MAIN ACTIVITY: EXPERIMENTING   **TIMING: 20 MINS**

LEARNING OBJECTIVES
- To be able to structure paragraphs for impact
- To be able to structure sentences for impact

EQUIPMENT
none

Read the sentences below.

A. Adults teach children to eat badly.

B. They give children sweets and chocolate as a treat or a reward.

C. We are made to eat vegetables.

D. Vegetables feel like a punishment.

E. We know vegetables are good for us.

F. We need to change the way we feed children.

G. We are harming children's health.

1. On a separate piece of paper, structure the ideas in the sentences above into a paragraph, aiming to achieve clarity and impact.
   You could think about:
   - linking the sentences
   - using short, single-clause or minor sentences
   - adding, changing or removing words or phrases
   - re-ordering the sentences.

You could use:

present participles	giving	making			
past participles	given	made			
adverbials	unfortunately	surprisingly	urgently		
conjunctions	and	but	because	although	even though

2. On a separate piece of paper, write a differently structured version of the paragraph, aiming to achieve clarity and impact.

AQA ENGLISH — Grades 5-9

| HOMEWORK ACTIVITY: CRAFTING FOR IMPACT | TIMING: 30 MINS |

LEARNING OBJECTIVES
- To be able to structure paragraphs for impact
- To be able to structure sentences for impact

EQUIPMENT
none

1. Write a paragraph in response to the Paper 2, Section B exam-style writing task below.

   > 'Schools and colleges need to do more to make learning fun. It would help students learn, and encourage them to want to learn.'
   >
   > Write a letter to your local newspaper in which you explain your point of view on this statement.
   >
   > **[40 marks]**

2. On a separate piece of paper, rewrite your paragraph, thinking carefully about how you could add clarity and impact to your writing by re-structuring your sentences and/or paragraph.

3. Write one or two sentences explaining the changes you have made and the impact of those changes.

33 ANSWERS

STARTER ACTIVITY: PLAYING WITH SENTENCES

1. Examples:
In the last few years, sales of fast food have rocketed as our time and attention-span have got shorter and shorter.
Sales of fast food have rocketed in the last few years as our time and attention-span have got shorter and shorter.
Sales of fast food have rocketed as our time and attention-span have got shorter and shorter in the last few years.

MAIN ACTIVITY: SPOT THE DIFFERENCE

1. Differences include: the range of methods linking ideas in the first section, e.g.
A: ideas presented in short, emphatic single-clause sentences
B: subordinating conjunction 'because'; relative pronoun 'which', explicitly linking the relationship between these points
C: non-finite verb 'crammed' emphasised at the start of the sentence; coordinating conjunction 'and' highlights the connection.
the various positions of, and consequently emphasis given to, the adverbial 'sadly'
the various methods used to create emphasis in the final section, e.g.
A: short, single-clause sentence
B: short single-clause sentence and minor sentence
C: short paragraph consisting of short single-clause sentence and minor sentence.
2. Student's own answers. Ensure they comment on some of the differences identified above.

MAIN ACTIVITY: EXPERIMENTING

1. Accept all valid responses. Example: Adults teach children to eat badly. Given sweets and chocolates as a treat or reward, children are made to eat vegetables and, even though we know they are good for us, it feels like a punishment. We urgently need to change the way we feed children. We are harming their health.
2. Accept all valid responses.

HOMEWORK ACTIVITY: CRAFTING FOR IMPACT

1. See exam-style mark scheme on pages 251–253.
2. Student's own answer. Ensure revisions suggest confident ability in manipulating paragraph and sentence structure.
3. Student's own answer. Ensure analysis demonstrates understanding of paragraph and sentence structure.

AQA ENGLISH — Grades 5–9

34 Writing to Present a Viewpoint: Selecting Vocabulary for Impact

LEARNING OBJECTIVES	SPECIFICATION LINKS
• To be able to select vocabulary for clarity and impact	• 3.1.2 producing clear and coherent text • 3.1.2 writing for impact

Starter Activity

- **A question of style; 5 minutes; page 222**
  Note that this lesson builds on the work completed in lesson 27. Explain that this lesson will focus on what makes a writer's vocabulary choice effective in the context of a writing task. Use the activity to discuss the advantages (and temptations!) of selecting ambitious or simpler vocabulary.

Main Activities

- **Clarity and ambition; 15 minutes; page 223**
  Discuss the potentially conflicting aims of selecting vocabulary that expresses your ideas well and demonstrates the breadth of your vocabulary. Use the activity to explore the balance between powerful simplicity, clarity, precision and sophistication. Emphasise that there are no rules for vocabulary selection: it must be judged in the context of the task.

- **Vocabulary and intention; 20 minutes; page 224**
  Emphasise that vocabulary choice should primarily be guided by intention – as should all choices the student makes as a writer. Highlight the importance, therefore, of identifying intention as a key element of planning. Make it clear that the intentions identified in the activity are examples, and that the student should be guided by their own intention in their writing.

Plenary Activity

- **Review and revise; 10 minutes**
  Ask the student to write one sentence in response to the exam-style writing task on the homework sheet, and then review and revise their vocabulary choices, focusing on intention, clarity, precision and sophistication.

Homework Activity

- **Crafting vocabulary; 30 minutes; page 225**
  Ask the student to write one or two paragraphs in response to the exam-style task. Emphasise the importance of reviewing and clearly revising vocabulary choices. The student may wish to refer to the ideas they gathered for this task in lesson 30.

Support Idea

- **Vocabulary and intention** Focus on those intentions/ideas that the student finds most accessible and achievable.

Extension Idea

- **Clarity and ambition; Vocabulary and intention** Encourage the student to review their choices frequently and weigh up a range of possible revisions.

Progress and Observations

ENGLISH
Grades 5-9

STARTER ACTIVITY: A QUESTION OF STYLE   **TIMING: 5 MINS**

LEARNING OBJECTIVES
- To be able to select vocabulary for clarity and impact

EQUIPMENT
none

Look at the two versions of a sentence written in response to the Paper 2, Section B exam-style writing task below.

> 'We need to think more about the food we put in our bodies and the effect it has on our lives. You are what you eat.'
>
> Write an article for a broadsheet newspaper in which you explain your point of view on this statement.
>
> **[40 marks]**

A. We should try to eat less rubbish and get off the sofa once in a while.

B. We should endeavour to ingest more nutritious cuisine and periodically commit ourselves to partaking in physical activity.

1. Which contains the most effective vocabulary choice? Tick it.

2. Write one or two sentences explaining your decision.

....

....

....

....

AQA ENGLISH — Grades 5-9

MAIN ACTIVITY: CLARITY AND AMBITION **TIMING: 15 MINS**

LEARNING OBJECTIVES
- To be able to select vocabulary for clarity and impact

EQUIPMENT
none

1. Compare these pairs of sentences. Which sentence in each pair expresses the writer's ideas most effectively? Tick the most successful sentence in each pair and underline the most effective elements in both sentences.

   i) A. Fast food is full of calories and not much else.

   B. Fast food is laden with carbohydrates but lacks significant nutritious value.

   ii) A. When a tasty burger is sitting in front of you, and it's smelling great, it's hard to say no.

   B. When you are faced with the temptation of a plump, succulent burger, and its delicious aroma wafts past your nostrils, it's virtually impossible to resist.

   iii) A. A ready meal looking brown and sloppy in its plastic tray is enough to make anyone want to learn how to cook properly.

   B. The appearance and odour of a ready meal, its unrecognisable ingredients festering in a murky puddle of gravy at the bottom of a plastic container, is an excellent incentive to encourage even the laziest person to improve their culinary skills.

2. Rewrite this sentence twice, using clear, powerful and precise vocabulary.

   When you make food yourself using real ingredients, you realise how nice food can be.

   ----

3. Review your sentences. Tick the most effective one and underline the elements that make it effective.

ENGLISH
Grades 5-9
AQA

MAIN ACTIVITY: VOCABULARY AND INTENTION	**TIMING: 20 MINS**

LEARNING OBJECTIVES
- To be able to select vocabulary for clarity and impact

EQUIPMENT
none

When making or revising vocabulary choices, it is important to think about your **intention**: the impact you want to have on the reader.

Look at this sentence.

> Picture the burger sitting in its polystyrene tray.

Now think about the impact that the next sentence could have on your reader. It could create:

Shock
What might be the shocking consequences of eating too many burgers?

Empathy
How could you encourage the reader to appreciate the temptations of a burger?

Intention

Disgust
How could you create a disgusting image of a burger in your reader's mind?

Humour
What aspect of this burger might amuse your reader? How it was made? How we are persuaded to buy them?

1. Write four sentences that could follow the sentence above. Make sure that each achieves a different impact.

   a) Shock

   ----

   b) Empathy

   ----

   c) Disgust

   ----

   d) Humour

   ----

2. Review your vocabulary choices. Can you add to or revise any of them to increase their impact?

ENGLISH
— Grades 5–9 —

HOMEWORK ACTIVITY: CRAFTING VOCABULARY   TIMING: 30 MINS

LEARNING OBJECTIVES
- To be able to select vocabulary for clarity and impact

EQUIPMENT
none

1. Write the opening of your response to the Paper 2, Section B exam-style writing task below.

> 'We need to think more about the food we put in our bodies and the effect it has on our lives. You are what you eat.'
>
> Write an article for a broadsheet newspaper in which you explain your point of view on this statement.
>
> [40 marks]

2. Review and revise your vocabulary choices.
   Think about:
   - expressing your ideas as clearly, powerfully and precisely as possible
   - achieving your intention.

   Remember to clearly show all the options you consider, and the choices you make as you revise your writing.

ENGLISH
Grades 5-9

34 ANSWERS

STARTER ACTIVITY: A QUESTION OF STYLE
1. A has clarity and power but its informality is potentially inappropriate.
B is unnecessarily and inaccessibly formal.
2. Student's own answer

MAIN ACTIVITY: CLARITY AND AMBITION
1. All responses are valid if justified. Examples might include:
i) Elements of both are effective, e.g. 'Fast food is laden with carbohydrates' (B) is precise, and 'not much else' (A) has blunt impact.
ii) B expresses the appeal of the burger far more explicitly.
iii) Elements of both are effective e.g. 'The appearance and odour of a ready meal, its unrecognisable ingredients festering in a murky puddle of gravy at the bottom of a plastic container' (B) is precise, and 'is enough to make anyone want to learn how to cook properly' (A) has blunt impact.
2. Example: When you cook a meal yourself using fresh ingredients, you immediately realise how delicious real food can look, smell and taste.
3. Student's own answer

MAIN ACTIVITY: VOCABULARY AND INTENTION
1. Student's own answers. Examples:
a) You may feel tempted now, but think how you will feel as your arteries clog with fat and your heart aches with the pain of pumping your thickened blood?
b) Imagine the crisp lettuce, the tangy sauce, the creamy mayonnaise, the spicy gherkin, all mingling with the perfectly salted fries, bursting with flavour on your tongue.
c) A fat-drenched lump of pulverised animal sits limp inside a soggy bun, getting soggier as it soaks up grease.
d) You look at the picture of a beautiful burger above the counter. You look again in disbelief at the unrecognisable blob lurking in the polystyrene tray in front of you.
2. Student's own answers

HOMEWORK ACTIVITY: CRAFTING VOCABULARY
1. See exam-style mark scheme on pages 251–253.
2. Student's own answer. Ensure clear evidence of review and revision is shown.

GLOSSARY
Emotive language
Language intended to prompt an emotional response in the reader

AQA ENGLISH — Grades 5-9

35 Writing to present a viewpoint: Planning a response

LEARNING OBJECTIVES
- To be able to plan and write an effective response to present a viewpoint

SPECIFICATION LINKS
- 3.1.2 producing clear and coherent text
- 3.1.2 writing for impact

STARTER ACTIVITY
- **The map; 5 minutes; page 228**
  Explain to the student that this lesson will consolidate all their learning on writing to present a viewpoint. Emphasise that this will be the map they will follow as they craft their response to the writing task. Note the similarities between this map and the one for narrative/descriptive writing.

MAIN ACTIVITIES
- **Planning; 15 minutes; page 229**
  Reiterate the importance of planning over the need to 'just get on with the writing'.
- **Beginning writing; 20 minutes; page 230**
  If the previous activity goes over time, focus this activity on the opening sentence or two of the response. Explain to the student that pausing, reviewing and revising during writing is an important part of crafting a successful response. Direct the student to recall some of the techniques and choices they have explored in the last six lessons while exploring structure, paragraphing, sentence forms and vocabulary choice.

PLENARY ACTIVITY
- **Review; 10 minutes**
  Work with the student to review the impact of their opening to the response. Encourage them to experiment with possible revisions to paragraphing, sentence structures and vocabulary choices.

HOMEWORK ACTIVITY
- **Complete your response; 30 minutes; page 231**
  Emphasise the importance of following the map established in the starter activity.

SUPPORT IDEA
- **Planning** Encourage the student to verbalise their thinking. Prompt where necessary.

EXTENSION IDEA
- **Planning; Beginning writing** Challenge the student to constantly review and revise throughout the planning and writing process, focusing on how effectively their response will achieve their identified intention.

PROGRESS AND OBSERVATIONS

ENGLISH
Grades 5-9
AQA

STARTER ACTIVITY: THE MAP **TIMING: 5 MINS**

LEARNING OBJECTIVES
- To be able to plan and write an effective response to present a viewpoint

EQUIPMENT
none

You are going to write your response to the Paper 2, Section B exam-style writing task below.

> 'People spend too much time complaining and moaning. If we all tried to be more positive and optimistic, everyone would be much happier.'
>
> Write an article for a broadsheet newspaper in which you explain your point of view on this statement.
>
> **[40 marks]**

Read this list of tasks you will need to complete to craft an effective response to the task. At what stage and in what order will you complete them?

1. **Tick to show whether you will complete each task before, during or after writing.**

2. **Number the tasks 1–10 to show the order in which you will complete them.**

No.	Task	Before	During	After
☐	Select precise vocabulary for clarity and impact.	☐	☐	☐
☐	Identify your viewpoint and intention.	☐	☐	☐
☐	Check your spelling, punctuation and grammar.	☐	☐	☐
☐	Review, select, structure and sequence your ideas.	☐	☐	☐
☐	Gather a range of ideas.	☐	☐	☐
☐	Think carefully about the introduction and conclusion to your response.	☐	☐	☐
☐	Structure your sentences for clarity and impact.	☐	☐	☐
☐	Think about how you will use paragraph structure in your writing.	☐	☐	☐
☐	Review and revise your choices of paragraph and sentence structure, and vocabulary.	☐	☐	☐
☐	Identify the form, purpose audience and central idea on which your writing will focus.	☐	☐	☐

AQA ENGLISH — Grades 5–9

MAIN ACTIVITY: PLANNING   **TIMING: 15 MINS**

LEARNING OBJECTIVES
- To be able to plan and write an effective response to present a viewpoint

EQUIPMENT
none

Use the space below to plan your response to the Paper 2, Section B exam-style writing task below.

> 'People spend too much time complaining and moaning. If we all tried to be more positive and optimistic, everyone would be much happier.'
>
> Write an article for a broadsheet newspaper in which you explain your point of view on this statement.
>
> [40 marks]

1. The central idea – try to think of two different ideas, and then choose the stronger.

2. Your viewpoint – what opinion are you going to share with the reader?

3. The details – note down the ideas you could explore in your response.

4. Review and select – discard any ideas that do not support your intention or your viewpoint.

5. Sequence and shape – finally, structure the ideas you have selected, thinking particularly about your introduction and conclusion.

ENGLISH
Grades 5-9
AQA

MAIN ACTIVITY: BEGINNING WRITING **TIMING: 20 MINS**

LEARNING OBJECTIVES
- To be able to plan and write an effective response to present a viewpoint

EQUIPMENT
none

1. **Write the opening of your response to the Paper 2, Section B exam-style question below.**

   > 'People spend too much time complaining and moaning. If we all tried to be more positive and optimistic, everyone would be much happier.'
   >
   > Write an article for a broadsheet newspaper in which you explain your point of view on this statement.
   >
   > **[40 marks]**

2. **Pause to review your writing so far.**
   You should think about:
   a) Structure – will your opening effectively engage and interest the reader?
   b) Paragraphs – could any of your paragraphs be restructured to add impact?
   c) Sentence structure – could any of your sentences be restructured to add impact?
   d) Vocabulary – could any of your vocabulary choices be more precise or have greater impact?

AQA ENGLISH — Grades 5–9

HOMEWORK ACTIVITY: COMPLETE YOUR RESPONSE   **TIMING: 30 MINS**

LEARNING OBJECTIVES
- To be able to plan and write an effective response to present a viewpoint

EQUIPMENT
none

1. **On a separate piece of paper, complete your response to the Paper 2, Section B exam-style writing task below.**

   > 'People spend too much time complaining and moaning. If we all tried to be more positive and optimistic, everyone would be much happier.'
   >
   > Write an article for a broadsheet newspaper in which you explain your point of view on this statement.
   >
   > **[40 marks]**

2. **When you have completed your response, review and revise it.**
   Think about your choices of:
   - whole text structure
   - paragraph structure
   - sentence structure
   - vocabulary.

35 ANSWERS

STARTER ACTIVITY: THE MAP

Before writing
1. Identify the form, purpose, audience and central idea on which your writing will focus.
2. Identify your viewpoint and intention.
3. Gather a range of ideas.
4. Review select, structure and sequence your ideas.
5. Think carefully about the introduction and conclusion to your response.

During writing
6. Think about how you will use paragraph structure in your writing.
7. Structure your sentences for clarity and impact.
8. Select precise vocabulary for clarity and impact.

During and after writing
9. Review and revise your choices of paragraph and sentence structure, and vocabulary.
10. Check your spelling, punctuation and grammar.

MAIN ACTIVITY: PLANNING
1. Student's own answers. Ensure two suitable ideas are suggested.
2. Student's own answer. Ensure a relevant point of view is identified.
3. Student's own answers. Ensure enough material is gathered.
4. Student's own answer. Ensure the most relevant material is selected.
5. Student's own answer. Ensure the material is structured effectively.

MAIN ACTIVITY: BEGINNING WRITING
1. See exam-style mark scheme on pages 251–253.
2. Student's own answers. Ensure revision of structure, paragraphs, sentence structure and vocabulary choices is thorough and carefully considered to convey the identified viewpoint and achieve significant impact.

HOMEWORK ACTIVITY: COMPLETE YOUR RESPONSE
1. See exam-style mark scheme on pages 251–253.
2. Student's own answer. Ensure revision of whole text, paragraph, sentence and vocabulary choices is thorough and carefully considered to convey the identified viewpoint and achieve significant impact.

ENGLISH
Grades 5-9

36 SPaG: Punctuation for clarity

LEARNING OBJECTIVES	SPECIFICATION LINKS
• To be able to use a range of punctuation accurately	• 3.1.2 producing clear and coherent text

Starter activity

- **What's missing?; 5 minutes; page 234**
  Explain to the student that the emphasis on (and reward for) accurate punctuation in the exam has increased. Fold the sheet in half. Ask the student to complete the task. Unfold the sheet and ask them to compare their response to the prompts. Identify any areas for further work and for close attention when proofreading.

Main activities

- **Commas; 20 minutes; page 235**
  Note that these two activities could be used as short, starter-style activities in other lessons.
- **Colons and semi-colons; 20 minutes; page 236**
  Note that these two activities could be used as short, starter-style activities in other lessons.
  Colons Fold the sheet to hide the correct answer. Focus on those phrases made redundant through the use of a colon, e.g. 'for example'. Note that this is not a 'rule': colons should only be used with careful attention to clarity of meaning. Reveal the correct answers and identify areas for further work.
  Semi-colons Emphasise that not all conjunctions can be replaced with a semi-colon, and that they should be used sparingly, with careful attention to clarity of meaning.

Plenary activity

- **Review; 5 minutes**
  Ask the student to review and evaluate the punctuation skills they have used in the lesson. Identify any areas for further work and for close attention when proofreading.

Homework activity

- **Test writing; 30 minutes; page 237**
  Advise the student to write only three or four sentences for each area of the test.

Support idea

- **Commas** Ask the student to read the sentences aloud and listen for the pauses that may suggest a comma. Remind them to check that every comma used is not a comma splice.

Extension idea

- **Throughout** Ask the student to verbalise their thought processes as they punctuate, explaining the reasons for their choices and the rules behind them.

Progress and observations

ENGLISH
Grades 5-9

STARTER ACTIVITY: WHAT'S MISSING? | **TIMING: 5 MINS**

LEARNING OBJECTIVES
- To be able to use a range of punctuation accurately

EQUIPMENT
none

Proofread and correct the text below. You should look for missing:
- full stops
- apostrophes
- speech punctuation.

I sat outside the headteachers office, I was innocent but I was sweating with fear and guilt. I stared down at the floor, I can still remember the piece of grey chewing gum welded to the blue carpet thinking I knew how it felt, trodden down and crushed.

The headteachers door opened.
'Come in said Mrs Flynn, staring at me with her piercing green eyes 'and hurry up. I have'nt got all day.'
'Sorry' I mumbled.

--- fold ---

I sat outside the headteacher's office. I was innocent but I was sweating with fear and guilt. I stared down at the floor. I can still remember the piece of grey chewing gum welded to the blue carpet thinking I knew how it felt, trodden down and crushed.

The headteacher's door opened.
'Come in,' said Mrs Flynn, staring at me with her piercing green eyes, 'and hurry up. I haven't got all day.'
'Sorry,' I mumbled.

ENGLISH
— Grades 5-9 —

MAIN ACTIVITY: COMMAS **TIMING: 20 MINS**

LEARNING OBJECTIVES
- To be able to use a range of punctuation accurately

EQUIPMENT
none

Use commas to separate items or clauses in a list. For example:

> I got out of bed, dressed myself, ate breakfast and went to the shops to buy corn flakes, milk, bread and sugar.

1. Why is there no comma before the last item or clause in these lists?

....

....

2. Write a sentence listing four things you will do this evening.

This evening, I will…

....

....

You should also use commas to…	Example
separate subordinate clauses when positioned at the beginning of a sentence	Although it was late, I could not sleep.
separate adverbials at the start of a sentence	Suddenly, I heard a noise.
separate non-essential information from the rest of a sentence.	It was, without a doubt, the sound of footsteps.

3. Add the necessary commas to the sentences below.

> When I got up I paused and listened carefully again. I knew without looking who it was. In the garden below my window they were waiting for me. Without stopping to breathe I ran downstairs and locked the door.

ENGLISH
Grades 5-9

MAIN ACTIVITY: COLONS AND SEMI-COLONS **TIMING: 20 MINS**

LEARNING OBJECTIVES
- To be able to use a range of punctuation accurately

EQUIPMENT
none

Colons can be used to introduce a quotation, a list of information, or an explanation.

1. Improve the sentences below by adding a colon and removing any words made redundant by it.

> Macbeth reveals his fears after murdering Duncan. For example, he says 'Methought I heard a voice cry, "Sleep no more!"'

> There are three things you can do to reduce the stress of GCSEs. These are to have enough sleep, do plenty of revision and make some time to relax.

> GCSEs are important. This is because they are the stepping stone to the next stage in your life.

------- fold -------

> Macbeth reveals his fears after murdering Duncan(:) 'Methought I heard a voice cry, "Sleep no more!"'

> There are three things you can do to reduce the stress of GCSEs(:) have enough sleep, do plenty of revision and make some time to relax.

> GCSEs are important(:) they are the stepping stone to the next stage in your life.

Semi-colons can replace conjunctions to show a strong relationship between two pieces of information. For example, compare these two sentences:

> I laughed but she didn't.   I laughed; she didn't.

Conjunctions can make the relationship between two pieces of information much clearer. If you use a semi-colon instead, make sure the connection is still clear.

2. On a separate piece of paper, write four sentences using each of the conjunctions below.
   a) but
   b) because
   c) although
   d) when

3. In which sentences could you replace the conjunction with a semi-colon? Tick them.

236

ENGLISH
— Grades 5-9 —

HOMEWORK ACTIVITY: TEST WRITING	TIMING: 30 MINS

LEARNING OBJECTIVES	EQUIPMENT
• To be able to use a range of punctuation accurately	none

1. **On a separate piece of paper, create a test with four separate sections to assess a student's understanding of punctuation.**

    You should include:
    - full stops, apostrophes and speech punctuation
    - commas
    - colons
    - semi colons.

    The test should take a student approximately 15 minutes to complete.

2. **On a separate piece of paper, create an answer sheet showing the correct answers to your test.**

ENGLISH
Grades 5-9

36 Answers

Starter activity: What's missing?
1. Answers are provided on the activity sheet. Note that there are two possible stylistic choices in the example: 'trodden down and crushed' could be punctuated as a minor sentence, e.g. 'Trodden down and crushed'; 'eyes, "and hurry up"' could be punctuated as a new sentence, e.g. 'eyes. "And hurry up"'.

Main activity: Commas
1. The comma preceding *and* at the end of a list (sometimes known as an Oxford comma) is optional.
2. Student's own answer. Example: This evening, I will do my homework, eat dinner, watch television and go to bed.
3. When I got up, I paused and listened carefully again. I knew, without looking, who it was. In the garden, below my window, they were waiting for me. Without stopping to breathe, I ran downstairs and locked the door.

Main activity: Colons and semi-colons
1. Answers are provided on the activity sheet.
2. to 3. Student's own answers. Ensure responses are carefully checked for clarity of meaning.

Homework activity: Test writing
1. Student's own answers. Ensure all four punctuation elements are covered.
2. Student's own answers. Ensure all answers are correct.

Glossary

Adverbial
A word or phrase that modifies a verb, adjective or another adverbial. Adverbials, such as *similarly*, *however* and *for example*, are used to link clauses within sentences and make links between sentences.

Coordinating conjunction
A word, such as *and*, *but*, *or*, that links two coordinate clauses. For example: *I ate dinner and went to bed*.

Subordinating conjunction
A word, such as *when*, *if*, *although*, that links a subordinate clause to a main clause. For example: *I ate dinner because I was hungry*.

Comma splice
When a comma is incorrectly used to join two sentences that should be separated by a full stop, it is called a comma splice.

Colon
Used at the end of a sentence to show an answer, elaboration or explanation follows

Semi-colon
Replaces a full stop or 'and' between two or more sentences that share a theme

ENGLISH
Grades 5–9

37 SPaG: Punctuation for Effect

LEARNING OBJECTIVES
- To be able to use a range of punctuation for effect

SPECIFICATION LINKS
- 3.1.2 producing clear and coherent text
- 3.1.2 writing for impact

STARTER ACTIVITY
- **Identifying punctuation for effect; 5 minutes; page 240**
  Identify and discuss the effect created by the punctuation in the extract. Ask the student to suggest other possible uses for, and effects of, these punctuation marks. Emphasise that punctuation for effect should be used sparingly.

MAIN ACTIVITIES
- **Exclamation marks and ellipses; 20 minutes; page 241**
  Note that these two activities could be used as short, starter-style activities in other lessons. Emphasise that, as with all punctuation for effect, overuse of exclamations and ellipsis weakens their impact and may become an irritation to the reader.
- **Dashes and brackets; 20 minutes; page 242**
  As the student completes questions 1 and 2, discuss whether the writer has overused dashes. In question 3, focus the student on the similarities between parenthetical commas, dashes and brackets, and the stylistic impact of each choice.

PLENARY ACTIVITY
- **Review; 5 minutes**
  Ask the student to summarise and evaluate their understanding of punctuation for effect, and assess their confidence in completing the homework task successfully.

HOMEWORK ACTIVITY
- **Punctuation practice; 30 minutes; page 243**
  Emphasise the importance of using (but not overusing) punctuation for specific effect. The student may wish to reuse some of the ideas they gathered for this task in lesson 28.

SUPPORT IDEA
- **Throughout** Encourage the student to read the examples aloud. How does punctuation change their reading, intonation or response?

EXTENSION IDEA
- **Throughout** Encourage the student to analyse the positive or negative impacts of alternative punctuation choices.

PROGRESS AND OBSERVATIONS

ENGLISH
Grades 5-9

STARTER ACTIVITY: IDENTIFYING PUNCTUATION FOR EFFECT   **TIMING: 5 MINS**

LEARNING OBJECTIVES
- To be able to use a range of punctuation for effect

EQUIPMENT
none

Punctuation helps to make your meaning clear. It can also be used for effect to add impact to your writing.

1. Circle three examples of punctuation used for effect in this student's writing.

> 'I… I don't know how to tell you this,' she said. Her face – usually smiling, often laughing – crumpled and she began to sob.
> 'What's wrong?' I said. 'What's happened to – '
> 'Everything's wrong!' she cried.

240

AQA ENGLISH — Grades 5–9

MAIN ACTIVITY: EXCLAMATIONS AND ELLIPSES   **TIMING: 20 MINS**

LEARNING OBJECTIVES
- To be able to use a range of punctuation for effect

EQUIPMENT
none

Exclamation marks are used to suggest volume or surprise. They are very easy to overuse.

1. In which of these sentences would you leave the exclamation mark? Underline them.

> I had never seen anything like it in my life! It was huge! Its huge teeth gleamed in the moonlight, its eyes were burning, its whole body tensed ready to pounce! I was terrified! I didn't want to scream but I couldn't stop myself!
> 'Help!' I screamed.
> I began to run but I could hear a noise behind me and, as I turned, I realised in horror that it was following me!

Ellipses are used to show a break or pause in the text.

An ellipsis can be used to suggest…	Example
an unfinished thought	But then again…
a hesitant pause or silence	'I… I don't know how to tell you this,' she said.
that the reader must infer what has been omitted.	We all know what that means…

2. Where in these sentences could you use an ellipsis? Mark each position with an X.

> 'What do you mean?' I said.
> 'I don't know,' she replied. 'All I know is, we've started something that, that we can't finish.'
> My brain began to race.
> Surely she didn't mean what I thought she meant.
> In the distance, I heard a noise. It was the sound of a car. And it was getting louder.
> That was when I realised. What we had done could not be undone. And we had no control over what would happen next.

3. Where in these sentences would you use an exclamation mark? Tick the positions.

ENGLISH
— Grades 5-9 —

MAIN ACTIVITY: DASHES AND BRACKETS   **TIMING: 20 MINS**

LEARNING OBJECTIVES
- To be able to use a range of punctuation for effect

EQUIPMENT
none

Read the sentences below, taken from one student's response to a Paper 2, Section B exam-style writing task.

> People say that thinking in a positive way makes positive things happen – but it doesn't.
>
> Thinking negatively means you will never be disappointed – and you might be pleasantly surprised if things turn out much better than you expect. Surprisingly – or perhaps not so surprisingly – you can't make things work out just by wishing for them.

1. **This student has punctuated their work using single and paired dashes. Annotate the text, noting their effect.**

2. **Complete the sentences below.**

   a) A single dash can be used to...

   ....

   ....

   b) Paired dashes can be used to...

   ....

   ....

Commas, paired dashes and brackets can be used to add supplementary information to a sentence, which can be removed without altering the meaning of the sentence.

3. **Compare three versions of the same sentence below. Which of the three versions is the most effective? Tick it.**

A. Moaning and whining, two of my favourite hobbies, make everything feel better.

B. Moaning and whining – two of my favourite hobbies – make everything feel better.

C. Moaning and whining (two of my favourite hobbies) make everything feel better.

242

ENGLISH
Grades 5–9

HOMEWORK ACTIVITY: PUNCTUATION PRACTICE   **TIMING: 30 MINS**

LEARNING OBJECTIVES
- To be able to use a range of punctuation for effect

EQUIPMENT
none

1. **On a separate piece of paper, write 150–200 words of dialogue and/or description in response to the Paper 1, Section B exam-style writing task below.**

   > Describe an occasion when you could not believe your eyes.
   > Focus on the thoughts and feelings you had at that time.
   >
   > **[40 marks]**

   Make sure you use some or all of the following punctuation for effect:
   - exclamation mark
   - ellipsis
   - single dash
   - paired dashes
   - brackets.

2. **Annotate the punctuation you have used for effect, noting your intention in each case.**

3. **Use the checklist below to check the accuracy of your punctuation.**

   - ☐ full stops
   - ☐ question marks
   - ☐ exclamation marks
   - ☐ apostrophes
   - ☐ speech punctuation
   - ☐ commas
   - ☐ colons
   - ☐ semi-colons
   - ☐ brackets
   - ☐ dashes
   - ☐ ellipses.

ENGLISH
Grades 5-9

37 Answers

STARTER ACTIVITY: IDENTIFYING PUNCTUATION FOR EFFECT
1. Examples: ellipsis to suggest hesitancy; paired dashes used parenthetically to add information; a single dash to suggest interruption; exclamation mark to suggest emphasis or volume.

MAIN ACTIVITY: EXCLAMATIONS AND ELLIPSIS
1. Only the indicating exclamation 'Help!' is necessary or effective.
2. Examples:
'What do you mean…?' I said.
'I don't know…' she replied. 'All I know is, we've started something that… that we can't finish.'
My brain began to race…
Surely she didn't mean what I thought she meant…
In the distance, I heard a noise. It was the sound of a car… and it was getting louder.
That was when I realised…
What we had done could not be undone… and we had no control over what would happen next…
3. Examples:
'What do you mean?' I said.
'I don't know!' she replied. 'All I know is, we've started something that, that we can't finish!'
My brain began to race.
Surely she didn't mean what I thought she meant!
In the distance, I heard a noise. It was the sound of a car! And it was getting louder!
That was when I realised. What we had done could not be undone. And we had no control over what would happen next!

MAIN ACTIVITY: DASHES AND BRACKETS
1. The single dash adds emphasis to the 'but' that follows it. The paired dashes separate additional information.
2. a) A single dash can be used to create a pause and add dramatic emphasis to the idea that follows it.
b) Paired dashes can be used to indicate an aside or supplementary information.
3. All responses are valid with justification. Arguably, brackets reduce the apparent significance of information, while paired dashes accentuate it.

HOMEWORK ACTIVITY: PUNCTUATION PRACTICE
1. See exam-style mark scheme on pages 251–253.
2. Student's own answers. Ensure answer shows confidence in manipulating punctuation for effect to achieve an intention.
3. Student's own answer. Ensure the student has checked their punctuation for accuracy.

GLOSSARY

Exclamation marks
Replaces a full stop to show surprise or shock

Ellipses
Used to show words have been missed from a quotation, or that a sentence is incomplete

Single dashes
Used to introduce an idea, list or explanation

Paired dashes
Used to separate non-essential information in a sentence, such as an inserted comment or explanation

Brackets
Used like paired dashed to separate non-essential information in a sentence

ENGLISH
Grades 5–9

38 SPaG: Spelling

Learning objectives	Specification links
• To be able to spell commonly misspelt words	• 3.1.2 producing clear and coherent text

Starter activity
- **Homophones; 10 minutes; page 246**
  Remind the student that 20% of the total marks available will be awarded for accurate use of spelling, punctuation and grammar. Explain that this lesson focuses on the most common spelling errors. Check their understanding of the term *homophones*. Use this activity to develop awareness of homophones and setting them as 'triggers' for double-checking during proofreading.

Main activities
- **Spotting spelling errors; 25 minutes; page 247**
  In the next activity, the student will evaluate their familiarity with the correct spelling of each word. When they have completed it, ask them to mark their responses using the table on the *Getting it right* activity sheet.
- **Getting it right; 10 minutes; page 248**
  Encourage the student to reflect on their confidence in the spelling of the words from the previous activity.

Plenary activity
- **Review; 5 minutes**
  Discuss the methods of learning spelling outlined in the homework sheet.

Homework activity
- **Learning spellings; 30 minutes; page 249**
  Ensure the quantity of spellings to learn is manageable within the time allowed. If not, suggest grouping them according to the specific area of difficulty, e.g. double letters, vowel choice/order.

Support idea
- **Homophones** Highlight the homophones in the text.

Extension idea
- **Spotting spelling errors** Remove the bold from the text.

Progress and observations

ENGLISH
Grades 5-9

STARTER ACTIVITY: HOMOPHONES **TIMING: 10 MINS**

LEARNING OBJECTIVES
- To be able to spell commonly misspelt words

EQUIPMENT
none

A homophone is a word that sounds the same as another word or words that are spelt differently and have different meanings. Can you identify all the homophones in this text?

> Their are no words to describe how your heart thumps when your weighting for bad news. Worse still, your mood effects everyone around you. Its as though you have shouted your negative thoughts allowed for everyone to here. Fear and anxiety spread like a disease; there contagious and deadly, to powerful to be resisted.

1. Annotate each homophone, noting all its partner homophones.

2. Correct any homophones that are spelled incorrectly in the text.

ENGLISH
— Grades 5–9 —

MAIN ACTIVITY: SPOTTING SPELLING ERRORS   **TIMING: 25 MINS**

LEARNING OBJECTIVES

- To be able to spell commonly misspelt words

EQUIPMENT

none

The text below contains more than 40 of the most common spelling errors in English.

> remembar
> remember
> remmeber

> happiness
> hapiness
> happines

> dificult
> difficult
> difficault

> achieve
> acheeve
> acheave

We should always **rember** that **happyness** is **difficalt** to **acheive** but easy to lose. It is a **precius posession**. However, my **freind**, Billy, is **quite wierd**. For example, he **truley believes** that **knowlege** is **completley unecessary**. **Unfortunatley**, this can lead to **arguments**. Billy is **really successfull** at **argueing because** he is not too **embarrased** to **interrupt** you **immediatley** and start shouting. This has **happened** on **severa**l **seperate occasions** and is **begining** to be a **persistant** problem that will not **dissappear**. This **differance** between Billy and the rest of my **freinds** has **finally** made us make a **dicision** that we would have **prefered** not to make. **Tomorrow** we will **definitley reccommend** that Billy takes a vow of **silence**. I am sure he will be **dissappointed** but it may be the **surprise** that teaches him a lesson – or more **likley**, it will be **buisness** as usual and he'll start an **argument**...

1. Look at the first four highlighted words in the text. Which is the correct spelling? Tick it and correct the text.

2. Now look at all the other highlighted words.

   a) Which are definitely spelled correctly? Tick them.

   b) Which might be misspelled? For each one:
- note two or three possible alternative spellings
- select the spelling you think is correct
- use it to correct the spelling in the text.

ENGLISH
— Grades 5-9 —

MAIN ACTIVITY: GETTING IT RIGHT   **TIMING: 10 MINS**

LEARNING OBJECTIVES
- To be able to spell commonly misspelt words

EQUIPMENT
- red, yellow and green coloured pencils.

Look at each of the tricky spellings from the previous activity

achieve	arguing	argument	because	beginning	believes	business
completely	decision	definitely	difference	difficult	disappear	disappointed
embarrassed	finally	friend	happened	happiness	immediately	interrupt
knowledge	likely	occasion	persistent	possession	precious	preferred
quite	really	recommend	remember	separate	several	silence
successful	surprise	tomorrow	truly	unfortunately	unnecessary	weird

1. Which words did you feel completely confident about? Colour them green.
2. Which words were you not sure about? Colour them yellow.
3. Which words were you sure you did not know? Colour them red.

There are some common patterns in these tricky spellings that can help you to learn them.
4. Add all the spellings you coloured yellow or red to the table below. Make sure you spell each word correctly.

When you add –ly, don't split it.	Think whether to double a letter or not.
Completley ✗	disappoint ✓ dissappoint ✗
Use the right vowels and/or put them in the right order.	**You just have to learn it.**
achieve ✓ acheive ✗	

248

ENGLISH
Grades 5–9

HOMEWORK ACTIVITY: LEARNING SPELLINGS	TIMING: 30 MINS
LEARNING OBJECTIVES	**EQUIPMENT**
• To be able to spell commonly misspelt words	none

1. Learn all the spellings you coloured yellow or red in the previous activity. Use the methods below to help you.

Repeat look-say-cover-write-check until you have learnt the spelling.

> **Look** at the word.
> **Say** each letter of the word aloud.
> **Cover** the word.
> **Write** the word.
> **Check** your spelling.

Find a word within the word. For example:

Break the word down into syllables and pronounce it how it's spelled. For example:

2. When you are confident with your spellings, write them out in the table below.

ENGLISH
Grades 5-9

38 Answers

Starter activity: Homophones

1. Homophones in bold, partners in brackets: **Their** (there, they're) are no words to describe how your heart thumps when **your** (you're) **weighting** (waiting) for bad news. Worse still, your mood **effects** (affects) everyone around you. **Its** (it's) as though you have shouted your negative thoughts **allowed** (aloud) for everyone to **here** (hear). Fear and anxiety spread like a disease; **there** (their, they're) contagious and deadly, **to** (too, two) powerful to be resisted.

2. there; you're; waiting; affects; it's; aloud; hear; they're; too

Main activity: Spotting spelling errors

1. remember; happiness; difficult; achieve
2. Full text with correct spellings in bold: We should always **remember** that **happiness** is **difficult** to **achieve** but easy to lose. It is a **precious possession**. However, my **friend**, Billy, is **quite weird**. For example, he **truly believes** that **knowledge** is **completely unnecessary**. **Unfortunately**, this can lead to **arguments**. Billy is **really successful** at **arguing because** he is not too **embarrassed** to **interrupt** you **immediately** and start shouting. This has **happened** on **several separate occasions** and is **beginning** to be a **persistent** problem that will not **disappear**. This **difference** between Billy and the rest of my **friends** has **finally** made us make a **decision** that we would have **preferred** not to make. **Tomorrow** we will **definitely recommend** that Billy takes a vow of **silence**. I am sure he will be **disappointed** but it may be the **surprise** that teaches him a lesson – or more **likely**, it will be **business** as usual and he'll start an **argument**...

Main activity: Getting it right

1. to 3. Student's own answers
4. Student's own answers. Ensure the student understands the patterns and spells the words correctly.

Homework activity: Learning spellings

1. Student's own work
2. Student's own answers. Ensure spellings are correct.

Glossary

Homophone
A word that sounds the same as another word or words that are spelt differently and have different meanings, for example *new* and *knew*

ENGLISH
Grades 3-5

MARK SCHEME: WRITING

CONTENT AND ORGANISATION

Marks		Criteria
19–24 marks	22–24 marks	**Content** • Register is skilfully controlled and fully appropriate for audience. • *Purpose is confidently achieved.* • Language is crafted with sophistication, and a considerable variety of vocabulary and language devices is used to fully achieve purpose and intention. **Organisation** • Structural choices are varied and skilfully managed. • A range of complex, developed ideas skilfully engages and directs the reader's response. • Paragraphing and discourse markers are skilfully managed for clarity and fluency.
	19–21 marks	**Content** • Register is fully appropriate for audience. • Purpose is fully achieved. • Language is deliberately crafted for effect and impact, and a considerable variety of vocabulary and language devices is used. **Organisation** • Structural choices are effective and varied. • A range of clearly linked and developed ideas engage the reader. • Paragraphing is consistently effective, with fluent use of discourse markers.
13–18 marks	16–18 marks	**Content** • Register is consistently appropriate for audience. • Purpose is consistently achieved. • A broad vocabulary and a range of language devices are clearly chosen for effect. **Organisation** • Structural choices are effective. • A range of clearly linked ideas engages the reader. • Paragraphing is effective, with a range of discourse markers.
	13–15 marks	**Content** • Register is broadly appropriate for audience. • Purpose is broadly achieved. • Vocabulary and language devices are clearly chosen for effect. **Organisation** • Structural choices are broadly effective. • A range of linked ideas engage the reader. • Paragraphing is usually effective, with a range of discourse markers.

ENGLISH
Grades 3-5

MARK SCHEME: WRITING

7–12 marks	10–12 marks	**Content** • Register is frequently appropriate for audience. • Purpose is frequently achieved. • Vocabulary and language devices are sometimes deliberately chosen for effect. **Organisation** • Structural choices are sometimes significant. • A growing range of relevant, linked ideas is presented. • Paragraphing is generally accurate, with largely appropriate use of discourse markers.
	7–9 marks	**Content** • Register is inconsistently appropriate for audience. • Purpose is inconsistently achieved. • There is some variety in vocabulary and language devices. **Organisation** • There is some awareness of structural conventions. • A range of relevant, linked ideas is presented. • Paragraphing is inaccurate, with inconsistently appropriate use of discourse markers.
1–6 marks	4–6 marks	**Content** • There is some awareness of audience. • There is some awareness of purpose. • Straightforward vocabulary and language devices are used. **Organisation** • There is some evidence of structural choices. • One or two relevant ideas are linked. • Paragraphing is inaccurate.
	1–3 marks	**Content** • There is a limited sense of audience. • There is a limited sense of purpose. • Limited, basic vocabulary is used. **Organisation** • There is little or no evidence of structural choices. • Limited, unlinked ideas are presented. • No paragraphing is used.
No marks		• No creditable response

ENGLISH
— Grades 3-5 —

Mark scheme: Writing

Technical accuracy

Marks	Criteria
13–16 marks	- Sentence demarcation is consistently accurate. - Meaning is fully supported with a range of punctuation, used highly accurately. - Sentence forms are highly varied and crafted for effect. - Standard English is used consistently and appropriately, with secure management of grammatical structures. - Vocabulary choices are sophisticated. - Spelling is highly accurate.
9–12 marks	- Sentence demarcation is usually accurate. - Meaning is usually supported with a range of punctuation, used with some accuracy. - Sentence forms are varied and crafted for effect. - Standard English is used generally accurately, with largely accurate management of grammatical structures. - A broad range of vocabulary choices is used. - Less common words are generally accurately spelled.
5–8 marks	- Sentence demarcation is largely accurate. - Meaning is largely supported with a range of punctuation. - Some variety of sentence forms is used. - Standard English is sometimes used, with some inaccuracies in agreement. - Vocabulary choices are varied. - Less common words are often accurately spelled
1–4 marks	- Sentence demarcation is infrequent. - There is limited evidence of deliberate punctuation. - A limited range of sentence forms is used. - There is limited use of Standard English, with frequent inaccuracies in agreement. - Common words are accurately spelled. - Vocabulary choices are straightforward.
No marks	- No creditable response

PROGRESS AND OBSERVATIONS

Published by Pearson Education Limited, 80 Strand, London, WC2R 0RL.

www.pearsonschools.co.uk

Text © Pearson Education Limited 2017
Series consultant: Margaret Reeve
Edited by Elektra Media Ltd
Designed by Andrew Magee
Typeset by Elektra Media Ltd
Produced by Elektra Media Ltd
Original illustrations © Pearson Education Limited 2017
Illustrated by Elektra Media Ltd
Cover design by Andrew Magee

The right of David Grant to be identified as author of this work has been asserted by him in accordance with the Copyright, Designs and Patents Act 1988.

First published 2017

20 19 18 17
10 9 8 7 6 5 4 3 2 1

British Library Cataloguing in Publication Data
A catalogue record for this book is available from the British Library

ISBN 9781292195391

Copyright notice
All rights reserved. The material in this publication is copyright. Activity sheets may be freely photocopied for use by the purchasing tutor. However, this material is copyright and under no circumstances may copies be offered for sale. If you wish to use the material in any way other than that specified you must apply in writing to the publishers.

The ActiveBook accompanying this book contains editable Word files. Pearson Education Limited cannot accept responsibility for the quality, accuracy or fitness for purpose of the materials contained in the Word files once edited. To revert to the original Word files, download the files again.

Printed in the United Kingdom by Ashford Colour Press Ltd

Acknowledgements
The author and publisher would like to thank the following for their kind permission to reproduce copyright material:

Extract on page 17 from *The Art of Eating* ('The Gastronomical Me') by M. K. Fisher. Copyright @ 1954, renewed 1982 by M. K. Fisher. Reprint by permission of Houghton Mifflin Harcourt Publishing Company and Daunt Books. All Rights Reserved. Extract on page 19 Copyright Guardian News & Media Ltd 2017. Extract on page 20 from *One Hundred Years of Solitude* by Gabriel Garcia Marquez. Published by HarperCollins and Agencia Literaria Carmen Balcells © 2014. Extract on page 21 from *The Ocean at the End of the Lane* by Neil Gaiman. Reproduced by permission of Headline Publishing Group and HarperCollins © 2013.

Photographs
Photodisc: Photolink 144, 151, 164, 183; **Image Source:** David Forman 153, 163, 177, 180, 182

All other images © Pearson Education

We would like to thank Tutora for its invaluable help in the development and trialling of this course.